PREJUDICE IN POLITICS

PREJUDICE IN POLITICS

Group Position, Public Opinion, and the
Wisconsin Treaty Rights Dispute

LAWRENCE D. BOBO

MIA TUAN

HARVARD UNIVERSITY PRESS

Cambridge, Massachusetts, and London, England · 2006

Library of Congress Cataloging-in-Publication Data

Bobo, Lawrence.
Prejudice in politics : group position, public opinion, and the
Wisconsin treaty rights dispute / Lawrence D. Bobo, Mia Tuan.
p.   cm.
Includes bibliographical references and index.
ISBN 0-674-01329-8 (alk. paper)
1. Ojibwa Indians—Public opinion.   2. Ojibwa Indians—Treaties.
3. Ojibwa Indians—Civil rights.   4. Indians, Treatment of—Wisconsin.
5. Racism—Wisconsin.   6. Politics and culture—Wisconsin.
7. Public opinion—Wisconsin.   8. Wisconsin—Politics and government.
9. Wisconsin—Race relations.   I. Tuan, Mia, 1968–   II. Title.

E99.C6B66   2006
305.897'3330775019—dc22   2005044862

For Marcyliena and Michael

CONTENTS

PREFACE

This project grew out of a deep concern that racial prejudice remains a serious problem in the United States, and indeed around much of the globe. Tensions and conflicts of a highly racialized nature, especially in the political realm, seem to be a durable feature of our social landscape. As social scientists, we set out to carefully theorize and test our ideas about the nature of prejudice. We believe that social scientists have a special obligation to help elucidate the causes and solutions to such dilemmas. We are not so naive as to think that systematic knowledge about a social problem is a sure and direct guide to successful reform and intervention. But we do feel that such knowledge greatly improves the chances for positive change as compared with reliance on uninformed judgment and speculation.

We are convinced that to mute and break down lines between ethno-racial groups, we must have clear and well-developed ideas about the basic nature of the processes involved in maintaining such distinctions. In taking stock of previous research, we found that several patterns stand out. First, the overwhelming majority of work from the United States is centered on black-white relations only. This is an important set of relations to understand, both for its historical prominence in the development of American culture and institutions and for the role the black-white divide still plays in our society today. Yet this plainly does not exhaust the sets of relations important in the American experience. Second, most of the previous research has intellectual roots in the sociocultural approach to prejudice exemplified by the work of distinguished social psychologist Gordon W. Allport. We have sought to build on these crucial foundations but also to advance beyond the traditional lines of emphasis in two respects. We focus on how the affirmation of treaty rights for the Chippewa of Wisconsin occasioned an intense and volatile period of political turmoil, putting an issue of relevance to Native American peoples—and arguably to disadvantaged indigenous groups around the world—at the center of attention. And we develop a full theoretical elaboration and robust empirical test of the theory of prejudice as a sense of group position, an approach inspired by the insights of sociologist Herbert Blumer.

Our work has convinced us that in most instances it is a mistake to think of racialized political controversy and conflict either as simply the irrational intrusion of prejudice into the political sphere or, in contrast, as a superficial distraction rooted in other more fundamental economic or situational factors. Our research leads us to believe that attitudes and material contingencies, identities and interests, the psychological and the sociological—all are engaged and constitutive elements of most circumstances of ethno-racial political tension and dispute. The search for the single psychological factor of importance is an intellectual and practical dead-end, as is the search for the single structural or economic factor of importance.

In this project we have incurred many debts. Original funding for the data collection came from three sources: the small grants program of the Spencer Foundation; the Robert M. La Follette Institute for Public Policy Studies at the University of Wisconsin–Madison; and the University of Wisconsin system's Institute on Race and Ethnicity. The data collection was carried out by the Literature and Sciences Survey Center at the University of Wisconsin, under the direction of sociology professor James Sweet and the day-to-day management of Robert Lee. These agencies, and especially these two individuals, are owed our thanks and appreciation.

Some elements of Chapter 1 appeared in Bobo's "Prejudice as Group Position: Microfoundations of a Sociological Approach to Racism and Race Relations," *Journal of Social Issues* 55 (1999):445–472, but are substantially modified from that publication.

A number of people took the time to comment on the original research proposal as it was developed and on the processes of questionnaire development and pre-testing. In addition to Jim Sweet and Bob Lee, we owe thanks to Franklin Wilson, Gary Sandefur, and Tom Heberlein of the University of Wisconsin–Madison sociology department. Several people commented on early drafts of various chapters or on the entire manuscript. We are especially indebted to Maria Krysan, Michael C. Dawson, Stephen Cornell, Jennifer Hochschild, Patricia Gurin, Thomas F. Pettigrew, Matt Snipp, and two anonymous reviewers for Harvard University Press. Jim Sidanius provided critical feedback and advice at a number of points in the project. And Michael Massagli provided invaluable assistance with LISREL modeling and the drafting of Appendix B.

Others played important roles in the project. Fred C. Licari was enormously helpful in the early pre-testing of the questionnaire and the preparation of the final data set and codebook. Estella Garcia was instrumental in preparing the original working paper issued by the La Follette Institute. Devon Johnson played an indispensable role in virtually all of the final data analyses for the book, and Victor Thompson provided needed assistance as we finished our work. They all deserve our thanks.

And of course our spouses have been enormously supportive during our long journey in bringing this project to fruition. Marcyliena Morgan, wife and pioneering linguistic anthropologist, and Michael Welch, husband and brilliant writer, were constant sources of inspiration, friendship, and encouragement to Larry and to Mia. You each have our love and respect.

PROLOGUE

This book addresses the interplay of ethno-racial prejudice and political controversy. From the project's inception, our approach to these issues was based on three interconnected objectives. Our first aim was to better understand the fundamental social-psychological processes involved in ethno-racial relations and conflict. In particular, we elaborate on and test the group position theory of prejudice. Our second aim was to put a divisive controversy over the rights of Native Americans—the fishing, hunting, and gathering rights of the Chippewa peoples of Wisconsin—on center stage. Our third aim was to use a social survey, a carefully designed study of public opinion, as our window into the dynamics of prejudice and political contestation. We hope to weave these objectives into an answer to the central question of this book: how and why does racial prejudice enter into politics in the modern United States?

There are many surface indicators suggesting that prejudice was an important factor in the Wisconsin treaty rights controversy, which erupted in the 1970s and persisted well into the 1990s. While attempting to fish using their traditional spearfishing methods, the Chippewa Indians faced angry crowds of whites who hurled such epithets as "Save a fish, spear an Indian," "Save two walleye, spear a pregnant squaw," and "Timber nigger." Numerous hostile confrontations took place at the boat landings where the Chippewa engaged in their age-old fishing traditions. A number of groups formed to fight against the Chippewa treaty rights. Political recall efforts against candidates apparently sympathetic to the Chippewa cause were launched. State officials pressured the Chippewa to either give up or "sell" their rights or face an open effort to abrogate the treaties. Many of these events and the bitter feelings they highlighted prompted a U.S. Civil Rights Commission report to point to racism as a key influence in the course of the dispute (U.S. Commission on Civil Rights 1989).

1

The controversy over Chippewa treaty rights, though waged mainly in the upper third of the state of Wisconsin and only occasionally breaking into national prominence ("Indian Fishing Dispute Upsets North Woods' Quiet," *New York Times*, April 24, 1988), bears striking similarity to a number of more broadly familiar disputes. Like the issues of school busing for desegregation and affirmative action in employment and higher education, the Wisconsin treaty rights dispute involved a long, contentious period of litigation. Like the issues of busing and affirmative action, the treaty rights issue was often understood as pitting the claims and status of a minority group against those of the majority white community. Like those earlier instances of black-white struggle, this modern case of "red-white" struggle occasioned bitter rhetoric, social protest and mobilization, and escalating ethno-racial tension. For these reasons and more, we take the Wisconsin treaty rights dispute as an important instance in which the possible role of prejudice in politics requires careful analysis.

BEYOND BLACK AND WHITE

One of our goals is to expand the substantive net cast by students of ethno-racial attitudes to include a political dispute in which the rights of Native Americans are the focus. While the great bulk of scholarship on prejudice in the United States is preoccupied with black-white relations, we feel there are a number of reasons to apply theories developed in the context of black-white relations to Indian-white relations. Disputes over Indian treaty rights have arisen in various states across the country. In Oregon, the Klamath Indians battle over water rights with white farmers ("Three Accused of Shooting Up Oregon Town; Water Dispute Cited," *New York Times*, December 21, 2001, p. 25). In Washington State, tensions flared after the U.S. Supreme Court affirmed the right of Washington tribes to harvest shellfish on private beaches ("Tribes' Shellfish Rights Affirmed by High Court," *New York Times*, April 6, 1999, p. 21). The Voigt decision that reaffirmed Chippewa fishing, hunting, and gathering rights in Wisconsin—it is called the Voigt case after Lester Voigt, who was secretary of the Department of Natural Resources when the decision was made—also applied to Chippewa tribes in Michigan and Minnesota. As one editorial writer put it: "In the East, there are disputes over land. It's water in the west. Fishing in the Northwest and Great Lakes areas. Voting Rights in South Dakota, New Mexico, Arizona, and Oklahoma. Taxation in Nebraska and Montana" ("Keep the Promises Made to the Indians," *USA Today*, September 14, 1987). Many of these areas experienced problems of rising ethnic tensions in connection with Indian treaty rights. The basic issue, in short, is one of national scope and importance.

In a close parallel, moreover, to the familiar school busing and affirmative action controversies, treaty rights disputes raise questions about the politics of group entitlement. Treaty rights have been denounced as special treatment and unfair favoritism for a specific racial group. Similar complaints have been lodged in the now well-worn debates over affirmative action. Some treaty opponents have also objected to government intervention that appears to place the rights of one group above those of another. This is similar to much antibusing rhetoric. The parallel even extends to the names social movement groups have adopted. One of the early anti–treaty rights groups in Wisconsin called itself Equal Rights for Everyone, and another, Protect America's Rights and Resources. The emphasis is much like that of ROAR—Restore Our Alienated Rights—a prominent antibusing group during the Boston school busing controversy. Another group, STA, or Stop Treaty Abuse, is reminiscent of BUSTOP, a parents' group that fought desegregation in Los Angeles. Hence conflicts over treaty rights are neither narrow nor anachronistic public policy concerns. They arise in many states and exhibit features increasingly characteristic of majority-minority political disputes all across the United States.

What is more, these disputes sometimes generate the same high tension and acute conflict seen in the cases of school busing and affirmative action. One dramatic artifact of the treaty rights conflict is a bar-room flyer advertising the "First Annual Indian Shoot" (Figure P.1). Perhaps even more dramatic is a flyer that features a hand aggressively pointing a gun at the reader with the phrase "Spear This!" emblazoned across the top and bottom (Figure P.2).

In Wisconsin, there is now a long history of litigation on the question of Indian fishing rights, spanning more than twenty years. A number of pro– and anti–treaty rights movement groups formed. The issue played a part in electoral recall efforts within the state ("Treaty Foes Fight [Rep.] Holperin," *Wisconsin State Journal*, January 7, 1990, p. 1a), elicited direct comment and involvement from state congressional representatives ("Indians Should Give Up Rights to Ease Tensions, [Cong.] Obey Says," *Milwaukee Journal*, October 14–17, 1984), and was one of the key issues in the 1986 Wisconsin gubernatorial contest. A number of confrontations,

First Annual Indian Shoot

TIME: Early spring, beginning of walleye run

PLACE: Northern Wisconsin lakes

RULES: Open shoot, off hand position only, no scopes, no sling, no tripods, and no whiskey for bait!

OPEN TO ALL WISCONSIN TAXPAYING RESIDENTS
Residents that are BLACK, HMONG, CUBAN or those on WELFARE, A.D.C., FOOD STAMPS, or any other GOVERNMENT GIVE-A-WAY program, are not eligible.   (Don't complain about discrimination, you'll have your own shoot later.)

SCORING: WISCONSIN RULES APPLY. POINT SYSTEM WILL BE USED.

> **PLAIN INDIAN** ....**5 POINTS**
>
> **INDIAN WITH WALLEYES**..**10 POINTS**
>
> **INDIAN WITH BOAT NEWER THAN YOURS** ....**20 POINTS**
>
> **INDIAN USING PITCHFORK** ....**30 POINTS**
>
> **INDIAN WITH HIGH SCHOOL DIPLOMA** ....**50 POINTS**
>
> **SOBER INDIAN**...**75 POINTS**
>
> **INDIAN TRIBAL LAWYER** ....**100 POINTS**
> **(Does not have to be spearing)**

JUDGES: Governor Tommy Thompson, Rev. Jesse Jackson

PRIZES: Fillet-O-Fish sandwiches and six packs of treaty beer

SPONSOR: Society Helping Individual Taxpayers Own Nothing (Known as SHIT ON)

ENTRY BLANK:
> I _____ will attend shoot.
> I _____ will_____ will not be taking scalps.

I BELIEVE SENATOR ROSHELL IS:

> ____ HONEST   ____ CORRECT
> ____ ACCURATE   ____ A SAINT
> ____ ALL OF THE ABOVE

I AM ENCLOSING $ ——————— FOR HIS RE-ELECTION

Bumper stickers reading "SAVE A FISH-SPEAR AN INDIAN" only $5.00 each. "T" shirts with same message only $10.00 each.

FIGURE P.1 Flyer found posted in a northern Wisconsin pizza restaurant.

FIGURE P.2 Flyer found posted in a northern Wisconsin tavern.

arrests, and violent protests occurred, including bombings ("Spearing Harasser Gets Year in Prison," *Capital Times*, January 6, 1990, p. 19). No quick or easy solution was achieved.

To be sure, the parallel to black-white relations should not be overdrawn. The circumstances of American Indians are unique in several critical ways. American Indians were incorporated into the United States through conquest, as compared with forced migration in the case of African Americans. Indian-white conflict emerged because of whites' desires for Native Americans' land. Black-white conflict historically rested on the exploitation of black labor power. Indians faced displacement and conquest. Blacks faced forced incorporation and oppression. The black and American Indian populations also differ in size, geographic location, and cultural traditions. Treaty rights and the reservation system, along with tribal systems of government, represent further differences in the experiences of the two groups. A core thrust of the African American struggle for civil rights has involved a push for integration and entry into the American mainstream. An important element of Native American aspirations has included the preservation of distinctive cultures, practices, and spheres of difference. Thus the parallel to issues in the black experience or to that of other groups should not be overstated.

With this in mind, however, it is crucial not to dismiss or overlook the similarities in experiences among minority racial groups in the United States. As distinguished historian Ronald Takaki (1979, p. xiv) aptly notes, whites have neither viewed nor treated racial groups within a social, political, or economic vacuum; rather, he writes, "What whites did to one racial group had direct consequences for others." African Americans and Native Americans both played fundamental roles in defining the development of America's social institutions and culture; white America was what red America and black America were not (Jordan 1968; Takaki 1979). According to prevailing ideology, whites were industrious, intelligent, and worthy, whereas Indians and blacks were not. It was the circumstances of these two groups that tempered Alexis de Tocqueville's (1969 [1848]) otherwise greatly hopeful assessment of American democracy. This simple fact underscores why theories developed to explain race politics in the case of black-white relations are applicable to understanding Indian-white relations.

ON THE INTRUSION OF PREJUDICE INTO POLITICS

The principal theoretical goal of this work is to summarize and evaluate the current theoretical models of the effects of prejudice on politics. In response to a series of disputes that grew out of the civil rights gains of African Americans, scholars spanning sociology, political science, and social psychology have investigated the controversies over school busing, affirmative action, and black electoral office seeking. Theories about the controversies surrounding each issue have fallen largely into three categories.

The predominant take on explaining mass public opinion on these issues has been rooted in *theories of racial prejudice* (Kinder and Sanders 1996; McConahay 1986; Sears 1988; Sears et al. 1997). In the main, this work has suggested that a largely irrational antiblack animus continues as a potent political force. To be sure, the surface content of publicly articulated prejudice has softened from the blunt racism of the Jim Crow era, becoming ever more sophisticated and polished. The changing form of prejudice in politics is perhaps best captured in the contrasting images of, on the one hand, a snarling Alabama governor George Wallace vowing in 1963 to defend segregation to his last breath and, on the other hand, the smoothly telegenic Louisiana state legislator David Duke in 1990, condemning the unfairness of quotas and the fraud against decent, taxpaying citizens perpetrated by "welfare queens." According to the theories of racism, however, the wellsprings of dissent over busing, affirmative action, and black electoral candidates are still the same. They may be found in an emotional and unreasoning form of racial prejudice held by many white Americans.

The reach of these theories now extends well beyond issues of black-white relations. Analysts have used the models to understand public responses to issues of bilingualism in Latino-white relations (Citrin et al. 1990; Huddy and Sears 1995), and the framework has also been brought to bear on the increasingly important questions of immigration policy and multiculturalism (Sears et al. 1999). At their core, the theories point to the modern relevance of long-standing individual-level prejudice models (Allport 1954; Katz 1991; Pettigrew 1982; Selznick and Steinberg 1969). Antiminority feelings and beliefs learned early in life, through normal processes of socialization and human cognition, come to guide whites' political thought and action when, as adults, they are confronted with issues of interethnic relations.

A clear alternative theoretical view emphasizes the role of *clashing values and dispassionate reason* in controversies such as those around busing and affirmative action. Social policies that run against such deeply rooted American values as individualism and self-reliance, the argument goes, are destined to be disputed. And rightly so, from this perspective, since cherished political and moral principles are undermined by government recognition of ethnic-group or collective claims on social resources (Glazer 1975; Roth 1990; Sniderman and Piazza 1993; Sowell 1984; Tetlock 1994; Thernstrom and Thernstrom 1997). A closely related theory blends a concern for traditional values with more practical considerations. This view suggests that, for many whites, the governmental enforcement of minority group rights raises challenges to the notion of majority rule and is perceived as entailing objective, pragmatic costs that would be rejected if only common sense prevailed (McClendon 1985; Rieder 1985; Stinchcombe and Taylor 1980; Taylor 1986). By implication, such policies are wrong-headed and simply defy reason. Thus the bulk of white resistance to racial change is not merely race-neutral but in fact derives from broadly important, color-blind principles on which the republic was founded: individualism and the work ethic, on one hand, and reason and majority rule, on the other.

A third theoretical view emphasizes the role of *simple self-interest* in these controversies (Kluegel and Smith 1986; Rieder 1985; Waldinger 1996). There is, in short, an objective basis for hostility between members of different racial groups due to an underlying clash of material, economic, and political interests. For instance, in the case of school busing, parents with children in the public schools should be those most likely to object to school busing for desegregation because they are the ones directly affected by the policy. Self-interest theories are clear about the determinants of hostility: the bulk of whites' resistance to racial change is due to direct and personal vulnerability to displacement, loss, or the costs of adaptation resulting from change in their social environment.

For all the differences among them, these three theoretical approaches have significant similarities. All three give short shrift to what we regard as the basic sociological ideas of ethno-racial stratification and the force such persistent inequality exerts on the dynamics of group relations, identities, and politics. Several sociological analysts have thus, not surprisingly, been critical of them. These analysts have attempted to give serious weight to racialized social identities and political values, while simultaneously drawing attention to a more historically grounded, instrumental, and collective basis for white reactions to minority-group pressures for a greater share of economic, political, and social resources (Bobo 1983, 1988a,b; Kaufmann 2004; T. Lee 2002; Quillian 1996; Smith 1981; Taylor 1998; Wellman 1977).

It is not merely valuable on intellectual and practical grounds to understand modern racial politics in a more sociological fashion: it is essential. Some recent major works in political science that grapple with the impact of race on politics offer little in the way of sustained analysis of how race and ethnicity have shaped American institutions, culture, and identity (Carmines and Stimson 1989).[1] Beyond a minimal recognition that racism has constrained the attainments of blacks, Native Americans, Asians, and Latinos, there is sometimes a stunning inattention to the part that race and ethnicity play in social stratification and therefore in politics. For example,

Sniderman and Piazza's *The Scar of Race* (1993) suggests that race only really became "politicized" in the post–civil rights, affirmative action era. From many different angles of approach this is a curious observation. Race has cast a long shadow over the development of American political institutions (Fredrickson 1999; Gerstle 2001; Klinkner and Smith 1999; R. Smith 1993). Captured in this shadow are such pivotal turning points in American history as the drafting of the Constitution (Ellis 2001); the Civil War; the adoption of the Thirteenth, Fourteenth, and Fifteenth Amendments to the Constitution (Fredrickson 1971); the very nature of New Deal social provisions (Lieberman 1998; Quadagno 1994); the reforms of the Great Society and the War on Poverty (O'Connor 2001); and the current waves of welfare curtailment (Gilens 1999) and attacks on affirmative action (Kinder and Sanders 1996; Sidanius et al. 2000).[2] With regard to the issues that will dominate our attention in this volume, it is impossible to see the historical dispossession of Native Americans of their lands, their near genocidal decimation, the forced imposition of a tribal reservation system in the mid-nineteenth century that has lasted to the present, and the current levels of poverty and desperation in which many American Indians live as events stemming from a lofty and essentially race-neutral American past. Racial prejudice and discrimination were not minor mis-strokes on an otherwise vast equalitarian canvas (Fredrickson and Knobel 1982; R. Smith 1993; Takaki 1979).

It is not our purpose to suggest that American history must be understood as a great "racial" project and narrative, though such an emphasis would not be wholly out of place (Horsman 1981; Omi and Winant 1986). We are suggesting, however, that the general and persistent pattern in the academy has been to systematically marginalize race and, when not so marginalized, to misunderstand the frequently pivotal role of race in U.S. political dynamics. The rapid proliferation of discussions of "identity" and the emphasis on the intersection of "race-class-gender" have been, at best, a mild and at times counterproductive anodyne (Brubaker and Cooper 2000) to the otherwise dominant dismissive approach to racial dynamics.

What we do mean to suggest is that the material, political, and socio-emotional advantages that flow from ethno-racial stratification are not mere contextual details or social embroidery. The major premise of our work is that ethno-racial dividing lines are as basic to human social organization as class, gender, and age. Ethno-racial boundaries intertwine with and condition the experience of class, gender, and age differentiation.

Once ethno-racial inequalities have been built into the foundation of a particular social order, those cleavages may have quasi-autonomous and permeative effects on social identities, group cultures, living spaces and activities, and the larger life prospects of both individuals and groups.

This premise rests, in part, on a wide body of social-psychological research on the processes of perception and stereotyping, group identity, and discrimination. Research on categorization and stereotyping has made clear the apparent cognitive habit, if not necessity, of employing grouping strategies to simplify a ceaseless flow of psychological stimuli (Fiske 1998). The categories we use prefigure much of what we perceive, what we believe we know, and, therefore, how we are likely to behave (Bodenhausen, Macrae, and Garst 1998). The long and influential body of work on social identity theory (Tajfel 1969, 1981, 1982) makes it clear that humans possess a strong capacity to act on the basis of group categories and identities. These actions are likely to follow a pattern of in-group favoritism, if not necessarily to out-group discrimination and hostility. And a very powerful recent line of work labeled "social dominance theory" has further generalized social-psychological ideas about categorization and group identity to include the creation and maintenance of social hierarchies within social systems (Sidanius and Pratto 1999). For our purposes, the upshot of these developments is that ethno-racial distinctions are particularly well suited to drawing consequential lines of individual identity and behavior, and of social organization.

We treat the central role of ethno-racial divisions in the organization of social life as a foundational assumption rather than as a matter of sustained analysis and inquiry in its own right. There is as yet no single work that articulates this position. However, a number of scholars have operated from viewpoints that have important similarities to our own (Blauner 1972; Bonilla-Silva 1997; Omi and Winant 1986; Stone 1985; Winant 2000). To be sure, like most sociologists we understand racial and ethnic categories and identities as social constructions. Although frequently incorporating references to physical and biologically inherited characteristics such as skin color, facial features, hair texture, and so on, race and ethnic designations are above all else subjective creations (Cornell and Hartmann 1998). They vary enormously in content, salience, and consequences. As a result, what we take to be racial and ethnic distinctions are profoundly, historically contingent and malleable phenomena (Zuberi 2001).

Yet it would be a mistake to regard such categories and identities as intrinsically fleeting, weakly rooted, or insubstantial. The socially constructed and contingent character of race and ethnicity no more renders such ideas of superficial consequence in social life than the socially constructed character of "paper money" vitiates the purchasing power of a twenty-dollar bill or the socially constructed character of borders and nations vitiates the lines governments draw between citizens and noncitizens. Once a set of categories and identities has been institutionalized—in particular, when that institutionalization has involved sharp differentiation and inequality between groups in their access to and control of power, wealth, and prestige—then ethno-racial divisions become powerful forces in a social order (Dawson 2000; Kim 2000; Sidanius and Pratto 1999).

This premise has immediate implications for theories of the role of racial prejudice in politics. Any theory about the impact of prejudice on politics that fails to begin with the twin facts of racialized identity and racialized social status is, all else equal, fated to misunderstand the dynamics of prejudice as a social force. As Winant (2000, p. 181) argues, theory must be able to link the "micro- and macro-aspects of racial signification and racialized social structure. Such a multileveled and interconnected account is a general obligation of social theory in the present." Most theories springing from political psychology do indeed take racialized identities very seriously. Orthodox prejudice theories, however, are not seriously informed by the fact of racialized social statuses and conditions. As a result, the central role played by ethno-racial group interests, which are the inevitable product of ethno-racial stratification, has virtually no place in orthodox accounts of how and why prejudice influences politics. Blauner articulated the core idea behind our position more than two decades ago:

> Because economic and status privileges are bulwarks of racial stratification, racism cannot simply be viewed as a set of subjective irrational beliefs that might be overcome through more and better contact, communication, and understanding. When such a focus on prejudice forms the dominant approach to racial conflict—as it does in America today, even among social scientists—then the fact that whites, blacks, Chicanos, and other third world groups have distinct objective interests is overlooked. Ethnic and racial groups are first and foremost interest groups. (1972, p. 28)

Given sharply differentiated ethno-racial statuses, it is a fundamental error to conceive of the attitudes and beliefs undergirding a system of privilege and "dis-privilege" as thoroughly devoid of rational or instrumental bases.

The point here is perhaps more readily expressed in terms of a different type of socially constructed identity—namely, nationalism. As distinguished sociologist Rogers Brubaker has argued:

> We should not in fact have to choose between an instrumentalist and an identitarian approach to the study of nationalism. That this is a false opposition becomes clear when we think about the cognitive dimension of nationalism. Considered from a cognitive point of view, nationalism is a way of seeing the world, a way of *identifying interests,* or more precisely, a way of specifying interest-bearing units, of *identifying the relevant units in terms of which interests are conceived.* It furnishes a mode of vision and division of the world, to use Pierre Bourdieu's phrase, a mode of social counting and accounting. Thus it inherently links identity and interest—by identifying *how we are to calculate our interests.* (Brubaker 1998, pp. 291–292, emphasis in original)

National identities forge a connection between, on the one hand, an emotion-inflected sense of self, place, and belonging, and, on the other hand, material instrumentalities in the real world. The same logic applies in the case of race-based social distinctions, a point we elaborate on in Chapter 1.

In contrast, most theories springing from sociology take racialized social conditions and statuses very seriously. Mainstream sociological analyses, however, are less well informed by the individual psychological fact of racialized social identities (e.g., Steinberg 1995). As a result, the central role played by individual social-psychological processes of identity and attitude formation and their effects on behavior have at best a secondary, if not tertiary, place in orthodox sociological accounts of ethno-racial inequality and conflict. One unfortunate consequence of the assault on orthodox theories of prejudice by Blauner, Wellman, and others has been a failed attempt to understand ethno-racial inequality in strictly institutional and macrosocial terms. That is, such an approach neglects individual psychological functioning and agency (see the critique in Bobo 2000b). Research and theory can and should exhibit a mutual concern for institutional and macro-level social processes and individual, micro-level processes of identity, attitude, belief, and behavior, as well as the meso-level conditions and processes that serve to connect the two.

Many scholars, even some of those operating squarely in the orthodox prejudice or value-based approaches, have seen merit in better reconciling these alternative points of emphasis. All too often, however, the research advancing a more sociological or collective view of prejudice has been found wanting (for critical views of a sociological approach, see Sears and Kinder 1985; Sniderman and Carmines 1997; Sniderman and Tetlock 1986a). Perhaps fairly so. The main weakness of this school of thought, we believe, has been the piecemeal character of the research advancing a more sociological, group-level, and "collectivized prejudice" theory. The work has been piecemeal in at least two respects. First, comparatively little attention has been devoted to meaningful, substantive elaboration and empirical testing of this type of theory of prejudice. Mary Jackman's ambitious work *The Velvet Glove* (1994) is the one major exception to this pattern. But she reaches beyond ethno-racial divisions to develop a theory of paternalism as the linchpin of intergroup ideologies in class, gender, and racial contexts. Second, and more important, this perspective has simply not become a core research agenda for scholars in the fashion observed with the orthodox prejudice and value-based theories. In many ways this reflects the current intellectual fashions and biases within sociology more than it does a problem or defect in the core insight offered by the collective prejudice perspective.

Thus our objective is to extend and test such a collectivized prejudice theory. As is the case for a number of other scholars, our starting point is Herbert Blumer's theory of prejudice as a sense of group position (Blumer 1958a). In many ways Blumer's approach to prejudice, though developed only in a very brief essay, is regarded as a classic statement. His ideas about the nature of prejudice have influenced sociohistorical analyses (Almaguer 1994; Wilson 1973) and qualitative studies of interethnic attitudes and relations (Blauner 1989; Bonilla-Silva 2003; J. Lee 2002; Wellman 1977), as well as quantitative research spanning social psychology (Bobo 1983; Bobo and Hutchings 1996; Jackman 1994; Quillian 1996; Smith 1981; Taylor 1998), demography (Fossett and Kiecolt 1989), and political science (Giles and Evans 1986; Glaser 1994, 2003). It is thus surprising that comparatively little serious effort at theoretical elaboration has been undertaken to expand on Blumer's ideas, much less to design and collect new data. His notion of prejudice as "a sense of group position" has functioned most often as a pivotal sociological insight or "sensitizing" concept (Lal 1986, 1995) and a good deal less often as the kernel of a new paradigm on prejudice. Such paradigm building requires rigorous and innovative application. We argue that our group position theory of prejudice offers the most promising framework for the effective and balanced theoretical linkage of a concern with ethno-racial stratification and group interests, and a concern with human subjectivity, identities, and attitudes. Much of our ambition is to push group position theory toward this fuller realization.

ON SURVEYING SOCIAL LIFE

A third goal of this project is to take up the group position theory within the context of survey-based research. There is an important irony here, inasmuch as Blumer was a vigorous critic of survey research as a tool for understanding society (see essays in Blumer 1969). Blumer's critical posture was as much in evidence in his work on group position as it was in his various essays challenging the attitude construct, public opinion polling, and quantitative or "variable analysis." We believe that most of Blumer's criticisms of the methods and concepts on which our work depends were misdirected. Yet the concerns he raised are useful. They lead us to be more explicit about several important concepts and assumptions. Also, the concerns raised by Blumer are by no means passé, having been invoked more recently by others (Bonilla-Silva 1997; Esposito and Murphy 1999). They are still accepted in some sociological circles, even though an impressive body of research argues against them (see Bobo 2001; Schuman 1995).

Blumer questioned whether the attitude construct was viable for analyzing human social behavior. On the basis of its conceptual and empirical vagueness, and its limited role in shaping human behavior, Blumer thought it best that scholars eschew reliance on the attitude construct (1955a). He also thought the effort to conceptualize variables and subject them to quantitative analysis was of only small utility (Blumer 1956), that "variable analysis" lent itself to barren, decontextualized research. Such research was, in Blumer's view, particularly inappropriate where the task was to understand complex and variegated matters of human interpretative processes and the social construction of meaning that underlies action.

Prior to publishing these challenges to the attitude construct and to quantitative social analysis, Blumer had also raised doubts about the sociological merits of "public opinion and public opinion polling" (1948). Most polls or surveys are based on general population samples. As such, according to Blumer, they cannot represent what we know of the functional organization of society into differing social groups, organizations, resource levels, and vastly differing levels of access and influence in decision making. As he put it: "In my judgment the inherent deficiency of public opinion polling, certainly as currently done, is contained in its sampling procedure.

Its current sampling procedure forces a treatment of society as if society were only an aggregation of disparate individuals. Public opinion, in turn, is regarded as being a quantitative distribution of individual opinions" (1948, p. 546). His main objection to public opinion polling, then, boils down to a distinction between "mass opinion" and influential or "elite opinion." For Blumer, an examination of the latter, how it forms and who contributes most directly to its formation, would be more worthy of sociological investigation.

Studies of prejudice came in for particularly harsh criticism from Blumer. In a broad-gauge review of studies of race relations in the United States, published in 1958, Blumer took a thoroughly skeptical posture toward research on prejudice, stereotyping, and interethnic attitudes: "Parallel to the variety of studies of 'stereotypes' a great deal of measurement of the 'attitudes' of races toward one another has been undertaken. This is chiefly a continuation of the form of study which was so common in the period 1938–1945. Since such attitude measurement studies of the past decade add nothing of significance, though they may yield a lot of 'data,' there is no need to refer to any of them" (1958b, p. 423). He drew attention, in particular, to a series of substantive and methodological challenges to *The Authoritarian Personality* (Adorno et al. 1950), the then preeminent theory of prejudice, as well as to evidence questioning a connection between prejudiced attitudes and discriminatory behavior (LaPiere 1934).

Examinations of attitudes, accordingly, made unwarranted assumptions about the importance of stereotypes and negative feelings to actual patterns of intergroup relations. By virtue of focusing attention on an analysis of the researchers' constructs of presumed importance (that is, prejudiced attitudes), rather than on the actual processes of group contact and relations, Blumer concluded that a welter of disconnected empirical findings and perspectives had emerged in social-psychological studies of prejudice. He argued: "Original premises become watered down by increasing qualification. The effort to bring them together gives rise to a shallow eclecticism in the form of a mere ordering of very diverse views. A good example is Allport's comprehensive discussion of prejudice" (Blumer 1958b, p. 435). And with this one citation, Blumer's scorn for this genre of research reached so far as to completely dismiss Allport's seminal work, *The Nature of Prejudice* (1954).

Blumer was not entirely alone in offering near polemical criticism of studies of prejudice. Arnold Rose once claimed: "no study of prejudice, using any definition or theory, helps us much in understanding what is going on in the desegregation process today. The explanation is apparently to be looked for in terms of legal, economic, political and social structural forces" (1956, p. 176). More recently, Wellman (1977) developed a trenchant review and critique of psychological theories of prejudice and argued that Blumer's group position offered a far more telling analysis of the nature of contemporary antiblack prejudice among white Americans.

In sum, the full weight of Blumer's criticisms makes it easy to grasp why some of those concerned with his ideas about group position pursued either an entirely qualitative approach (Wellman 1977) or an entirely sociohistorical approach to analyzing the nature of prejudice (Almaguer 1994). While Blumer's objections to studies of attitudes, prejudice, variables, and public opinion have some validity, they do not warrant the conclusions Blumer and many others reached. There is no single research methodology appropriate to generating useful sociological knowledge or to testing sociological theories. All research methodologies have limitations or weaknesses. The shortcomings, for instance, of more observational and ethnographic approaches are ably reviewed elsewhere (Attewell 1974; Davis 1987; Duneier 1992; Law and Lodge 1978; Wacquant 2002), as are the limitations of sociohistorical analysis (Kiser and Hechter 1991, 1998; Lieberson 1991). And we are all familiar with the external validity questions and other problems that bedevil otherwise powerful laboratory experiments (see Sears 1986). A full recitation of these limitations would be at least as debilitating against each of the other approaches as are Blumer's criticisms of the approach adopted here. Hence it is more important at this juncture to acknowledge the limitations of any given approach, to clarify the appropriateness of the chosen method for the questions at hand, and to triangulate among methodologies as much as possible.

Social psychologists have long understood attitudes to involve "a favorable or unfavorable evaluation of an object or an affect for or against an object" (Schuman 1995, p. 68). Just as social objects such as racial and ethnic groups or political issues are highly complex phenomena, so too are the attitudes or evaluations made of such objects. Important social attitudes are thus likely to be internally differentiated and influenced by a number of what John Zaller (1992) has aptly termed "considerations." Such evaluations or, in short, attitudes, are formed, tested, and influence behavior, and they are subsequently modified, extinguished, or reinforced through social interaction and experience (Kelman 1974). Attitudes thus are not unidimensional, fixed, and static orientations.

We are mindful that attitudes are but one input to behavior. Situational factors and constraints, as well as individual characteristics, all affect the likelihood that an attitude will play itself out in behavior. Yet there is now a strong body of literature showing that attitudes can exert substantial effects on overall patterns of behavior toward a social object or issue (Brannon et al. 1973; Fishbein and Ajzen 1975; Schuman 1995; Weigel and Newman 1976).

Both the object of an attitude and the nature of the evaluation expressed have often been understood in narrow terms (as in an individual's favor-or-oppose reaction to a specific political candidate). Such a narrow reading of the meaning of attitudes is indeed part of what Blumer reacted against. Blumer also reacted against a tendency to focus analytical attention merely on responses to questions. To be sure, the task of measuring attitudes in surveys involves individuals' responses to questions (Bradburn and Sudman 1988). Such questions entail the use of symbols (for example, words and phrases such as "treaty rights" or "American Indians") that the researcher hopes are meaningful to those interviewed. Responses to questions are important and constitute an intrinsic element of all the analyses we conduct (Schuman and Kalton 1985). And as Schuman (1982) once observed, the great strength of survey research derives, in fact, from its wedding of the everyday human practice of asking questions of others and taking seriously the responses we are given to the sophisticated technology of representative sampling: as a result, we thus learn not about a haphazardly selected and disparate set of individuals but about important populations. We collect information about attitudes, beliefs, values, and behaviors, it is essential to emphasize, to shed light on the social processes and conditions in society. In this case, we probe attitudes to understand the conflict and controversy over the fishing, hunting, and gathering rights of the Chippewa Indians of Wisconsin.

Attitudes themselves are not the end of our concerns. We are not interested in attitudes qua attitudes, nor do we simply conceptualize public opinion as a socially uprooted and unorganized "mass opinion." Much of the importance of such preferences derives from the influence they may have on individual behavior and, in particular, whether such attitudes achieve consequential political expression. Carefully conceptualized and designed studies have shown impressive correlations between attitudes and behaviors (Weigel and Newman 1976), including in the domain of interracial behaviors (Brannon et al. 1973; Jackman 1976; Sidanius and Pratto 1999). Among the more striking results in this vein has been clear and convincing evidence of a connection between individual racial attitudes and voting behavior (Kinder and Sears 1981; Sears, Citrin, and Kosterman 1987). In some districts, for example, school board members who favored desegregation involving busing were voted out of office and replaced by leaders of the local antibusing group (Sears and Allen 1984). Negative racial attitudes strongly influenced voting choices in Tom Bradley's first (unsuccessful) and second (successful) bids to be elected mayor of Los Angeles (Kinder and Sears 1981). Similar patterns were observed in his unsuccessful bid to become California's first black governor (Pettigrew and Alston 1988). The same dynamics have played out in many other political contests and contexts (Kaufman 1998).

A connection between the racial attitudes and the candidate choices of voters has been observed in many mayoral contests in which candidates of different races have run against one another (Pettigrew 1971). White candidates with clear ties to minority causes and interests run the risk of significant prejudice-based voting against them (Citrin, Green, and Sears 1990). National surveys continue to show at least 8 percent of the adult white population openly saying they would not vote for a qualified black presidential candidate nominated by their own party (Schuman et al. 1997). Indeed, even issues lacking manifest racial content, such as California's historic property tax reduction initiative (Prop. 13), appeared to elicit a real measure of prejudice-based voting (Sears and Citrin 1985). None of this is to suggest that prejudice is the bedrock of public opinion in the United States. Instead, it is now clear that, through the democratic electoral process, attitudes of prejudice, to the extent they are widely shared and become linked to important political choices, can powerfully influence outcomes of direct concern to the interests of members of minority groups.

Attitudes matter for more than referenda voting and candidate choices in elections. Several studies have found that racial attitudes also play a part in social movement participation (Begley and Alker 1982; Taylor 1986; Useem 1980). Taylor (1986) found a connection between racist attitudes and willingness to engage in antibusing protest actions in his Boston study. Summarizing the results of his analysis of the effects of racial attitudes and the willingness to engage in antibusing actions, he wrote: "For any of the measures considered [willingness to defy a court order, to boycott of public schools early in the process and late in the process], those who are racist and/or fearful of racial concentration are much more likely than those who are not to favor taking action against desegregation" (p. 59). Begley and

Alker's (1982) survey of white South Boston residents found that those who felt economic deprivation relative to blacks were much more likely to engage in antibusing confrontations with blacks. None of this is to equate opposition to race-targeted policies with racism, since other factors are also at work. These and other studies do show, however, that interethnic attitudes are consistent contributors to individual and collective behaviors in ethno-racial political disputes. Such a connection is especially likely where there is an organizational base for articulating grievances and mobilizing those with negative attitudes (Useem 1980; Walsh 1981).

Blumer's complaint against studies of "public opinion" goes astray in at least two other basic ways. His emphasis on elite opinion and behavior misses the obvious point, especially in a formally democratic social order, that political leaders are elected. Elected officials must, therefore, be concerned with monitoring and not falling too far out of step with the views of their constituents. To be sure, issues vary in their salience and intensity of feeling for individuals in a complex society. Individuals and groups differ, likewise, in the level of organization and resources they possess to bring their influence to bear. Nonetheless, one can hardly hope to comprehend the actions of influential decision makers in or outside of formal government structures without comprehending one of the most basic inputs to their thinking—namely, constituent opinion and preferences (Hutchings 2003). Indeed, to argue otherwise is not merely empirically dubious in the light of substantial evidence of leadership responsiveness to public expectations, it is to adopt an untenable, unidirectional, top-down model of modern political and social organization. The relation between public opinion and social outcomes is complex and mediated in basic ways by organizations and formal leadership structures, but this does not render public opinion sociologically unimportant.

Analyses of mass public opinion, therefore, are constituent elements of any full account of the sociology and politics of ethno-racial relations and conflict. Studies of attitudes can contribute to an understanding of the life course of a political issue, a fact nowhere more vividly shown than in the passage of major civil rights legislation. A comprehensive analysis of available survey data by Page and Shapiro (1992) showed that policy changes at the federal level often follow and are congruent with major shifts in public opinion. This is particularly true of civil rights issues. Burstein (1985) carried out a detailed and sophisticated examination of the part public sentiment played in the passage of equal employment opportunity

(EEO) legislation. He concluded that congressional support for EEO legislation "was strongly related to public attitudes about treatment of minorities and women in the labor force and to state adoption of EEO and equal pay laws; as attitudes about blacks, Jews, women, and other groups became more egalitarian and as more laws were passed, congressional support soon increased" (Burstein 1985, p. 66).

The full scope of our research aims to grasp and map the meanings that the issue of Indian treaty rights took on, the feelings and beliefs that grew up around the controversy, the behaviors and responses that it occasioned, and, above all else, the role that prejudice played in the Wisconsin treaty rights controversy. We hope to better understand the general processes at work when such controversies arise. We will achieve this by specifying the relevant attitudes and their dimensions and contours, as well as their social location, effects, and a host of other complexities, in this instance, of the apparent intrusion of prejudice into the politics of Chippewa treaty rights.

We offer a final reflection on Blumer's criticisms of survey-based social research and the concepts and devices usually contained in the survey researcher's "tool kit." In responding to Blumer's criticism of public opinion research, Theodore Newcomb commented that Blumer had attacked a highly caricatured view of the field. Newcomb's first reason for arguing that Blumer's critique had missed its mark was "that he was not quite selective enough in his aim. I wish he had not tried to direct his fire toward all the people who, to use his phrase, use polling as a device, all at once. The most conscientious of them differ so much from those who are less so that I can hardly think of what it is that they have in common" (Newcomb 1948, pp. 551–552). Julian Woodward (1948) in his response to Blumer identified four possible changes in the conduct of "polls" that, if made routinely, would greatly blunt the bite of Blumer's criticisms. These changes were to measure the intensity of opinion, to measure individuals' organizational and group memberships, to conduct fuller multivariate analyses of the connections between personal background factors, group memberships, and opinions, and to pursue a more direct concern with the impact of political leaders. A similar list of design and analysis requirements was outlined by the eminent survey researcher Paul Sheatsley (1983). We have taken both sets of directives to heart.

The design and content of the survey on which this book is based and the overall project involved a deliberate effort to capture the inherent complexity of the opinions under examination, as well as the sociohistorical roots of the controversy itself. To more completely contextualize this research, the survey, described in fuller detail later in the book, oversampled individuals living in areas where the controversial treaties have legal force and where the overt conflict was most intense. What is more, attitudes and opinions were not reduced to responses to a single, simplistic item or two. We adopted a multidimensional conceptualization of interethnic attitudes and sought to develop multi-item measures of key theoretical constructs derived from several different models. We routinely sought to understand the frames of reference that underlie attitudes by asking the people with whom we spoke to explain in their own words why they expressed a particular point of view. We sought, as well, to understand the personal salience and centrality of the treaty dispute to the people with whom we spoke. We also tested levels of knowledge regarding the treaty rights. We included in the surveys several measures of direct behavioral involvement in the treaty dispute.

As a result, we assess the contours, bases, and potential effects of public opinion on the treaty rights in what we hope is a fine-grained and nuanced manner. The analysis and interpretation of these rich data are embedded in a deep, though no doubt incomplete, appreciation of the long history of Indian-white relations and of the specific legal and political events attendant to the Wisconsin treaty dispute.

The greatest limitations on our work, about which we should be very direct, are twofold. First and foremost, we were not able to sample opinions among any significant number of American Indians, including the Chippewa themselves. This poses a serious theoretical and substantive problem for us—a problem that is difficult to overcome, since the Chippewa were also largely voiceless in the mainstream press, save for a small number of tribal leaders. It must be conceded that, in the main, our work is an analysis of whites' opinions and reactions. In this fashion our work carries on an unfortunate bias toward examining only the views of dominant group members.

Second, we did not survey mainstream political elites. Samuel Stouffer's classic public opinion study, *Communism, Conformity, and Civil Liberties* (1955), provided a powerful exemplar of how important it is to view mass public opinion in the light of elite thought and action. Fortunately, we do have much greater insight today through the mainstream media and other public records into how political elites responded to the treaty rights dispute. In addition, the survey contained questions about the assessment and evaluation of relevant political figures.

PLAN OF ANALYSIS

Chapter 1 develops the major theoretical models to be examined. In particular, it sketches in fuller detail our extension of the group position theory. Chapter 2 lays the historical, legal, and contemporary social foundation for the modern Wisconsin treaty rights controversy. In this chapter we discuss how whites' sense of group position vis-à-vis Native Americans has taken shape through time. Chapter 3 lays the groundwork for an examination of public opinion on the treaty dispute. Here we establish the general salience of the issue, the levels of information and knowledge, and the basic distribution of opinion in response to the treaty dispute. We also review the evidence on whether self-interest and classic models of prejudice help to explain views in the treaty rights dispute. Chapter 4 compares and then reassesses the viability of three theoretical models of why prejudice enters politics. We examine the empirical viability of the injustice frame, symbolic racism, and group position models. Chapter 5 examines political action in the treaty dispute. This includes mapping public responses to the antitreaty protests, how personally central or important the issue became in general, and the actual extent of involvement on the issue. In Chapter 6 we summarize the empirical results and draw out the full theoretical implications of our research.

Chapter 1

LINKING PREJUDICE AND POLITICS

Racial and ethnic conflict are often conspicuous features of the American political landscape. U.S. courts and policymakers at all levels of government, as well as the mass of ordinary American people, continue to grapple with matters of "racial politics." Modern controversies range from disputes over affirmative action, minority business set-asides, and political districts drawn to assure minority group representation, to English-language-only referenda, bilingualism, multiculturalism, and immigration policy. These issues have shown a remarkable capacity to generate intense emotions, seemingly endless litigation, social protest, and collective action efforts, as well as direct debate and action by elected officials. In short, political issues with a strong racial component seem endemic in the modern American experience.

Less conspicuous but no less important than these issues affecting the large African American, Asian American, and Latino populations are political disputes over the rights and prerogatives of Native Americans. In some states, battles are waged over water rights ("Two Arizona Tribes Plan to Sue U.S. over Water Rights," *Wall Street Journal*, January 8, 1982, p. 35; "Three Accused of Shooting Up Oregon Town; Water Dispute Cited," *New York Times*, December 21, 2001, p. 25). In other states the issues of mining and timber harvesting, whether on or off the reservation, have become divisive. Citizens and legislators in many states have had to address gambling facilities on reservation land ("Costly Fight Rages in California over Indian Gambling Measure," *New York Times*, October 13, 1998; "Veto of Indian Gambling Bill Overturned," *New York Times*, June 21, 1994). One of the most common modern disputes concerning American Indians revolves around access to and consumption of certain natural and wildlife resources, especially fishing and hunting rights ("Michigan Pact Resolves Battle over Limits on Indian Fishing," *Wisconsin State Journal,* August 8, 2000; "Minnesota Prepares for Walleye Spearing. They're Hoping to Avoid Conflict on the Lakes," *Wisconsin State Journal,* April 6, 1997).

Between 1974 and 1992 the state of Wisconsin was embroiled in controversy surrounding the off-reservation fishing, hunting, and gathering rights of the Chippewa Indians. Litigation surrounding the controversy, which pitted the "people of the State of Wisconsin" in the office of the state attorney general against the Chippewa, lasted nearly two decades and left a legacy of twelve key court decisions. A variety of social protest and organizing efforts sprang up in connection with the treaty rights dispute. Intense media coverage, at first in the upper part of Wisconsin where the treaties have legal force and later statewide as the intensity of the conflict escalated, spanned several years as well. The conflict became a matter of widespread and deeply felt concern for most of the people of Wisconsin. In no small part this issue became so divisive and drew such sustained attention and concern because it involved racial politics. It engaged fundamental ideas and expectations about who was entitled to what, with racial group identity and membership providing the significant dividing line. And in this instance, the rights of the minority racial group largely— though not entirely—prevailed over the claims, objections, and vigorous protests of members of the dominant racial group. The Wisconsin treaty rights controversy raised to prominence the possibility that prejudice was once again playing a heavy role in attempts to undermine the protection of minority group rights.

ON THE ROLE OF PUBLIC OPINION

This book, first and foremost, is a study of how prejudice enters public opinion and politics where issues of race relations are concerned. The contours of public opinion inevitably play a role in how ethno-racial controversies are framed, played out, and ultimately resolved. Public opinion can exert both indirect and direct effects on the outcome of racial political struggles. Indirectly, public opinion is one gauge of the social climate in which a minority group seeks to exercise its rights and improve its status and living conditions. If public opinion runs heavily against the claims and aspirations of a minority group, then there will likely be many different ways in which those claims face at least indifference, if not open rebuff and challenge. Courts and (especially) legislators also attend to prevailing public opinion. Court decisions that are radically out of step with public preferences run the risk of undermining the legitimacy and authority of the courts. Legislators who do not monitor and attend to constituents' preferences run the risk of offending those who hold the key to their reelection. And public opinion matters in one further indirect way: it can become a powerful "third party." Partisans on one side of an issue can heavily influence public dialogue and potential decision making if they can show that public opinion is on their side or decisively shifting in their favor.

The force of public opinion can also be felt in more direct fashion. Attitudes and issue preferences influence voting decisions. This is true both with campaigns for elective office and with more specialized referenda or ballot initiatives. Through these mechanisms, the weight of public opinion is manifest in who holds important elective offices and, on occasion, the direct passage of laws. For all of these reasons, studies of public opinion on matters of "racial politics" are now a small industry.

ON RACIALIZED POLITICS

By racial politics we mean those issues of public debate and controversy in which the rights, statuses, resources, and privileges of groups defined by racial or ethnic criteria are contested. This contestation may involve groups pressing claims on one another or, as is more often the case, it may directly engage formal governmental structures such as the courts, administrations, and legislative bodies. The key element is that the rights, statuses, resources, and privileges of racially or ethnically defined groups are a major component of the issue under debate.

In some instances the racial component may be explicit. This was certainly the case in the conflict over school busing for desegregation that was so much a part of the political scene in the 1970s. It was also true of the long-running debate over affirmative action in access to higher education and in the workplace, which rose to acute prominence in the 1990s. The same explicit character is seen in the intensifying debate over immigration policy today. The treaty rights dispute in Wisconsin is, likewise, a case of explicit, or manifest, racial politics. It involves legally valid and affirmed treaties between the Chippewa peoples and the United States government. It involves the contested rights, status, resources, and privileges of those identified as members of the Chippewa Indians as distinct from those not so identified.

There can be, we should note, significant matters of racial politics of a more implicit, latent, or hidden variety. In general such implicitness arises, in part, because the significance of ethno-racial group membership bleeds over into many other domains of life under a racially stratified social order. Hence, a great many important material as well as symbolic allocational decisions may implicate an ethno-racial hierarchy without invoking an explicit claim. Perhaps the most commonly recognized issue of this type concerns the debate over social welfare policy and provision. Both historically and in the present, a substantial element of the debate in the United States over the social welfare guarantees that government ought to provide concerns the types of resources to be made available to minority communities (Fox 2004; Lieberman 1998; O'Connor 2001; Quadagno 1994). Studies of public sentiment bear this out, revealing, for instance, that antiblack attitudes play a major role in white Americans' support for the welfare state (Bobo and Smith 1994; Gilens 1999). We take note of the possibility of implicit racial politics not merely for the sake of completeness but to underscore the point that once racial inequality is institutionalized, allocational decisions of both a material nature (such as affirmative action mandates or the exercise of off-reservation fishing, hunting, and gathering rights) and a symbolic one (establishing a national holiday honoring Dr. Martin Luther King or terminating the use of aspects of Indian culture as mascots and cheerleading devices for sports teams) are immediately rife with the potential to animate racial prejudice as a force shaping public opinion on the issue at hand.

THEORIES OF RACIALIZED POLITICS

Our purpose in this chapter is to review the existing theoretical perspectives on how and why racial prejudice enters into modern politics. Prior research has been dominated by four basic models: self-interest, race-neutral principles and the sense of injustice, orthodox prejudice and symbolic racism, and group position.

THE VIEW FROM SELF-INTEREST MODELS

The most common explanation for the appearance of ethno-racial antagonism in politics is simple self-interest. Those individuals with something tangible to lose as a result of social change are the most likely to become psychologically and behaviorally engaged in contesting efforts to enforce or enhance the rights and statuses of minority groups. By this logic, for example, those individuals whose workplace is directly touched by affirmative action mandates should be in the forefront of opposition to diversifying the workforce; those in low-wage, highly competitive sectors of the economy should most strongly recoil against lax immigration policies; and, in our case, those whose living standard and lifestyle might be materially affected by the Chippewa's off-reservation fishing, hunting, and gathering rights should take the most vigorous stand against the exercising of those rights.

One explanation for the negative reaction among many whites to the reassertion of Native American treaty rights has indeed hinged on such claims of an objective clash of interests. The argument holds, in one variant, that those individuals who are most at risk of tangible, material loss, such as small business owners involved in the tourism industry, are the most likely to object to ethno-racial change because it hurts their pocketbooks most directly. During the heyday of the Wisconsin controversy, angry accusations that the Chippewa were driving away tourists because they were taking all the fish for themselves were commonplace.

A second variant of the self-interest model includes objections to racial change on the basis of social class. The claim here is that, owing to an acute sense of scarcity and economic need, persistently marginal segments of the class hierarchy will be particularly ripe for expressing hostility to minority group advances. Those who are economically vulnerable because of low skill and education levels or few economic resources should, as an expression of their weak economic posture, express hostility to something like the treaty rights. Individuals strongly positioned in the economy, by virtue of skill or education levels or income, should be less inclined to see advancements for others as impinging on their own opportunities. This claim, too, has strong plausibility with respect to the treaty rights dispute. The area known as the North Woods of Wisconsin, where the dispute was rooted, is a less affluent part of the state, and economic grievances were frequently voiced against the Chippewa's pursuit of their rights (Satz 1991).

THE VIEW FROM RACE-NEUTRAL PRINCIPLES AND
SENSE-OF-INJUSTICE MODELS

A second type of explanation for racialized politics points to several principled or at least race- and ethnicity-neutral grounds for objecting to ethno-racial policy change. Three loosely interconnected approaches argue that whites' opposition to enforcing the rights or enhancing the status of minority groups and their members springs from a feeling of being treated unjustly: (1) pragmatic costs and burdens (McClendon 1985), (2) value contradictions (Sniderman and Carmines 1997; Sniderman and Piazza 1993), and (3) violations of notions of majority rule (Stinchcomb and Taylor 1980; Taylor 1986). The race-neutral case against change is often voiced in terms of the ostensibly pragmatic harm from enforcing minority group rights. For instance, a frequent argument against school busing for desegregation was that it wasted educational resources on student transportation that could have been used more effectively to improve educational quality. Similarly, one of the most frequent complaints against relatively open and flexible immigration policies has been the supposed drain on social programs and tax resources created by a heavy influx of new immigrants. The value contradictions claim holds that individuals rise or fall largely on the basis of their own efforts and talents. Thus social policies that interfere with this principle of meritocracy and equality before the law are likely to generate significant resistance and outrage.

In terms of the issue at hand, one of the primary grounds given for objecting to Chippewa treaty rights was a concern that local sportfishing tourism would be undermined if the Indians exercised their rights. Sports anglers would be turned away from fishing in the woods of northern Wisconsin if the Chippewa consumed a large fraction of the fish. Moreover, many charged that the Chippewa practice of spearfishing during the spawning season would permanently harm the underlying natural resource. Though neither charge was valid, these claims were common among publicly voiced objections to enforcing the treaty rights (Satz 1991; Strickland, Herzberg, and Owens 1990; U.S. Commission on Civil Rights 1989).

At the same time, the race-neutral case against minority group claims may reach beyond a narrow concern with pragmatic harms to include an assertion that cherished alternative principles and values may be violated. The most familiar argument of this kind, no doubt, is the charge that affirmative action policies violate the American ideals of individualism and meritocratic advancement. Among the putatively "principled" grounds for objecting to Chippewa treaty rights in Wisconsin was the concern that all individuals should be equal before the law. To wit, the recognition of treaty

rights applicable only to members of specific Native American tribes created pernicious group distinctions in the society.

THE VIEW FROM ORTHODOX PREJUDICE MODELS

A third set of explanations points to individuals' learned negative feelings
and beliefs as the fundamental force animating ethno-racial antagonism.
An immediately plausible account of whites' opposition to minority group
claims can be summed up in one word: *prejudice.* Traditional conceptions
of prejudice define it as involving negative feelings and beliefs about minority groups and their members, with these underlying orientations pre-
disposing the prejudiced person to engage in discriminatory behaviors
(Allport 1954; Pettigrew 1982; Simpson and Yinger 1985; Williams 1965).
Even a cursory review of media coverage and writing on the treaty dispute
provides grounds for expecting that prejudice classically understood—that
is, as involving hostile feelings and stereotyped perceptions—played some
part in the controversy. Facing protesters shouting anti-Indian epithets
and voicing the coarsest of stereotypes was common for the Chippewa
who attempted to exercise their rights (Satz 1991).

An important recent variant of the orthodox prejudice approach is the
symbolic racism model. David Sears and colleagues (see Sears 1988 for a
review) proposed the concept of "symbolic racism" to describe a qualitative change in the content of significant racial attitudes and to explain the
widespread resistance to black candidates for political office, school busing, and strong forms of affirmative action. Specifically, they argued that
such early learned, traditional American values as individualism and the
work ethic were increasingly becoming linked with early learned negative
feelings toward blacks. In the modern period, these racial attitudes have
formed a potent resentment of blacks that has found expression in discontent with blacks' level of welfare dependency and with other forms of "special" or "preferential" treatment and favoritism. These beliefs may relate to
or grow out of what symbolic racism proponents term "old-fashioned" bi-
ological and segregationist racism, but they are not so coarse.[1] And relative
to classical prejudice theory's concern with affect and stereotyping, the
concept of symbolic racism is held to be the more proximate and critical
determinant of major racial policy attitudes.

Furthermore, symbolic racist attitudes are based in early childhood socialization and sociocultural learning rather than in any tangible personal stake or group-based instrumental contingency. The main tests of the symbolic racism model attempted to pit symbolic racism against self-interest and realistic group-conflict models (Kinder and Sears 1981; McConahay 1982; Huddy and Sears 1995). The purpose of these tests was to show that opposition to school busing or to black candidates for political office rested in psychological predispositions, not in the material needs of individuals or realistic struggles for social resources between racial and ethnic groups.

The treaty rights dispute is well suited to a test of symbolic racism. American Indians are one of the minority groups that mainstream American culture has traditionally held in disdain. There are long-standing and widely accessible anti-Indian stereotypes in the culture, stereotypes disseminated through many means but especially through such popular media as Western movies, cartoons, and dime novels. When any new political issue surfaces that that involves American Indian people, according to prejudice theories, many whites will respond in terms of the underlying psychological predispositions they have toward Indians. Neither real, practical aspects of the issue nor concrete individual interests will play much of a role in shaping responses to new efforts to protect and enhance the rights of American Indians. Instead, the deeply rooted cultural stereotypes and antipathies that constitute anti-Indian prejudice will come to the fore and guide the political thinking and behavior of many whites.

THE VIEW FROM THE GROUP POSITION MODEL

We propose and seek to develop a fourth explanation for racialized politics, one that is inspired by Herbert Blumer's group position theory of prejudice. We develop the group position theory as a framework for effectively integrating the valuable contributions of the individual self-interest and orthodox prejudice models with a more sociological concern with the historical development of systems of racial inequality.

There is an intrinsically collective or group-based dimension to issues of racial politics. The inescapably group or collective nature of racial political controversies poses an immediate difficulty for the theoretical interpretations we have considered thus far. Interpreting racial controversies merely in terms of *individual* self-interest, *individual* values, or *individual* feelings of prejudice elides the intrinsically ethno-racial, supraindividual, and *relational* nature of issues that constitute "racial political controversies," whether the specific issue be affirmative action, immigration policy, or treaty rights. By the same token, attempting to reduce racial politics to class politics, while expressly concerned with economic groups in some specific historical social relation to one another, profoundly distorts the thoroughly and manifestly racialized character of the social group relationship in question.

In a five-page essay published in 1958 that has since become a classic, Herbert Blumer (1958a) criticized theories of prejudice that focused narrowly on individual feelings of like and dislike. He proposed that "prejudice" fundamentally inhered in a "sense of group position," with this sense of group position having indissoluble collective properties to it. Prejudice required the recognition and use of racial categories. Individuals had to place themselves and others into different categories. This differentiation of categories, perforce, established a relationship between members of the categories. Of necessity, ideas and feelings about racial groups have implications for appropriate relations between members of those categories. One could not have an idea or orientation to blacks in the United States, for example, without immediately invoking—at least implicitly—the comparison or connection with white Americans. As Blumer put it: "Fundamentally racial feelings point to and depend on a positional arrangement of racial groups" (Blumer 1958a, p. 4). The focus of theory and research should, therefore, be the collective process of defining racial groups and their statuses. This collective process ranges from, at the simplest level, individual interaction and discussion of what makes "them different from us" to, at a more significant and consequential level, the assertions and positions put forward by organized leadership or elite segments of ethnoracial groups who have access to the "public ear" and control of other power resources.

The group position model of racial prejudice, we suggest, effectively blends core ideas from orthodox prejudice models with a sociological understanding of group relations. The former, as emphasized above, directs attention to the social learning of negative feelings and beliefs about ethno-racial groups and their members. The latter directs attention to the historical development of group relations and to the collective or group interests that naturally flow from the institutionalization of a racially or ethnically stratified social order. Group position theory weds these perspectives by directing attention to a historically emergent and variable set of racialized identities, modes of social organization, group interests, and status expectations.

Group position theory shifts analytical attention away from processes internal to the individual while still recognizing that individual racial prejudice is a powerful social force. This approach stands in contradistinction to both the symbolic racism approach (Kinder and Sanders 1996; Sears 1988) and more conventional sociological models of ethnic antagonism (Bonacich 1972, 1973). The former attempts to develop a purely psychological and ideational account of racial politics. The latter typically seeks to reduce such conflict to purely objective, ultimately class-based material struggles. Both models, we believe, develop distorted analyses of racial conflict.

Blumer maintained that racial prejudice was best understood as a general attitude or orientation involving normative ideas about where one's own group should stand in the social order vis-à-vis an out-group. His main focus was on prejudice among members of a dominant group. We continue that emphasis here. It is worth noting, however, that the main concepts and dynamics identified by Blumer may be fruitfully applied to how members of a subordinate group may come to view members of a dominant group. These ideas may also be usefully applied to relations among and between nondominant groups in a multiethnic social setting (Bobo and Hutchings 1996; J. Lee 2002).

Under group position theory, then, dominant group outlooks exhibit four features. The first is a feeling of superiority on the part of dominant group members. The second is a belief that the subordinate group is intrinsically different and alien. The third involves a sense of proprietary claim over certain rights, statuses, and resources. The fourth involves a perception of threat from a subordinate group seen as harboring a desire for a greater share of dominant group prerogatives. Each feature requires some elaboration.

From our perspective, Blumer's discussion of feelings of superiority and beliefs that a subordinate group is alien and different is but a reformulation of readily familiar notions. These notions can be restated as the orthodox prejudice models' concern with intergroup affect or feelings and with negative stereotyping. The bedrock assumption of the group position model is that dominant group members must make an affectively important distinction between themselves and subordinate group members. This affective distinction is linked to ideas about the traits, capabilities, and likely behaviors of subordinate group members.

Yet such ethnocentrism and stereotyping fall well short of making prejudice a dynamic social and historical force. As Blumer explained: "The combination of these two feelings of superiority and of distinctiveness can easily give rise to feelings of aversion and even antipathy. But in themselves they do not form prejudice" (Blumer 1958a, p. 4). The dynamic factors in prejudice begin with the feeling of proprietary claim or first rights to scarce and socially valued goods and resources. A wide range of claims might be recognized in the sense of group position. This includes such relatively tangible claims as access to or control of land, property, jobs and businesses, political decision making, educational institutions, and recreational resources. But it also includes claims on such relatively intangible things as positions of prestige and access to "areas of intimacy and privacy" (p. 4). Thus the sense of group position is a very general orientation or broad-spectrum view on where the dominant group should stand *relative* to the subordinate group.

These feelings of proprietary claim or ideas about the rights, resources, and statuses dominant group members are duly entitled to enjoy come to have social effect when confronted with feelings of perceived threat. The sense of group position is most readily revealed and becomes consequential insofar as dominant group members believe that subordinate group members are encroaching on their rightful prerogatives. It is the conjunction of presumed prior access or claim and perception of threat to that claim that arouses the belief that a subordinate group is "getting out of place": "The dominant racial group construes the crossing of the line or preparations to cross the line as threats to its status, its power, and its livelihood. It thus develops fears, apprehensions, resentments, angers, and bitternesses which become fused into a general feeling of prejudice against the subordinate racial people or peoples" (Blumer 1955b, p. 13). Herein lies the intrinsically positional nature of racial prejudice. "The source of race prejudice," Blumer argued, "lies in a felt challenge to this sense of group position" (1958a, p. 5).

Several efforts to draw on the group position model exist in the research literature and merit consideration here. On the whole, these efforts have faced one of two limitations. First, previous research has been restricted to indirect tests of the core mechanisms of racial prejudice. Second, those studies not relying on indirect tests have typically been secondary analyses with less than ideal measures of core concepts (Fossett and Kiecolt 1989; Quillian 1996; Taylor 1998).

Responding to the same modern social trends observed by the symbolic racism researchers, several sociologists have attempted to apply and test a theory of group position. Wellman (1977) was the first to do so. He conducted in-depth interviews with selected white respondents from a larger survey of racial attitudes conducted in the San Francisco Bay Area. Although respondents generally espoused racially egalitarian ideals, Wellman found fairly uniform opposition to concrete policy changes that would improve the position of blacks relative to that of whites. He noted some generational and class-based differences in how this opposition was justified (for example, the working-class whites talked more in terms of self-interest, and middle-class whites talked more in terms of principles of individualism). Nonetheless, he concluded that both exhibited white racism in resisting blacks' demands for change and equality. The rationalization of the resistance, he found, involved "a culturally sanctioned, rational response to struggles over scarce resources" (Wellman 1977, p. 35). Such a response was most sensibly interpreted, Wellman argued, within Blumer's group position framework.

Some research springing more directly from survey analyses also drew on the group position model. Most of this work emphasizes the importance of group *proportions* in a hypothetical contact setting to the dominant group's willingness to enter such a setting. Smith (1981) conducted analyses of trends in whites' levels of support for desegregated schooling. Specifically, he analyzed a set of questions that asked whites about their willingness to send their children to a school where, first, a few of the children were black; second, where about half of the children were black; and, finally, where more than half of the children were black. He found that whites' openness to integration plummeted as the proportion of black children in the question increased. Moreover, the results showed that in the case of a majority black school, a white persons' level of education and the region of the country ceased to influence responses. These patterns, according to Smith, suggested a collective racial response to integration that was based on a shared sense of group position.

But the sense of group position involves more than styles of explaining opposition to policy change beneficial to minority groups, and it involves more than numerical dominance in contact situations. Both ways of testing group position theory are indirect. In the case of Wellman's in-depth interviews, one must infer perceptions of threat to a preferred group status or position. In the case of the studies arguing from numerical dominance, one must infer that lower proportional representation is understood as a loss of relative status on the important dimensions of concern.

With the exception of Wellman, none of this work attempts theoretical elaboration or specification of the group position model. There are three features of the group position theory that we believe should be more explicitly incorporated into the group position model. The first concerns the nature and effects of ethno-racial identities. The second concerns the role of affect and emotions in the sense of group position. And the third concerns the pivotal role of interests and interest groups in race relations.

First, we maintain that racial and ethnic identities are quasi-autonomous social forces, ranking with economic and other institutional dynamics in shaping human social organization. Blumer most effectively makes this point in his essay "Industrialization and Race Relations," published in 1965. After reviewing the core features of the process of industrialization and the presumed social effects thereof, he debunks one of the principle claims about the impact of industrialization made by mainstream economists and sociologists: namely, that it would inevitably erode the parochial and anachronistic effects of ethno-racial ties in ordering social life (see also Omi and Winant 1986; Stone 1985).

From our perspective, early modes of social organization constrain and condition the presumed rationalizing force of economic modernization. This is especially likely to occur where patterns of racial identity, belief, and social organization have been institutionalized. Indeed, accommodation to an established racial order may become economically rational under such conditions. As Blumer explained:

> Rational operation of industrial enterprises which are introduced into a racially ordered society may call for a deferential respect for the canons and sensitivities of that racial order. This observation is not a mere a priori speculation. It is supported by countless instances of such decisions in the case of industrial enterprises in the Southern region of the United States, in South Africa and in certain colonial areas. . . . It is a mistake, accordingly, to assume that the rational motif of industrialism signifies an automatic undermining of a racial order into which industrialism enters. To the contrary, the rational imperative in industrial operations may function to maintain and reinforce the established racial order. (Blumer 1965b, p. 233)

Blumer thus credited race with a powerful capacity to influence, shape, and condition the economic and class dynamics of a society. He did so, it must be emphasized, without denying the importance of economic and class dynamics (Blumer 1955b). Instead, he avoided the more conventional sociological error of reducing race to merely its economic manifestations. Racial and ethnic attachments and modes of social organization have social underpinnings that reach beyond the economic.[2]

Blumer expected that the existing racial order would be built into new or transforming economic institutions. Minorities would be excluded from important positions, locked into lower-level positions, or afforded only highly constrained mobility opportunities in a modern economic order. In part, he expected that those occupying key hiring and managerial ranks would act on the basis of their preexisting orientations or, at least, in response to pressure from workers and customers. This behavior would be greatly reinforced by other features of the institutionalized racial order, such as racially segregated communities, racially segregated friendship networks and spheres of informal interaction, and racially homogeneous family units.

At a minimum, from the racialized group position perspective, economic transformation could not alone undermine a racial order that had other social bases and so many other social manifestations. Only theories that reduced racial identities to an economic base could advance such a prediction. Such an analysis misunderstood the underpinnings both of ethno-racial identities and the dynamics of a racialized social order. Instead, a near opposite pattern should obtain where the racial order asserts itself within the economic sphere. Again, consider the claim that "the intrinsic structural requirements of industrialism need not, contrary to much *a priori* theorising, force a rearrangement of the relations set by the racial system. We have here, indeed, somewhat of a paradoxical situation in that while industrialization may alter greatly the social order, it may leave the racial system that is embedded in that order essentially intact" (Blumer 1965b, p. 234). Since ethno-racial attachments are not reducible to economic or material bases, there is neither a logical reason nor a historical basis for expecting otherwise profound economic transformations to fundamentally erode a racial order.

None of this, however, amounts to adopting a primordial or essentialist view of racial identities. Indeed, we reject such a claim in favor of a socially constructed view of racial identities. We recognize that systems of racial inequality can and often do undergo great change. But from the perspective of group position theory, change in a racial order springs from a direct assault on that racial order by largely noneconomic and political forces. "The evidence seems to me," Blumer wrote, "to lead overwhelmingly to the conclusion that such changes do not arise from inner considerations of industrial efficiency. Instead they arise from outside pressure, chiefly political pressures" (1965b, p. 247).

Such a political challenge to the racial order, to a widespread and deeply rooted collective sense of group position, is most likely to take shape "when the process of running definition does not keep abreast of major shifts in the social order" (Blumer 1958a, p. 7). The breakdown of what Blumer terms "running definition" most often occurs when social trends enhance the power resources under direct control of minority groups or important allies of minority groups, without encountering effective dispute and challenge from dominant group members. A lack of effective, ongoing protection for a privileged group position may have several sources. One cause Blumer recognized was an opaque or only dimly perceptible connection between some social trends and the long-term power balance between groups. A clear example of this would be the demographic shift of the black population from the South to non-South states and from rural to urban areas that resulted in blacks' greater financial resources, political influence, and leadership strength—a change in resources within the black community that provided the foundation for a sustained social protest movement (McAdam 1982; Morris 1984). A subordinate group's capacity to challenge the dominant group thus might greatly change and improve for reasons and in ways not readily apprehended as a threat to the existing racial order.

Likewise, a shift in the interests and needs of a major external party to a set of social relations may work in favor of a subordinated racial group. Two cases in point are the gradual but decisive change in the federal government's stake in the Jim Crow institutions of the American South in response to ideological struggles against communism during the cold war (Dudziak 2000; Franklin and Moss 1988; Sitkoff 1981) and the development of biracial unionism in the face of effective use of blacks as strike breakers (Wilson 1978). Bobo, Kluegel, and Smith (1997) provide just this sort of group position analysis of changes in whites' attitudes toward blacks in the United States.

In sum, the sense of group position, the psychological but collectively created and shared instantiation of a racialized social order, is a potent social force in its own right. It is reducible neither to the psychological attributes of individuals nor to some putatively more fundamental economic and material base. It is socially constructed and therefore variable across situations and over time. But it is also a key factor in shaping a person's sense of place and identity, and sense of right and wrong, within a social order. The sense of group position thus comes to guide thought and action in a fashion that intersects with and conditions the influence of other important social cleavages based on economics or class (or gender or age, for that matter), rather than simply yielding to such alternative bases of social differentiation and stratification.

The second feature of group position theory we wish to highlight and incorporate in our model is that ethno-racial attachments and the sense of group position have core nonrational or socioemotional elements. The theory of group position is sometimes discussed as though it were a purely instrumental argument about the nature of racial prejudice (Almaguer 1994; Giles and Evans 1986; Quillian 1995; Taylor 1998). The historical origins and tenacity of ethno-racial attachments cannot be accounted for in terms of purely rational and material forces. First and foremost, there is nothing natural or rational about the elemental fact of attachment to a particular set of socially constructed ethno-racial identities. It would be both incorrect and dangerous to regard such social categories as "Indian" or "white" as intrinsically meaningful. Nature did not create these distinctions, nor did it endow them with social significance. Nor did an institutional economic form such as slavery create sensitivity to skin color and cultural differences or to the black-white divide in the United States (Jordan 1968), though the slavery era profoundly affected it (Fredrickson 1971; Takaki 1979). There is a more complex human social and interpretative process at work, a process that involves both individual psychological factors and broader sociohistorical factors. The interplay of such forces has long been the foundational concern of sociological social psychology (House 1981; Kohn 1989; Turner 1988). Even once articulated and put into social practice, such categories are not forever fixed in meaning and import.

Blumer himself did not seriously explore or theorize about the emergence of basic ethno-racial categories or attachments. He did note that such identities take shape through a historical process and are decisively influenced by the initial terms and conditions of contact of different groups (Lieberson 1961). But the categories that come to assume significance—or, more important, why any particular ethno-racial marker or set of markers comes to powerfully shape human identity and expectations—were not the focus of Blumer's attention. Instead he focused on understanding how the sense of group position functions once a set of racial group relations had been largely institutionalized.

There are at least two other ways in which a purely objective and instrumental reading of group position theory goes astray. The sense of group position, first and centrally, is a *normative* construct. To wit:

> Sociologically it is not a mere reflection of the objective relations between racial groups. Rather it stands for "what ought to be" rather than for "what is." It is a sense of where the two racial groups *belong.* . . . In its own way, the sense of group position is a norm and imperative—indeed a very powerful one. It guides, incites, cows, and coerces. It should be borne in mind that this sense of group position stands for and involves a fundamental kind of group affiliation for the members of the dominant racial group. (Blumer 1958a, p. 5, emphasis in original)

This normative character of the sense of group position immediately separates it from a purely instrumental interpretation. The sense of group position is not merely a sort of descriptive codification of what is; it is also, and more important, a prescriptive view of the way things should be.

Second, the sense of group position functions along two important axes. One axis involves the more obvious dimension of domination and oppression, of hierarchical ordering and positioning. A second critical axis, however, involves a dimension of exclusion and inclusion, of socioemotional embrace or recoil. The exclusion and inclusion dimension, again, invokes the affective or emotional basis of the sense of group position. Blumer spoke directly, although briefly, to this point in his original essay. As noted above, he drew attention to aspects of the sense of proprietary claim that included "certain areas of intimacy and privacy" (Blumer 1958a, p. 4). He also expressly held that "on the social psychological side [the sense of group position] cannot be equated to a sense of social status as ordinarily conceived, for it refers not merely to vertical positioning but to many other lines of position independent of the vertical dimension" (p. 5).

Even Blumer's discussion of perceptions of threat identified an emotional component. He explained the nature of feelings of threat in the following way: "Race prejudice is a defensive reaction to such challenging of the sense of group position. It consists of the disturbed feelings, usually of marked hostility, that are thereby aroused. As such, race prejudice is a protective device. It functions, however, shortsightedly, to preserve the integrity and the position of the dominant group" (Blumer 1958a, p. 5). The theory expressly recognizes a concern with group integrity, not merely positional status. Challenges to this conception of where the dominant group should stand relative to the subordinate group are experienced as emotionally involving and upsetting.

Part of the point here is that restrictions imposed on a subordinate group reach beyond the conventional material-status dimensions defined by position within the economic and political order. Blumer made just this point most forcefully in "The Future of the Color Line" (1965a). In this essay he spoke directly to the exclusion-inclusion dimension of the sense of group position and applied it to an understanding of the substantial but delimited successes of the black civil rights movement. In large part, his message was that even profound change in some aspects or dimensions of a racial order, and the sense of group position surrounding it, may not erode other core aspects of the sense of group position.

In this essay Blumer defined "the color line" in a fashion that identified the American black-white divide as an important instance of the functioning of the sense of group position. Blumer suggested that the color line

> is a line which separates whites from Negroes, assigning to each a different position in the social order and attaching to each position a differential set of rights, privileges, and arenas of action. It defines the approach of each racial group to the other, it limits the degree of access to each other, and it outlines respective modes of conduct toward each other. The color line stems from a collective sense held by whites that Negroes as a racial group do not qualify for equal status, and that because of their racial difference Negroes have no claim to being accepted socially. Thus, the color line expresses and sustains the social position of the two groups along two fundamental dimensions—an axis of dominance and subordination, and an axis of inclusion and exclusion. (1965a, p. 322)

The color line, so understood, involved all of the elements incorporated into group position theory. It involved an abstract idea about groups in relation to one another. This abstract idea was a shared, collective sense of position, not merely individual feelings of like or dislike. The color line also had implications for many different domains of social interaction and experience. In sum, in Blumer's analysis, "the sense of group position is the central ingredient of the color line" (p. 323).

The color line, like the sense of group position, has many layers or levels. The levels of economic status and political status are themselves complex and multilayered. Thus, for example, the elimination of racial exclusion policies in access to employment would hardly mean that blacks would find an easy route to positions of high pay, authority, and prestige. More important, the economic and political dimensions of the racial order are not the only forms of restricted life chances facing African Americans, nor are they the sole factors undergirding racial prejudice as a social force.

Blumer said that for this reason the civil rights movement had failed to bring about a fundamental change in the color line. He argued that

> the area of civil rights constitutes only a part, even though a highly sig-nificant part, of the larger region from which the Negro has been barred by the color line. The contested area of civil rights is, as previously stated, but the outer band of the color line. Inside it lies the crucial area of eco-nomic subordination and opportunity restriction—an area of debar-ment of Negroes which is exceedingly tough because it is highly compli-cated by private and quasi-private property rights, managerial rights, and organizational rights. Still further inside the color line are the varied cir-cles of private associations from which the Negro is grossly excluded. Thus, the successful achievement of civil rights merely peels off, so to speak, the outer layer of the color line. (1965a, p. 350)

Reaching into the inner layers of the color line, those layers that involve feelings of exclusivity and the most intimate areas of private life, would first require profound success in peeling back the more public layers of the color line. Blumer was doubtful that this would happen. In particular, he saw grounds to expect ongoing racial strife and discord because of the emerging economic, political, and social isolation of many urban black communities. That is, he expected that the racial sense of group position would continue to assert itself. There had been only partial success in changing the color line in the political and economic spheres. How the color line affected the private spheres of community, friends, home, and family ties had not been touched at all.

In effect this points us to an "inner citadel of the color line." The inner citadel involves the exclusion-inclusion dimension of the sense of group position. This inner citadel is "a matter of personal attitude and thus falls inside the area of individual determination" (Blumer 1965a, p. 335). As such, it is unusually resistant to external pressure for change. The broad theoretically important gravamen of these elaborations on the normative character of the sense of group position, of the nature of perceived threat, and of the intersecting dimensions that define the sense of group position is that there is a powerful socioemotional component to the sense of group position; a component that cannot be regarded as rooted in objective, material, and clearly instrumental needs.

And third, having sketched the socioemotional component of the sense of group position, it must be stressed that there is at the same time a crucial instrumental character to racial prejudice. Once a set of racial inequalities has been institutionalized, there are meaningful interests that attach to such group positions in a hierarchical and deeply racially stratified social order. To acknowledge a strong socioemotional dimension to the sense of group position is by no means to mitigate or deny a central place for collective or racial group interests in the dynamics of prejudice, and recognition of this is a major factor distinguishing group position theory from orthodox prejudice theories.

On its face, the mere thesis of race prejudice as a sense of group position immediately invokes the imagery of hierarchy, inequality, and oppression. It calls to mind the differing statuses, positions, and interests constituted in a social order divided by race. Indeed, the emphasis on areas of felt proprietary claim and on perceptions of threat as the central features of racial prejudice, again, raise to a prominent place the stake or interest dominant group members have in a particular racial order.

Yet equally clear is the importance of the role of interests and of organized interest groups in shaping race relations. Such factors play a powerful role in the ongoing process of recreating and defending the sense of group position. Organized segments of ethno-racial groups with clear interests may act to influence public discourse and to influence significant political outcomes. As Blumer put it:

> Their self-interests may dictate the kind of position they wish the dominant racial group to enjoy. It may be a position which enables them to retain certain advantages, or even more to gain still greater advantages. Hence, they may be vigorous in seeking to manufacture events to attract public attention and to set lines of issue in such a way as to predetermine interpretations favorable to their interests. The role of strongly organized groups seeking to further special interest is usually central in the formation of collective images of abstract groups. (1958a, p. 6)

To be sure, the social dialogue that creates and sustains the collective sense of group position involves abstract collective notions; takes shape in the sphere of broad public discourse, especially around highly salient "big events" that capture mass attention; and is disproportionately shaped by the articulated views of elite social actors. Yet this discourse about and emergent sense of group position is nonetheless intimately wedded to the interests and actions of interest groups with an instrumental stake in the racial order.

This thread of concern with interest and power can be easily missed, however, because Blumer accorded it separate and sustained discussion only briefly. Aside from his discussion of the sources of pressure for change in the sense of group position that we noted above, he was most explicit about the central role that should be given to matters of interests and power in a 1958 review essay. After critiquing most of the available research on race relations and finding the social-psychological research especially wanting, Blumer sketched out what he called the "elements of a new theoretical framework." This new framework has three core features of relevance to us. First, Blumer insisted on a focus on actual behavior of groups in contact with one another. Second, he identified two levels or domains of interaction between groups. Contact could, of course, involve immediate or direct face-to-face encounters between members of different racial and ethnic groups. And contact could also take an indirect form in which most of the interaction involves elite segments of racial/ethnic groups (such as when the NAACP lobbies Congress for legislation). Third, he called for careful analysis of the configuration of interests and organized power or control resources in studying any situation of racial/ethnic group relations. As Blumer argued:

> A deeper and more realistic analysis of the "situation" would move along the line of isolating the structure of interests and the structure of control in the situation. Studies of the structure of interests would seek to identify the relevant people of the racial groups who have interests in the situation, and in learning what these interests are—which individuals, associations, and institutions have interests in maintaining the relationship, which are indifferent to it, and which have interests which incline them towards a change in the relationship—where such individuals, associations, and institutions are placed in relation to each other; and what their respective positions of power or strategic advantage are. (1958b, p. 437)

Paying attention to matters of interests and power serves to better identify the sustaining conditions of racial group relations. "A study of the sustaining conditions in terms of how they function," Blumer suggested, "must necessarily deal with such matters as vested interests, entrenched power, the inertia of institutions, the use of social codes, devices of intimidation, an established opportunity structure, and the responsiveness of office-holders and decision-makers" (p. 437).

In this respect, the sense of group position involves significant elements of a "realistic group conflict" theory (LeVine and Campbell 1971). The theory is expressly concerned with (1) groups who occupy unequal positions in a social order and the interests that attach to those positions, (2) perceived threats to groups' interests, and (3) resulting meaningful struggles over access to various material and symbolic resources. It is instructive to note that many other students of intergroup attitudes and conflict would concur in this understanding of realistic conflict. For instance, Henri Tajfel argued: "The conflict for the scarce resources of rank, status, prestige, or winning a contest is 'realistic' when it is institutionalized, i.e., when it is explicitly defined as a contest or determined as such by the norms of the situation" (Tajfel 1982, p. 12). This is a view shared by distinguished sociologist Robin M. Williams, Jr. (1965), and, to an important degree, by Gordon Allport as well. To borrow Allport's own phrase: "All we are saying here is that clashes of interest and values do occur, and that these conflicts are not in themselves instances of prejudice" (1954, p. 229).

The subtle and more significant point, however, is that the melding of group identity, affect, and interests in most real-world situations of racial stratification make the now conventional dichotomous opposition of "realistic group conflict versus prejudice"—or, in Brubaker's terms, "instrumentalist versus identitarian" approaches—empirically nonsensical (Brubaker 1998). From the group position perspective, both elements are present, as Eliot Smith has stressed in his important work (E. Smith 1993; Smith and Ho 2002). Likewise, Allport, the premier prejudice theorist, maintained that most instances of intergroup conflict will likely involve elements of both affect and interests, of feelings and reason. Thus the current habit of pitting realistic group conflict theory against prejudice as mutually exclusive accounts of modern racial politics is, upon close inspection, distressingly and distortingly simplistic (see Bobo 1988a). As Allport maintained, "Realistic conflict is like a note on an organ. It sets all prejudices that are attuned to it into simultaneous vibration. The listener can scarcely distinguish the pure note from the surrounding jangle" (1954, p. 233). In many concrete group conflict situations, the social context is defined by the presence of both affect-laden identities and orientations *and* sharply unequal positions and interests defined along those group boundaries. We will show in the next several chapters that the same intermingling of forces is at work in the Wisconsin treaty rights controversy.

CONCLUSIONS

Taken as whole, then, we believe that our formulation of group position theory is the only model of prejudice as a social force that integrates concerns with group identity and attachment, negative stereotyping, and group interests and competing claims to significant social resources that operate in a racially stratified social order. It is the only model that effectively links the individual psychological aspects of prejudice to the historical and collective dimensions of prejudice. It is the only model that effectively links the unreasoning and emotional dimensions of prejudice with the resoundingly instrumental and interest-based dimensions of prejudice. The empirical analyses reported in the subsequent chapters of this volume make a convincing case for this interpretation.

We put these several theories, including the group position model, to the test using a statewide telephone survey conducted in the state of Wisconsin. The Chippewa Indian Treaty Rights Survey (CITRS) was conducted by the Letters and Science Survey Center at the University of Wisconsin, Madison. The field period for the study lasted from July 23, 1990, to October 1, 1990. The sample was made up of two components, a statewide element and an element drawn from the nineteen counties that fall entirely or largely within the territory covered by the Chippewa treaties.[3] The length of the interview averaged twenty-eight minutes, and the survey yielded 784 completed interviews, with an unadjusted response rate of 61.1 percent. The sample characteristics closely parallel data from the 1990 U.S. Census.

We wish to emphasize at this point the extent to which the survey involved a broad-gauge examination of public opinion on the treaty rights dispute. Table 1.1 displays information on the number of survey items used to tap a range of constructs—and the chapters in which we will discuss those specific results—that are important to a complete understanding of popular engagement with and responses to the treaty issue. As should be immediately obvious, the Chippewa Indian Treaty Rights Survey goes well beyond a narrow and simplistic assessment of issue attitudes.

TABLE 1.1   Selected summary of Chippewa Indian Treaty Rights
            Survey characteristics

Total sample size	$N = 784$	
Treaty county	$N = 345$	
Nontreaty county	$N = 439$	
White, non-Hispanic respondents	$N = 714$	
Average length of interview	28 minutes	
Response rate	61.1%	

Topical coverage	*Number of items*	*Chapter*
Salience items	2	3
Issue knowledge	3	3
Treaty rights issue attitudes	3	3
Anti-Indian affect	1	3
Anti-Indian stereotypes	3	3
Self-interest	2	3
Injustice frame	4	4
Symbolic racism	4	4
Group competition	3	4
Perceived political threat	3	4
Issue importance	2	5
Behavior involvement	4	5
Open-ended probes	3	3, 4

Systematic attention is paid to issue salience, knowledge, and self-interest. There are multiple item measures of key concepts from each theoretical account of racial policy views, ranging from the classical prejudice-theory concern with affect and stereotyping to the injustice frame, symbolic racism, and group position (that is, group competition and perceived political threat) models. In addition, the survey contains a number of behavioral measures of actual involvement in the treaty dispute and three strategically placed open-ended questions designed to give us fuller access to the frames of reference of respondents when analyzing answers to key questions.[4] (Certain survey questions discussed in the following chapters appear in Appendix A.)

This extensive coverage in the survey itself reflects our effort to fully ground and richly detail our analysis of the racial politics of the treaty rights dispute. Our examination of core attitudes in the treaty dispute begins in Chapter 3. Before turning to those empirical results and our tests of competing theories, it is essential that we properly situate and frame our work by developing a basic sense of the history of white–Native American relations in general, and of the Wisconsin treaty dispute specifically. Chapter 2 provides this historical foundation.

Chapter 2

RETURN OF THE CHIPPEWA:
FOUNDATIONS OF THE TREATY RIGHTS CONTROVERSY

In March of 1974, Fred and Mike Tribble, members of the Lac Courte Oreilles Chippewa band, challenged Wisconsin State Department of Natural Resources prohibitions against off-reservation fishing and were subsequently arrested by state game wardens. This led the tribe to bring suit in 1975 to affirm its fishing, hunting, and gathering rights, which were guaranteed under earlier treaties with the U.S. government. There had been three key treaty agreements. In agreements made in 1837 and 1842, the Chippewa sold large landholdings (14.33 million acres) in Wisconsin, Michigan, and Minnesota to the U.S. government. The 1854 Treaty of La Pointe established the current reservation areas. As part of these treaties, the Chippewa bands retained the right to fish, hunt, and gather in the ceded territory.

The Chippewa Indians initially lost their suit against the state of Wisconsin. In 1978 federal judge James Doyle sided with the state, concluding that the tribes had lost their off-reservation rights when they accepted the reservations. What became an eight-year court battle effectively came to an end, however, on January 25, 1983, when a federal appeals court in Chicago reversed Judge Doyle's ruling and instructed him to define and uphold the Chippewa treaty rights. This decision was affirmed by the U.S. Supreme Court's refusal to hear the case. A series of rulings have subsequently reaffirmed the basic treaty rights of the Chippewa but also delimited their scope.

The Chippewa treaty rights controversy erupted largely in response to these rulings. Wisconsin residents opposed to the recognition of treaty rights clashed head-on with the Chippewa and their supporters, resulting in ugly confrontations involving taunts and racial epithets; the throwing of rocks, beer cans, and bottles; and fistfights and shoving matches. During the height of the controversy, great concern was expressed by both sides that if tensions did not subside, someone would be injured or even killed. Less confrontational forms of protest, such as petition drives to pressure Congress to modify or rescind treaties ("PARR Circulating Petition Urging Change in Treaty Rights," *Lakeland Times*, April 27, 1988, p. 24), as well as recall efforts to unseat politicians perceived to be sympathetic or "soft" on the issue of treaty rights, were also pursued ("Anti-Treaty Group Vows Obey Recall Campaign," *Capital Times*, March 12, 1990, p. 23; "Treaties' Foes Fight Holperin," *Wisconsin State Journal*, April 7, 1990, p. 1).

The Chippewa's demand to exercise their traditional and preserved fishing, hunting, and gathering rights was not a spontaneous grab for resources. By the same token, the controversy that arose in the wake of court rulings upholding those rights was no mere atomistic spasm of reaction. Both events emerged from the long and vexed history of intense conflict and mistrust that has characterized Indian-white relations. It is not possible, then, to develop a sociological understanding of the Wisconsin treaty rights controversy in the absence of a fuller historical account of Native American relations with the dominant white society.

Such a historical backdrop is also a necessary component of our theoretical concern with prejudice as a sense of group position. The sense of group position is shaped in important ways by the initial terms of contact between groups. As Lieberson and others have argued, the patterns of interaction, power, status, and identity established early on in a set of group relations can exert long-lasting force as those relations unfold through time (Lieberson 1961; Stone 1985). The initial terms of contact influence how group relations are played out and reconstituted in each new era. Although we do not attempt to present a primary or detailed history here, it is essential to our argument about group position that the historical development of Indian-white relations in general, and the situation of the Chippewa in particular, be brought into clearer relief. From our perspective, the ultimate wellsprings of modern attitudes toward Native Americans and responses to their demands to exercise their treaty rights reside in the historical pattern of relations and the sense of group position among white Americans, created over the course of Indian-white interactions.

Our first task in this chapter is to provide a broad overview of the Native American experience. As will be clear, Native Americans since this country's inception have played the role of the proverbial "thorn" in white America's side, first as obstacles to its grand expansion plans into the New World, and more recently as troublemakers intent on reclaiming rights guaranteed to them in "antiquated" treaties (Cornell 1988; Jorgensen 1978). A second but critical task is to trace the development of Native American stereotypes. The evolution of these stereotypes is a major part of the story of whites' changing sense of group position relative to Native Americans. And the stereotypes serve an instrumental function in justifying behavior toward Native Americans. Our third task is to review the immediate legal history of Chippewa treaty rights and the emergence of the Wisconsin controversy. At its core, the dispute has raised questions concerning what America owes, if anything, to the descendants of the native people who first inhabited this country, and whether those inhabitants merely "occupied" it or held some deeper claim to the land on which their forebears once resided.

HISTORICAL CONTOURS OF THE NATIVE AMERICAN EXPERIENCE

Relations between Indian peoples and white settlers, and later the U.S. government, have a complex history (Cornell 1988). While this history includes trade agreements, military alliances, and cooperative efforts, until the modern period the predominant tenor of U.S. policy toward Indians derived, by and large, from the barrel of a gun. As Enloe (1985, p. 81) has aptly stated: "Before 1849, it was the Department of the Army that had prime state responsibility" for Indian affairs. Given this fact, it is not surprising that such terms as conquest, oppression, and near-genocide have frequently been used to describe the Indian experience in the Americas (Steinberg 1989).

We have roughly divided the history of Indian-white relations in the United States into six partially overlapping periods or epochs: (1) fur trading; (2) land dispossession and Indian removal to reservations; (3) assimilation; (4) the Indian New Deal; (5) termination of federal responsibility; and (6) self-determination. Each period involves a characteristic mode of economic and political interaction between Indians and whites. Each period also brings different patterns of whites' beliefs about Indian peoples to the fore.

THE FUR TRADE AND AMERICAN INDIANS (MID-1500S THROUGH LATE 1700S)

Early on in their relations with white Americans, Native Americans enjoyed a modest degree of political and economic leverage over white settlers, owing to their pivotal role in the fur-trading business (Cornell 1988; Prucha 1984). The native people, for a short time, were instrumental in supplying a valued commodity in Europe, animal furs, thanks to their expert hunting skills and familiarity with the terrain. Nations such as England, Spain, France, and Russia heavily relied on Native Americans as the primary suppliers of beaver, fox, and other animal pelts so valued throughout Europe (Gibson 1976; Jennings 1975; Moloney 1967). Fur trading became a important arena in which European powers battled for economic and political control of the New World (Cornell 1988; Prucha 1984). Native Americans were viewed by competing European nations as necessary and valued allies in their quest for dominance.

Initially, tribal leaders were successful in limiting the degree of interaction between white traders and tribal members. Their concerns were grounded in fears of the incompatibility between what Vizenor (1972, p. 23) has called the "intuitive rhythms of the woodland life" and the profit-driven exploits of early European traders and settlers. It was well known among Indian as well as white leaders that the fur trade attracted unscrupulous frontiersmen who had no qualms about "debauch[ing] the Indian with liquor in order to cheat him out of his furs" (Prucha 1984, p. 21). Indian demand for and reliance on European products grew rapidly, however, and as the procurement of animal pelts came to dominate more and more of their daily routines, traditional activities such as plant cultivation and agriculture, as well as the production of traditional tools and handicrafts, were neglected (Vizenor 1984). Gradually the traditional routines and activities of the various tribes were undermined, thus moving them into a precarious relation of dependence with their white trading partners (Jennings 1975). This shift was instrumental in intensifying as well as institutionalizing a new pattern of Indian-white relations.

DISPOSSESSION OF AMERICAN INDIAN LANDS
(LATE 1700S THROUGH LATE 1800S)

By the close of the fur-trading period, Indian-white relations were characterized by widespread aggression and conflict as white Americans set their sights on Native American landholdings. As the westward expansion gained momentum, land became the most coveted prize to be acquired in the New World by white settlers and the European nations they represented. But as Nash (1974, p. 40) points out, the native people already inhabiting the New World posed a serious dilemma: "For Englishmen, as for other Europeans, the Indians' occupation of the land presented problems of law, morality, and practicality." For a brief period, Indians and colonists coexisted as uneasy neighbors, each wary of the other. Ultimately, however, this arrangement proved untenable as the colonists' insatiable demand for more and more land grew.

Some tribes voluntarily sold their land for a negotiated price. More often, however, a variety of less straightforward methods were used to take possession of Indian land. According to Jennings (1975, pp. 144–145) this included such practices as

> [allowing] livestock to roam into an Indian's crops until he despaired and removed. Even when the Indian uncharacteristically fenced his cropland, he found that there was something nocturnally mysterious that did not love an Indian's wall. The Indian who dared to kill an Englishman's marauding animals was promptly hauled into a hostile court. A second method was for Englishmen to get the Indian drunk and have him sign a deed that he could not read. A third method was to recognize a claim by a corrupt Indian who was not the legitimate landlord and then to "buy" the land from him. A fourth method, highly reminiscent of feudal Europe, was a simple threat of violence . . . A fifth method, which seems to have been a favorite in New England, was the imposition of fines for a wide variety of offenses, the Indian's lands becoming forfeit if the fines were not paid by their due date. The offenses ranged from unauthorized riding of an Englishman's horses to conspiracy against English rule.

As it became clear that the tribes had no intention of giving up their ancestral lands, conflict and tension became the dominant themes in Indian-white interactions (Deloria and Lytle 1983). Land acquisition, after all, was absolutely essential to the development of such key early American industries as cotton production in the South (Cornell 1988). Hostilities against Native Americans were typically triggered for instrumental reasons and rationalized on the grounds of the greater societal good of transforming the "wilderness into an agrarian society" (Takaki 1979, p. 103). White Americans' overarching concern with gaining access to Indian resources, then, played a pivotal role in shaping their attitudes and actions toward Native Americans. If Indians were acquiescent, white attitudes were favorable or benign. Resistance, however, resulted in a negative turn in attitudes and accompanying hostile treatment.

Native Americans experienced moments of success in temporarily halting the movement of settlers westward. Ultimately, however, they were unable to match the firepower and numbers of the white settlers, who came to see it as their God-sanctioned destiny to dominate, populate, and govern the New World (Horsman 1981). By the close of the nineteenth century the native population had dropped from what had been several million in 1492 to fewer than 300,000—a reduction of more than 90 percent in 400 years (Thornton 1987). Decimation through warfare, disease, and starvation gradually reduced the myriad tribes to essentially a totally conquered people who had no choice but to relinquish their collective landholdings (Jorgensen 1978).

Land transfers were most commonly executed through the signing of treaties between individual tribes and the federal government. Through these treaties, the U.S. government successfully appropriated Indian lands for use by railroad barons, industrialists, entrepreneurs, and homesteaders (Jorgensen 1978). But given the unequal power relationship, native people had little ability to influence treaty negotiations: "The actual document was always written in English and was generally interpreted by people who had a stake in a successful outcome of the proceedings, so the Indians were not always told the truth during these sessions" (Deloria and Lytle 1983, p. 5). In total, land transfers negotiated through treaties reduced the estimated 2 billion acres under Native American control prior to their first contact with Europeans to approximately 140 million acres (Jorgensen 1978).

Throughout this period in Indian-white relations, each side remained wary of the other. While the whites justified their suspicions by attesting to the "deceitful" and "treacherous" nature of the Indian character (Berkhofer 1978; Takaki 1979), native people actually had greater reason to distrust the "forked tongue" of the white man, given his record of broken promises and agreements. The following excerpt from a speech made by Canassatego, a representative of the Six Nations Iroquois Confederation, reveals the sense of resignation tribal leaders often felt during treaty negotiations:

We received from the Proprietors Yesterday, some Goods in consideration of our Release of the Lands on the West-side of Sasquehannah . . . We know our Lands are now become more valuable: The White People think we do not know their Value; but we are sensible that the Land is everlasting, and the few Goods we receive for it are soon worn out and gone . . . It is customary with us to make a Present of Skins, whenever we renew our Treaties. We are ashamed to offer our Brethren so few, but your Horses and Cows have eat the Grass our Deer used to feed on. This had made them scarce, and will, we hope, plead in Excuse for our not bringing a larger Quantity. If we could have spared more, we would have given more; but we are really poor; and we desire you'll not consider the Quantity. But few as they are, accept them in Testimony of our Regard. (Armstrong 1971, pp. 14–15)

In short, Native Americans stood to lose the most in the treaty negotiations. They were at a loss, however, to strengthen their bargaining position, owing to their diminishing economic and political influence in shaping Indian-white relations.

Thousands of white settlers and entrepreneurs poured into the western frontier in response to the federal government's successful acquisition of Indian land. Frontier communities quickly developed in response to the opportunities emerging with westward expansion and growth. Native Americans, meanwhile, were left with shrinking options: either assimilation to the ways and lifestyles of the white settlers, or removal to government-created and sponsored reservations.

President Andrew Jackson and other American leaders were initially hopeful that Indians who chose to remain together in their tribes would voluntarily relocate across the Mississippi. As it became clear that this would not be the case, Congress introduced the Indian Removal Act of 1830. In no uncertain terms, the bill made it clear that native people would have to make way for white settlers and relocate, by force if necessary. For the federal government, relocation was the perfect solution to the "Indian problem." Indian resistance to assimilation was widespread among the various tribes. Furthermore, assimilation at the tribal level took too long and required more money than the federal government was willing to appropriate. Removal simultaneously allowed the government to delay addressing the "Indian problem" while also "buying time" for assimilation to occur.

The removal process was devastating for the tribes. Leaving their ancestral homelands deeply scarred the Indians' feelings of self-worth and sense of honor (Deloria and Lytle 1983). Particularly for those weakened by sickness and old age, the actual journey to territories with unfamiliar climates and terrain was extremely difficult; many did not survive. By 1880, however, Indians who had chosen to remain with their tribes had moved onto federally defined reservations or onto parcels now called reservations, carved out of their original landholdings (Jorgensen 1978).

Ultimately, as Deloria and Lytle (1983, p. 7) argue, "the relocation of eastern Indians to reservations in the west did not solve the problem of Indian-white relations; it merely postponed it." Contrary to the expectations of federal officials, reservation life did not hasten assimilation for American Indians. Rather, their isolation from white settlers promoted and preserved distinct identities. Furthermore, reservations reinforced what Jorgensen (1978) has referred to as a relation of "domestic dependency," since they lacked self-governance and control of their own resources, and were unable to provide viable or long-term work opportunities for community members.

With passage of the Appropriation Act in 1871, treaty negotiations were brought to a close. The act read, in part: "Hereafter no Indian nation or tribe within the territory of the United States shall be acknowledged or recognized as an independent nation, tribe, or power with whom the United States may contract by treaty" (quoted in Cornell 1988, p. 49). Passage of the act was motivated less by an active desire to limit Native American sovereignty (which had already been severely curtailed by earlier treaties and agreements) than to resolve long-running arguments between the Senate and House of Representatives over the issue of which branch of the federal government held the authority to negotiate treaties. Irrespective of its original intentions, however, the Appropriation Act stands as a telling symbol of how Native Americans came to be phased out of the decision-making process in matters concerning their own lives. The act brings into clear relief their descent into nearly complete political powerlessness in dealing with the federal government; decisions were now to be made for Native Americans rather than by Native Americans.

ASSIMILATION PERIOD (LATE 1880S THROUGH THE LATE 1920S)

The federal government's policy of removing Native Americans to reservations was abandoned by the 1880s in favor of hastening their assimilation into the economic and social mainstream. The General Allotment Act (GAA) of 1887, also known as the Dawes Act, put into practice a renewed emphasis on Indian incorporation into American ways and lifestyles. In describing the GAA, President Theodore Roosevelt referred to it as "a mighty, pulverizing engine to break up the tribal mass" (quoted in White

1990, p. 3). Transforming American Indians into landowning farmers and, by extension, petty capitalists was seen as key to their assimilation and to ending the federal government's responsibility to them (Jorgensen 1978). Toward this end, tribal members received allotments of land formerly held in collectivity by the reservation. Supporters of the GAA were confident that American Indians, by cultivating their parcels, would join the ranks of America's farmers and crop growers in no time.

Once again reality did not align with aspirations, as federal interference actually left the tribes much worse off. The assigning of plots ill-suited for farming and the failure to provide sufficient financial assistance for buying tools, seeds, and livestock, coupled with a declining agricultural industry, ultimately doomed the GAA's stated mission of Indian assimilation. At the same time, however, the GAA proved highly useful for the interests of mining, timber, and agricultural production (Jorgensen 1978), since any remaining reservation land was made available for sale to white settlers and businessmen. According to Deloria and Lytle (1983, p. 10), "Indian landholdings were reduced from 138 million acres in 1887 to 48 million in 1934. Of this 48 million acres, nearly 20 million were desert or semiarid and virtually useless for any kind of annual farming ventures." Additional Indian landholdings were lost as a result of "debt, fraud, and deception or as a result of legislative alterations that facilitated individual sales" (Cornell 1988, p. 45). Rather than hastening assimilation, federal policy during this period furthered dependency and disempowerment for many Native Americans.

THE INDIAN NEW DEAL (LATE 1930S THROUGH MID-1940S)

The failure of the GAA to bring about Indian assimilation and self-reliance was made painfully clear by the harsh conditions that characterized reservation life by the early 1900s (Deloria and Lytle 1983). According to the Meriam Report, a survey commissioned by the secretary of the interior in 1928 to assess the social and economic status of American Indians, their quality of life had deteriorated precipitously. Widespread poverty, inadequate housing, poor health, and substandard levels of schooling were the norm. The report, conducted by the Institute for Government Research, harshly criticized the federal government for not providing enough guidance and financial support for implementation of the GAA and thus ensuring its failure. The report stated:

When the government adopted the policy of individual ownership of the land on the reservations, the expectation was that the Indians would become farmers. Part of this plan was to instruct and aid them in agriculture, but this vital part was not pressed with vigor and intelligence. It almost seems as if the government assumed that some magic in individual ownership of property would in itself prove an educational civilizing factor, but unfortunately this policy has for the most part operated in the opposite direction. (Meriam Report, p. 8, quoted in Deloria and Lytle 1983, pp. 12–13)

In response, the federal government launched a series of progressive programs, designed to improve conditions on the reservations, that came to be known as the Indian New Deal. These programs mirrored the larger New Deal policies being implemented nationwide under President Franklin D. Roosevelt's administration and included numerous infrastructure projects that generated work for tribal members. Passage of the Indian Reorganization Act (IRA) in 1934 formally curtailed the GAA allotment policy. Taking its place was a new policy advocating greater Indian autonomy and headed by such progressive thinkers as John Collier, who, as commissioner of Indian affairs, led many efforts for Indian community revitalization.

In many respects, passage of the IRA signified a major and radical change in U.S. policy toward Native Americans. In contrast to the GAA, which undermined tribal authority by dealing directly with individuals, the IRA sought to strengthen tribal governments (O'Brien 1989). Tribal governments were now formally recognized as well as modestly supported through a provision of a revolving credit fund from which loans could be made for tribal economic growth and development (Cornell 1988; Deloria and Lytle 1983; Tyler 1973). Furthermore, the IRA "authorized the return to tribal ownership of lands withdrawn for entry by homesteaders but never entered, and authorized the secretary of the interior to acquire additional lands for the tribes with funds provided for that purpose" (Cornell 1988, p. 92). Tribes were actively encouraged to adopt a corporate model for reservation governance, with elected tribal councils as board members to oversee all operations.

In other respects, however, the IRA was completely in keeping with Congress's practice of top-down governance and habit of determining for Native Americans what was in their best interests. Since the federal government now deemed Indian self-determination as a worthwhile policy, tribes were allowed and encouraged to form tribal governments. But how self-determining could these tribal governments actually be if they first required federal approval? In short, the significant extent to which the federal government kept an active hand in overseeing tribal self-determination indicated its fragility and vulnerability to changes in federal sentiment.

Ultimately the IRA put little real power in the hands of the tribes. While allowing them the opportunity to form tribal governments and holding out the possibility of greater tribal control over resources and cultural life, the IRA did not provide leaders with the authority to implement changes not sanctioned by the federal government. They were expected to follow the Western style of democratic governance instead of traditional models of tribal authority. For this reason as well as others, support for the IRA among the various tribes was mixed (Jorgensen 1978; Deloria and Lytle 1983). Some tribes refused outright to adopt the IRA, seeing it as the intrusion of an alien form of government (O'Brien 1989). Others had already adjusted to the dictates of the GAA and become accustomed to the notion of individual ownership. They saw the IRA as a return to communal and tribal life and therefore as a step backward.

While well intentioned, the IRA inadvertently contributed to greater confusion and in-fighting among many tribes and infused further distrust in Indian-white relations. Given the history of chicanery and broken promises on the part of the federal government, many American Indians, most notably the Navajo, were understandably skeptical and suspicious of the IRA and the government's intentions (Prucha 1984). They argued that the IRA actually promoted further Indian dependence on the federal government, since "tribal corporations" still had to answer to the government's Bureau of Indian Affairs (BIA). Nevertheless, through its acknowledgment of tribal communities and governments, the IRA did succeed in legitimizing the notion of tribal self-determination and rule even though it did not fully deliver on its promises.

TERMINATION (MID-1940S THROUGH EARLY 1960S)

Perhaps it is not surprising, given the erratic policy record of the federal government with regard to the "Indian problem," that this phase in American Indian history was distinguished by yet another reversal in policy. Federal receptivity to progressive social policies came to an abrupt close with the coming of the Second World War. In an effort to reduce domestic expenditures, the federal government began an aggressive campaign to cut "unnecessary" expenses. In this climate it was only a short time before the IRA came under attack. In the place of tribal revitalization, the federal government's new battle cry was tribal termination.

Leaders ushering in this new response to the Indian problem called for the complete dismantling of the reservation system and termination of all federal recognition of and responsibility to the tribes. Once again it was felt that the best solution was to force the Indians' rapid entry into the American social and economic mainstream. Tribal members would first have the opportunity to air grievances over past wrongdoings and seek financial redress through the Indian Claims Commission Act (ICCA) of 1946 (Lurie 1978). But the race against time was on: hearings began in 1947 to distinguish those tribes who were ready for immediate release from federal assistance from those who would need more time before their release (Deloria and Lytle 1983; Tyler 1973).

By 1952 official expression of the termination sentiment came in the form of House Concurrent Resolution 108, which stated that it was "the sense of Congress that, at the earliest possible time, all of the Indian tribes and the individual members thereof located within the States of California, Florida, New York and Texas, should be freed from Federal supervision and control and all disabilities and limitations specifically applicable to Indians" (quoted in Deloria and Lytle 1983, pp. 17–18). Soon after, bills were passed that officially began tribal termination. Two of the larger tribes to be terminated included the Klamath of Oregon and the Menominee of Wisconsin. According to Deloria and Lytle (1983, p. 18), the actual number of terminated tribes is unclear. Smaller tribes lacking political clout were especially vulnerable to termination. "Large tribes with treaty commitments and political sophistication (on the other hand) were not touched although they were very nearly frightened into submission."

But by the late 1950s, advocates of tribal termination faced a very different social climate. The civil rights movement ushered in not only new social justice policies but also new hope among historically oppressed groups. Spurred on by the actions of black community leaders, tribal leaders began fighting back against numerous federal government policies, including the termination program. And while it would take another dozen years before the termination policy was formally renounced, vital seeds were planted during this time that were responsible for shifting power relations between Indians and whites in the years to come.

SELF-DETERMINATION (1960S TO THE PRESENT)

The 1960s and 1970s witnessed a renewed interest in progressive social welfare programs and policies. The civil rights movement had infused the country with a greater sense of responsibility to historically oppressed groups, including native people. Given this receptive political climate, Native Americans benefited from many social welfare programs that came out of this era. These included the Indian Education Act (1972), the Indian Health Care Improvement Act (1976), the Self-Determination and Assistance Act (1975), and the Indian Child Welfare Act (1978).

At the same time that Indians were receiving greater benefits and social services, younger generations of Native Americans were becoming more aggressive and vocal in their protests over earlier wrongdoings and were making demands for redress. The black movement for civil rights served as a powerful model for inspiring and mobilizing other minority groups, and given the climate of protest so pervasive during the sixties and seventies, the spirit of activism understandably spread to native people as well. For Native Americans, there was the added issue of self-determination, a deep-felt wish to return to tribal authority in order to regain control of their own lives and affairs.

Starting with the American Indian Chicago Conference in June 1961, when representatives from ninety tribes met to articulate problems plaguing their communities on the reservations and in the cities, delegates began a campaign to reclaim authority in Indian matters. One product of the conference was a formal statement entitled the *Declaration of Indian Purpose,* in which delegates spelled out their concerns and their recommendations for addressing them (Prucha 1984). Panethnic efforts such as this conference helped to raise public awareness among Indians and non-Indians alike of the issues plaguing native communities. Flush with their success in using the mass media to broadcast their concerns, tribal representatives began their push for even greater autonomy as well as for redressing broken promises on the part of the federal government.

It was in this spirit that Native Americans began to make their mark on America's political landscape by asserting rights guaranteed to them in treaties their ancestors had signed a century earlier. Major treaty disputes were waged over water, timber, oil, mineral, land, and fishing rights. Three signal events, the Northwest fishing rights movement, settlement of the Alaska native claims dispute, and restoration of the Menominee tribe to federal status, reflect the growing sense of Native American empowerment during this period.

In treaties negotiated in 1854 and 1855, Northwest tribes agreed to sell significant landholdings in what was to become the state of Washington to the federal government. During the negotiations, however, tribal leaders were insistent that the treaties uphold their right to continue fishing on the ceded lands. The tribes were dependent on fishing for personal consumption as well as to maintain their livelihood. Isaac Ingalls Stevens, then governor of the Washington Territory and chief negotiator during the proceedings, agreed to their request and promised the tribes "the right of taking fish at usual and customary grounds and stations," a declaration he had written into each of the treaties (Cohen 1986). His promises were short-lived, however, as Native Americans quickly found themselves in competition with local fishermen and commercial canneries. In an effort to control the burgeoning fishing industry, state agencies began to limit steelhead trout and salmon fishing, regulations that tribal fishermen gradually found themselves subject to as well. Northwest tribes that appealed to the courts to uphold their treaty rights received a mixed reception. While generally affirming that the tribes did possess such rights, the courts legitimated the state's role in regulating those rights. This included forbidding the practice of traditional fishing methods, such as spearing and gill netting, as well as restricting off-reservation fishing rights to times when Washington's regular fishing seasons were open.

In practice, tribal fishermen continued to fish by traditional methods and in their customary locations. Such activities, however, were often practiced surreptitiously and under threat of arrest by state fisheries wardens. In the 1960s Northwest tribes successfully began a campaign of public protest by holding "fish-ins" to draw attention to the limitations placed on their fishing rights, highly publicized events in which tribal members fished in open defiance of state restrictions. The state of Washington responded by arresting the Indian fishermen and seizing their gear. The issue got more publicity in the wake of the arrests and from the many resulting court cases. Eventually, in the fall of 1970, the Justice Department responded to the pressure of the growing controversy and filed suit against the state of Washington on behalf of fourteen tribes, for violating their treaty rights. The case, *U.S. v. Washington,* came before Judge George H. Boldt in August 1973. After months of deliberation, Judge Boldt decided in February 1974 that the tribes were entitled not only to fish off-reservation but to collect 50 percent of the allowable fish harvest. The Boldt decision, as the ruling came to be known, set off a new round of hostility between the tribes and commercial and sport fishermen. Anti-treaty protests, illegal fishing, and court appeals followed in the wake of the ruling. Eventually the Supreme Court heard the case in 1979, and to the great disappointment of treaty protesters, the Court upheld Judge Boldt's interpretation of the treaties.

Settlement of the Alaska Native Claims Settlement Act of 1971 stands as another symbol of the growing empowerment of Native Americans. Historically, Indians, Eskimos, and Aleuts living in Alaska had been excluded from federal policies established for dealing with Native Americans because of their geographical remoteness from the rest of the nation. This all changed, however, with the discovery of Alaska's rich oil, gas, and mineral resources in the second half of the nineteenth century and the early part of the twentieth (Prucha 1984). The native people of the region quickly found themselves struggling to protect their land and traditional hunting and gathering practices in the face of rapid white encroachment and land development. The issue of aboriginal land claims came to a head when Alaska achieved statehood in 1959. As part of the statehood act, Congress granted the newly recognized state the right to select approximately 103 million acres of "public domain" land for the state's use (Prucha 1984; Berger 1985). The native people, outraged by this blatant disregard of their aboriginal claims, responded by filing suits against the state, effectively freezing up any further land development until some settlement could be reached. Over the ensuing years, efforts were made to reach a compromise, but no breakthrough was reached until the discovery of rich oil reserves in 1968 and the proposed construction of a 900-mile pipeline to transport the oil. With this discovery and the added pressure by oil companies eager to begin construction came a strong incentive on the part of state and federal officials to settle the question of native claims quickly. In December 1971 the Alaska Native Claims Settlement Act became law, granting Alaska's native people legal title to approximately 40 million acres of land (roughly 10 percent of the Alaskan territory) and a $962.5 million compensation package in exchange for extinguishing all claims on the state (Berger 1985).

Debates have been waged over the long-term consequences and implications of the settlement. Owing to the complicated nature of the settlement, which required the formation of twelve regional corporations and more than two hundred village-level corporations, dividends have been slow to reach individual shareholds (native Alaskans), and by the time they have reached them the amounts have been quite small. Moreover, as Berger (1985, p. 28) argues, "For a great many of these so-called investors, receipt of income from this investment, negligible though it may be, threatened their eligibility for welfare programs." The promises of the Native Claims Act have fallen short of many Alaskan natives' expectations. But despite its many shortcomings, the controversy surrounding the treatment of Alaskan natives by state officials and the resulting Native Claims Act symbolized the growing acknowledgment by state and federal officials that the rights of native people could no longer be blatantly disregarded.

According to Prucha (1984, p. 1135), the restoration of the Menominee in Wisconsin to federally recognized tribal status in 1975 "showed that in the era of self-determination and Indian rights it was possible for an Indian community with determined leaders to reverse congressional action and policy." During the termination period, the Menominee, along with the Klamath in Oregon and other less-known tribes, were officially cut from all federal responsibility. Instead of successfully assimilating tribal members into the social and economic mainstream, however, tribal termination was disastrous in its consequences. Most members of the Menominee were thrown into even deeper poverty and social despair, and in-fighting increased as tribal members debated the pros and cons of selling off their land assets.

While some members attempted to make the best of the new situation, a strong and vocal group consisting of Menominee as well as other Indian groups formed to protest and reverse the termination policy. Their efforts were successful, largely owing to the receptive climate in the 1960s and 1970s to the rights of historically oppressed groups. In December 1973 President Richard Nixon signed House Resolution 10717, officially restoring the Menominee to federal trust status. As with the Alaska native claims settlement, however, all was far from rosy for the Menominee after their victory. Internal dissension continued to plague the tribe as questions emerged concerning leadership and what social, political, and economic course the tribe should follow. Nevertheless, their successful restoration to tribal status was a crucial event in the movement for Indian self-determination and is remembered as a testament to Indian self-empowerment.

As these three events demonstrate, Native Americans sensed a new dawn in their capacity to influence both the federal and state governments to respond to their demands for recognition and self-determination. Their collective struggle to regain social, political, and economic control over their lives and to get the federal government to acknowledge and atone for atrocities committed in the past was seen as coming closer to fruition. While not without its flaws, internal conflicts, and setbacks, Indian self-determination provided a long and desperately needed sense of empowerment for native people across the nation. More and more tribes successfully brought suit to reassert their treaty rights and recover lands taken from them. The Chippewa treaty rights controversy, not surprisingly, has its origins during this period as well.

These eras in Indian-white interaction are not merely a historical sequence of events and institutionalized relations. Each period also involves distinctive ways of conceptualizing Native Americans and appropriate Indian-white relations. They involve common ideas, albeit malleable and changing, about who Native Americans are and what they are entitled to claim and expect in interacting with white society. To put it simply, these eras involved a particular sense of whites' group position relative to native people, and understanding them brings into sharper relief what those images and expectations were.

In the following section, we discuss the often instrumental ways in which the "Indian" has been understood and portrayed by white America, the economic and political sources of those portrayals, and how they have changed over time. The processes in which these stereotypes have evolved and shifted are critical to how white Americans have understood themselves and their changing sense of group position relative to Native Americans. Fundamental shifts in the predominant white image of Native Americans exhibit a functional connection to changes in the types of needs or claims on resources pressed by whites, and to the nature of resistance put forward by Native Americans. As the theory of group position maintains, prejudice becomes a potent societal force insofar as members of a racial or ethnic group hold a sense of proprietary or legitimate claim to rights, resources, or privileges and perceive themselves as facing resistance, challenge, or threat from members of another group.

STEREOTYPES AND THE SENSE OF GROUP POSITION AS A SOCIAL FORCE

The savage, bloodthirsty Indian. The uncivilized Indian. The noble Indian. The conquered Indian. The stone-faced, cigar store Indian. The devoted Tonto. The militant, Red Power Indian. The innocent Indian. The spiritual Indian. The drunken, welfare-dependent Indian. The reservation Indian. The medicine-man Indian. The ecological Indian. As this laundry list of well-known stereotypes illustrates, Native Americans have been depicted in a variety of contradictory ways throughout our history. Popularized through such media as film, television, literature (fictional and historical), and newsprint, these stereotypes speak to the complex ways in which Native Americans have been understood by white America. The ease and rapidity with which one image has shifted to another illustrates how responsive the stereotypes have been to the changing economic, social, and political exigencies of this country's leaders and white citizenry.

From the outset, it is important to recognize that Native Americans have historically been perceived by white Americans as the proverbial "other" (Berkhofer 1978). During less hostile times, this perception has been understood in benign or even favorable terms, as in stereotype of the kind and noble Indian (in contrast to the calculating white) or, more recently, the environmentally conscious and spiritual Indian (in contrast to the shallow and materialistic white). More typically, however, the perception has been negative and has involved some combination of undesirable traits. Typically during such times of negative Indian stereotyping whites have thought of themselves as being industrious, hard working, and honest. This polarity in perception, as Bataille and Silet (1983) argue, was particularly pronounced during the early, formative years of America's development: "So much of White America's mythos was contained in the legends of the West and of its 'taming' and 'conquest' that it was emotionally threatening to portray Indians in any other way. The very experience of the westward movement, the very rationale for the subjugation of the continent, depended on the adversary relationship between Whites and Indians" (pp. 13–14).

The notion of a universal "Indian," however, simplistically reduced the immense cultural and linguistic differences among the myriad native tribes who had preceded the coming of the white man. Those native people did not conceive of themselves as Indians; they were Anishinabe, Tankiteke, Wiwanoy, Narragansett, or one of any thousands of other independent tribal identities. For purposes of convenience and lack of sensitivity to group differences, however, whites consolidated the native tribes into a single "Indian" category. Commonly, the cultural practices and habits of one tribe were treated as exemplary of all others (Berkhofer 1978).

THE INNOCENT INDIAN

The origin of the term *Indian* can be traced back to Christopher Columbus's fateful journey in search of an all-water route to the Orient. Believing he had landed in India (that is, Asia), Columbus referred to the native people he encountered as "Indians" (Berkhofer 1978; Cornell 1988; Fixico 1993). Columbus's initial accounts and images of native people were, for the most part, quite favorable. He regarded them as timid and childlike, eager to please and pure of heart. Rather than inspiring fear and contempt, the native people generally invoked thoughts of innocence and compassion.

Columbus's accounts, in turn, were supported by later reports from other European explorers: "We were entertained with all love, and kindness, and with as much bountie, after their manner, as they could possibly devise. We found the people most gentle, loving and faithful, void of all guile, and treason" (statement made by Arthur Barlow, member of the first expedition to Roanoke Island, in Nash 1974, p. 43). These idyllic images were well suited to the purposes and interests of European explorers during their early expeditions. After all, only a "friendly" Indian could be a trading Indian. Natives were portrayed as a people who would not stand in the way of European investors and explorers in their search for fortune, an image that allayed fears of angry natives intent on ousting intruders (Jennings 1975).

This benign image of the innocent Indian did not persist for very long, however, before it underwent a swift and drastic transformation. Describing native people as childlike and carefree also meant that they could be seen as lazy or not industrious, as evidenced by their lack of material accumulation and disinterest in dominating the lands they inhabited. At first white settlers expected that native people would give up their "base" ways in exchange for the superior Christian life and the benefits of "civilization" (Axtell 1974; Deloria and Lytle 1983; Horsman 1981; Jennings 1975; Pearce 1957; Steinback 1977). This idea gradually faded, however, as it became clear that the Indians were quite happy with their own cultures, values, religion, and ways of life. By daring to reject the European lifestyle, native people ended the honeymoon period with white settlers. They increasingly came to be seen as unreasonable and as standing in the way of "progress" and "civilization," especially as whites' demand for their lands grew (Berkhofer 1978; Jennings 1975; Nash 1974). More important, Native Americans came to be seen as unsalvageable, unable or unwilling to learn the ways of the white man. Rather than living lives guided by civility, industry, and rationality, Native Americans were doomed to remain "creatures of passion," instinctive, and totally lacking in self-control (Takaki 1979).

THE UNCIVILIZED INDIAN

This revised image of the Indian as backward, primitive, and un-American served to justify colonists' changing policies toward them and to assuage their guilt over seizing lands that did not technically belong to them (Axtell 1974; Bataille and Silet 1983; Nash 1974, pp. 40–41). After all, since these people were not Christian and did not conform to white norms of civility and propriety, the settlers could hardly be blamed for taking away lands that the Indians merely "occupied" rather than "owned."

Like the frontier land itself, the native people had to be dominated and brought under the control of the white man's hands (Takaki 1979). They were viewed as wild creatures who roamed the earth like other wild animals. In contrast, the colonists saw themselves as possessing the fortitude, drive, and moral virtue necessary to transform the developing nation into a world power. Native Americans simply had no place in the vision that whites had created of what America was to become. With this realization, then, came an odd peace of mind, brought about by a sense of moral inevitability concerning what needed to be done with the indigenous people.

> Humanity has often wept over the fate of the aborigines of this country, and Philanthropy has been long busily employed in devising means to avert it, but its progress has never for a moment been arrested, and one

by one have many powerful tribes disappeared from the earth. To follow to the tomb the last of his race and tread on the graves of extinct nations excite melancholy reflections. But true philanthropy reconciles the mind to these vicissitudes as it does to the extinction of one generation to make room for another. (President Andrew Jackson in his second annual message to Congress, in Takaki 1979, p. 103)

As this passage conveys, whites perceived Native Americans as regrettable but necessary casualties in the march toward progress. If the Indian had only accepted the ways of the white man and joined him in his efforts to transform and control the wilderness, his fate would not have taken such a downward turn. By choosing to remain an uncivilized dweller on the earth, he had sealed his own fate.

THE HOSTILE AND SAVAGE INDIAN

Not surprisingly, hostilities grew as Indian-white relations entered this new phase. No longer was the Indian perceived as a gentle wanderer of the land; now he was a savage and warlike aggressor. Little mention was made of the fact that early confrontations were usually triggered by whites rather than Native Americans, or that the Indians were understandably trying to resist being forced off of their ancestral homelands. With the advent of open conflict, white settlers could claim moral justification for the slaughter of Native Americans, as this leader of the Chesapeake Bay colony did after an Indian attack:

Our hands which before were tied with gentleness and faire usage, are now set at liberty by the treacherous violence of the Sauvages . . . So that we, who hitherto have had possession of no more ground than their waste and our purchase at a valuable consideration to theire owne contentment gained; may now by right of Warre, and law of Nations, invade the Country, and destroy them who sought to destroy us; whereby wee shall enjoy their cultivated places, turning the laborious Mattacke into the victorious Sword . . . and possessing the fruits of others labours. Now their cleared grounds in all their villages (which are situate in the fruitfullest places of the land) shall be inhabited by us, whereas heretofore the grubbing of woods was the greatest labour. (Quoted in Nash 1974, p. 62)

Indian-white conflict was now interpreted as a struggle between good and evil, between innocent and righteous whites in their quest to settle on the western frontier and blood-hungry Indian savages intent on scalping white men, women, and children, a depiction that provided the moral legitimacy for aggressive and increasingly unapologetic policies toward native people (Horsman 1981; Takaki 1979).

The incidents surrounding the Powhatan tribe's 1622 "massacre" of Virginia colonists offer one example of a typical chain of events in the Indian-white conflict. With the success of the tobacco industry in the Chesapeake Bay region and its dependence on the continuing availability of fertile land for cultivation (Nash 1974), tensions between white settlers and Indians living in the area were inevitable. Those tensions came to a head in 1622 when Indian leaders decided it was time to take a stand, defend their way of life, and discourage further white encroachment. The Powhatans attacked and killed nearly one-third of the settlers in the area. But this attack served only to give other white settlers in Virginia the moral justification they needed for a ruthless and avenging policy toward native people. According to Nash (1974, p. 63): "In the aftermath of the Indian attack of 1622 an unambiguously negative image of the Indian pervaded the Virginian mentality . . . Hereafter, the elimination of the Indians could be rationalized far more easily, for they were seen as cultureless, unreconstructible savages rather than merely as hostile people whose culture, though different in some respects from the English, fitted them admirably for survival in the Chesapeake area." This pattern of interaction would repeat itself again and again. White encroachment heightened the need for Indian self-preservation and acts of self-defense, which confirmed whites' beliefs regarding the savage and warring nature of the Indian and justified their aggressive and unapologetic policies toward them.

Implicit in all Indian-white interactions from the viewpoint of the colonists was the belief in the superiority of European (that is, white) civilization and its destiny to spread across the continent (Pearce 1957). As Horsman (1981) and others argue (Nash 1974; Steinback 1977), white Americans increasingly came to feel that they were a "chosen" people, a superior breed favored by God to take control of and dominate the world. Only "American Anglo-Saxons could bring the political and economic changes that would make possible unlimited world progress" (Horsman 1981, p. 189). Moreover, it was their moral responsibility to spread their superior culture across the New World (Nash 1974). Armed with this sense of superiority and purpose, the colonists were able to justify any and all actions taken to fulfill their "racial destiny," including the pain and suffering they inflicted on native people.

Even when the Indian was viewed in more generous terms, he was never seen as an equal to the white man. Rather, he was an innocent "Red child" in need of guidance and care from his "White father" (Takaki 1979). As proof of their superiority, colonists pointed to the widespread diseases afflicting the native people, noting that this was another sign of God's intervention on their behalf. During the early stages of Indian-white contact, at least the possibility of assimilating the native people was considered a viable option. With the overall deterioration in relations, however, such assimilative policies were abandoned in favor of isolation and removal (Nash 1974). This was the sentiment that ushered in the reservation system and the image of the "reservation Indian."

THE CONQUERED INDIAN, AKA THE RESERVATION INDIAN

The image of the drunken and indolent Indian continues themes found in earlier Native American stereotypes. Like the "innocent Indian" and the "savage Indian," the "reservation Indian" remains at heart un-American and "other" (Berkhofer 1978):

> Living neither as an assimilated white nor an Indian of the classic image, and therefore neither noble nor wildly savage but always scorned, the degraded Indian exhibited the vices of both societies in the opinion of White observers. Degenerate and poverty-stricken, these unfortunates were presumed to be outcasts from their own race, who exhibited the worse qualities of Indian character with none of its redeeming features. Since White commentators pitied when they did not scorn this degenerate Indian, the image carried the same unfavorable evaluation overall as the bad or ignoble Indian. (p. 30)

More than any other stereotype, however, the image of the reservation Indian epitomizes white America's belief in the descent of Native Americans into powerlessness and dependency. This stereotype conveys most clearly the notion of Native Americans as a conquered people forced to relocate on government-created and sponsored reservations (Vizenor 1972). The image of the reservation Indian reflects their marginalized status as relics of an earlier era living in a society that no longer has a place for them.

Juxtaposed against this picture stands that of the paternalistic white

American whose duty and responsibility it is to care for dependent Indians (Trimble 1988). For some whites, the stereotype conjures feelings of compassion and remorse based on some sense of guilt or acknowledgment of earlier wrongdoings against Native Americans. For others the image is more likely to generate feelings of resentment and anger rooted in the belief that the reservation Indian is undeservedly being supported by white taxpayers. The reservation Indian is seen as lazy—content to live off of monthly welfare checks instead of earning his or her own paycheck. Most important, the reservation Indian is seen as the recipient of special services and opportunities that he or she does not deserve.

THE TREATY-ASSERTING INDIAN

Of the various stereotypes used to characterize American Indians today, the treaty-asserting Indian is the most likely to arouse sharp animosity among segments of white America. This image is reminiscent of the hostile and savage stereotype of earlier days, in that natives are understood as being dangerous and unpredictable. The difference, however, is that the treaty-asserting Indian is less a physical threat than an economic and political threat.

Like the reservation Indian stereotype, this characterization elicits strong feelings of resentment among segments of white America because of the perception that Native Americans are making unfair claims and demands on public resources. Indians' assertions of treaty rights are seen as unjust since they are based on antiquated treaties that have no place in modern society. Furthermore, the individuals benefiting from treaty rights, they argue, hardly qualify as Indians, given the extensive miscegenation that has occurred over the years. Opponents of treaty rights argue that they are denied the same rights—and are thus unfairly discriminated against— simply because they are non-Indian or, more important, because they lack the proper Indian blood quantum. To their mind, treaty rights create a special class of people who receive benefits above and beyond the general population, a belief well captured in the following excerpt from an article about the Chippewa treaty dispute, published in a northern Wisconsin newspaper:

> Many of the [spearfishing] settlement points brought scornful laughter
> and comments from the crowd. For example, when one person asked
> what the tribal people would do with the money they make through eco-

nomic development, others in the crowd said, "Go to the bars," or "Buy liquor."

There was also scornful laughter whenever the negotiators explained about the add-ons for job training, labor, a halfway house and natural resources for the Native American people.

"We've done nothing but give them money over the past 80–100 years," one woman said. The result is alcoholism, drug abuse and illiteracy, she said. "This has failed. I can't see giving $50 million to watch it fail again."

"We know there is a lot at stake here," Long [Boulder Junction businessman] said. "The bottom line is that we are going to be living together, we are going to be neighbors. It's going to be extremely detrimental to all of us to continue to breed hate between people. It's going to do nothing but further damage the area."

A crowd member replied, "When they [Native Americans] start to pay taxes, work 40 hours a week and abide by the same laws we abide by now, we're more than willing to be good neighbors," a response that brought another round of applause from the crowd. (*Lakeland Times,* October 10, 1989, p. 2)

As is evident in this article, many treaty opponents have excused themselves from any sense of responsibility for either creating or ameliorating the current Indian condition. Indian poverty, illiteracy, and other ills are seen as caused solely by the poor work habits, lifestyles, and values of Indians themselves. Whites, in contrast, are the real victims, thanks to a judicial system that continues to expect them to provide for the comfort and well-being of a small and undeserving group. Indians' demands for treaty rights simply add further insult to injury in this view, and serve as a telling symbol of how white Americans' rights have come to take second place behind those of a militant minority.

Neither the historical uses and shifts of whites' stereotypes of Native Americans nor the recent mobilization of negative imagery in response to the Chippewa treaty rights dispute can be adequately understood according to conventional models of prejudice. Learned negative feelings and stereotypes, although plainly elements of the process, cannot alone account for the shift in whites' views of Native Americans. As we have seen, benign early images of Indians as trading partners eventually gave way to starkly opposed images of savages and barbarians standing in the path of permanent white settlement and expansion. The former imagery suited a goal of peaceful trading relations, whereas the latter was conducive to violent domination whenever Indians resisted white encroachment. The manifest historical legacy of struggle and conflict, as well as the functional imperative or goal at the root of the shifting attitudes make reducing these processes to simply a matter of psychological affect and stereotyping completely untenable.

To explain these events and processes we need to, first, incorporate a concern with group claims, rights, and statuses and, second, acknowledge the dynamic force introduced into group relations by a perceived challenge or threat to a preferred group's rights, statuses, or privileges. In short, the group position model, with its express concern with group claims, sense of entitlement, and perceived threat to such claims (above and beyond negative feelings and stereotypes) provides the best account of prejudice as a social force in Indian-white relations.

THE WISCONSIN TREATY RIGHTS CONTROVERSY

The Chippewa treaty rights dispute has a long and complicated history dating back to the early nineteenth century. In 1837, the United States sought to secure significant landholdings from the Wisconsin Chippewa for the large-scale harvesting of pine timber (Strickland, Herzberg, and Owens 1990). When the Chippewa initially agreed to cede their lands to the federal government in exchange for annuities, provisions, and the settlement of outstanding debts, they did so with the confidence that they retained their right to fish, hunt, and gather on those lands. According to Satz (1991) and others (Strickland, Herzberg, and Owens 1990), the Chippewa sincerely believed that the federal government and its white citizenry sought access to the ceded lands' resources rather than the land itself. In fact, the Chippewa repeatedly expressed their concern during the negotiation process that they retained the right to "make sugar from the trees" and "get their living from the lakes and rivers." They signed the treaty with the understanding that their traditional hunting, fishing, and gathering practices would remain unchanged. In the near future, this assumption would prove to be false.

Five years after the first treaty, the federal government again sought to obtain land from the Chippewa, this time, however, for the purposes of mining the rich copper deposits reported to exist along the shores of Lake Superior. The chief U.S. negotiator for this treaty, known as the 1842

Treaty at La Pointe, was Acting Superintendent of Indian Affairs Robert Stuart. Given the immense financial reward tied to the outcome of the negotiations, Stuart relied on less than honorable tactics in dealing with the Chippewa. He downplayed the value of the land, suggesting instead that the federal government, in its great benevolence, was actually performing an act of charity toward the Chippewa. According to Satz (1991, p. 37): "Stuart informed the Indians assembled at La Pointe, using language very similar to (Governor) Dodge's at St. Peters in 1837, that their Great Father in Washington 'knows that you are poor, that your lands are not good, and that you have very little game left, to feed and clothe your women & children—He therefore pities your condition, and has sent me to see what can be done to benefit you.'" While there is little documentation conveying the Chippewa's perspective on the proceedings, they no doubt felt a sense of resignation over their inability to influence the negotiations. After all, like other Indian tribes before and after them, the Chippewa could not offer any real opposition or resistance during the negotiation process, given the balance of power heavily in favor of the U.S. government. Whites largely dictated the terms and conditions under which land cessions took place, with only minor adjustments stipulated by the Indian parties. Whites determined the timing of treaty negotiations and often rushed Indian leaders to sign documents they had not had sufficient time to peruse. Whites decided to treat diverse Indian bands as monolithic groups and expected them to behave as such, as illustrated, in the case of the Chippewa treaties, by this statement made by Stuart: "Your Great Father will not treat with you as Bands, but as a Nation" (quoted in Satz 1991, p. 37). Given these conditions, the Chippewa could only appeal to the conscience and sense of morality of white leaders to enter into the negotiation process honorably and to respect the conditions and terms laid out in the treaties. For their part, leaders such as Stuart and Henry Dodge, chief negotiator during the 1837 treaty, reassured the Chippewa that they should have no fear of being evicted from their ancestral lands any time soon. Rather, they would be able to live on ceded lands and continue to practice their customs for many years to come.

Unfortunately, as the Chippewa soon discovered, the promises made by white leaders were short-lived at best. An obscure phrase in Article 5 of the 1837 treaty (which created a legal loophole that would come back to haunt the federal government nearly 150 years later) read: "The privilege of hunting, fishing, and gathering the wild rice, upon the lands, the rivers and the lakes included in the territory ceded, is guaranteed to the Indians, during the pleasure of the President of the United States." Less than twenty years later, in 1850, President Zachary Taylor indeed found it to be his pleasure to terminate Chippewa fishing, hunting, and gathering rights and to order their removal to unceded lands.

> The privileges granted temporarily to the Chippewa Indians of the Mississippi, by the Fifth Article of the Treaty made with them on the 29th of July 1837, "of hunting, fishing and gathering the wild rice, upon the lands, the rivers and the lakes included in the territory ceded" by that treaty to the United States; and the right granted to the Chippewa Indians of the Mississippi and Lake Superior, by the Second Article of the treaty with them of October 4th 1842, of hunting on the territory which they ceded by that treaty, "with the other usual privileges of occupancy until required to remove by the President of the United States," are hereby revoked; and all of the said Indians remaining on the lands ceded as aforesaid, are required to remove to their unceded lands. (President Zachary Taylor, quoted in Satz 1991, p. 55)

The Chippewa vigorously opposed their removal, and with the aid of missionaries, newspapers sympathetic to their plight, and other supporters, they were successful in suspending the order a year after it was issued.

While President Taylor's removal order was never carried out, it created a state of ambiguity regarding the legal status and rights of the Chippewa. The Chippewa continued to exercise their treaty rights on the ceded lands after President Taylor's removal order, but at the start of the twentieth century, Wisconsin state officials effectively curtailed those rights when they determined that conservation regulations were applicable to the Chippewa (U.S. Commission on Civil Rights 1989; Arey 1991). The Chippewa filed numerous suits to protest this decision as well as the arrests of tribesmen caught hunting and fishing off the reservation. Their efforts were unsuccessful, however, until the arrest of the Tribble brothers in 1974, which began a new round of litigation. While they initially lost that suit in 1978, the Chippewa eventually emerged triumphant, thanks to the 1983 landmark ruling by the U.S. Court of Appeals, Seventh Circuit. The decision in *Lac Courte Oreilles etc. v. Voigt*, or LCO I (700 F.2d 341 [1983]), a ruling that came to be known as the Voigt decision, was that the original treaties could be terminated only in the event of "misbehavior" on the part of the Chippewa against non-Indian settlers. Because President Taylor's executive order for Chippewa removal was not based on Indian "misbehavior," the appeals judges ruled the order invalid, thus reaffirming the rights guaranteed to the Chippewa in the original treaties and setting the stage for anti-treaty backlash.

Eight subsequent court rulings and a final summary judgment were issued in the ensuing eight years to define the scope and range of Chippewa fishing, hunting, and gathering rights. In LCO II (760 F.2d 177 [1985]), issued April 24, 1985, Judge James Doyle affirmed the Chippewa's right to off-reservation hunting and fishing but refined his LCO I ruling by excluding privately owned land. In LCO III (653 F.Supp. 1420 [W.D. Wis. 1987]), issued February 18, 1987, Judge Doyle, ruling on such issues as resource commerce, methods for harvest, and harvest restrictions, stated:

> (1) Indians were not confined to hunting and fishing methods their ancestors relied upon at treaty time, but could take advantage of improvements in hunting and fishing techniques, and could trade and sell to non-Indians in modern manner from current harvests; (2) usufructuary rights reserved by Chippewa Indians in 1837 and 1842 treaties had been terminated as to all portions of ceded territory which were privately owned as of times of contemplated or actual attempted exercise of those rights; but (3) allocation of resources in which rights had been reserved between Indians and non-Indians were currently unwarranted.

Upon Judge Doyle's untimely death in 1987, the subsequent LCO cases were assigned to Judge Barbara Crabb. In LCO IV (668 F.Supp. 1233 [W.D. Wis. 1987]), issued August 21, 1987, Judge Crabb, ruling on the issue of whether the state held any authority to regulate Chippewa treaty rights, wrote:

> The state may regulate the tribes' off-reservation treaty rights where the regulations are reasonable and necessary to prevent or ameliorate a substantial risk to the public health or safety, and do not discriminate against the Indians. A public health and safety regulation is reasonable if it is appropriate to its purpose. Such a regulation is necessary if it meets a three-part test. First, the state must demonstrate that there is a public health or safety need to regulate a particular resource in a particular area . . . Second, the state must show that the particular regulation sought to be imposed is necessary to the prevention or amelioration of the public health or safety hazard. And third, the state must establish that application of the particular regulation to the tribes is necessary to effectuate the partic-

ular public health or safety interest. Moreover, the state must show that its regulation is the least restrictive alternative available to accomplish its health and safety purposes.

In LCO V (686 F.Supp. 226 [W.D. Wis. 1988]), issued June 3, 1988, Judge Crabb set out to quantify the phrase "modest standard of living" issued by Judge Doyle in LCO III regarding the amount of resources the Chippewa could harvest. Her ruling in effect gave the Chippewa carte blanche to harvest as much as they desired: "I conclude that plaintiffs have established the monetary measurement of a 'modest standard of living' and have proven that they could not achieve this standard even if they were permitted to harvest every available resource in the ceded territory and even if they were capable of doing so. In other words, the modest living standard imposes no practical limit on the amount of the natural resources that can be harvested by tribal members."

In LCO VI (707 F.Supp. 1034 [W.D. Wis. 1989]), issued March 3, 1989, Judge Crabb ruled on the request made by the state for authority to regulate the Chippewa's fishing harvest of walleye and muskellunge within the ceded territory. Judge Crabb granted the Chippewa the right to self-regulation, provided they enacted a management program in accordance with "biologically sound principles necessary for the conservation of the species being harvested":

> For the reasons that follow, I conclude that defendants have failed to show that plaintiffs are incapable of regulating their members' off-reservation walleye and muskellunge harvest, but that defendants have shown that plaintiffs can conduct that harvest without harm to the walleye and muskellunge only if plaintiffs enact and implement certain conservation-based measures and procedures as set forth in this opinion. If plaintiffs do this, then defendants cannot regulate tribal members' rights and activities in harvesting walleye and muskellunge within the ceded territory, except to the extent agreed to by the parties in their pretrial stipulations.

The treaty protest movement reached its zenith around the time of LCO V and VI. Perhaps out of their perception of the unfairness of the rulings, treaty opponents vigorously stepped up their activities, and hostilities toward the Chippewa increased during this same time period.

The final three LCO cases significantly tailored back the earlier rulings handed down by Judge Crabb. In LCO VII (740 F.Supp. 1400 [W.D. Wis.

1990]), issued May 9, 1990, Judge Crabb sharply delimited the scope of the Chippewa's rights by ruling that all the resources within the ceded territory must be shared equally by Indians and non-Indians. Furthermore, she ruled that the Chippewa could exercise their rights only on public lands. Hunting rights were also scaled back. Chippewa requests for deer hunting during summer months were rejected, and the practice of "shining," hunting for deer at night with lights, was prohibited. In a further setback, Judge Crabb ruled in LCO VIII (749 F.Supp. 913 [W.D. Wis. 1990]), issued October 11, 1990, that the Chippewa could not seek financial remuneration from the state of Wisconsin for the years of denial of treaty rights. And in LCO IX (758 F.Supp. 1262 [W.D. Wis. 1991]), issued February 21, 1991, Judge Crabb ruled that the rights guaranteed to the Chippewa did not include the commercial harvest of timber. A final judgment was pronounced on February 28, 1991, highlighting the major findings of the earlier nine LCO rulings. While both sides had the opportunity to bring suit, neither the state nor the Chippewa challenged the summary judgment, effectively bringing the Chippewa treaty rights litigation to a close.

Other politically significant highlights during this period of litigation include efforts by the state to negotiate out-of-court settlements with individual Chippewa bands. It was hoped that, in exchange for cash and other forms of social and economic assistance, the Chippewa would "lease out" their harvesting rights to the state for a negotiated period of time. The first of these negotiations began in April 1987. After months of prolonged bargaining, subtle coercion, and threats on the part of state negotiators to encourage the Indians to accept a settlement, Attorney General Donald J. Hanaway offered the Mole Lake reservation ten million dollars in exchange for a ten-year lease. Wisconsin congressman James Sensenbrenner, Jr., threatened to call for the complete abrogation of off-reservation usufructuary rights in Wisconsin as well as to hold back state legislation for the creation of job opportunities on the reservations unless the Chippewa cooperated (Satz 1991). Despite the money and the state's strong-arm tactics, the Mole Lake band turned down the offer in January 1989. Later that same year the state proposed another ten-year negotiated settlement, offering the Lac du Flambeau reservation up to fifty million dollars to stop the off-reservation exercise of their treaty rights ("Dec. 31 Deadline Set for Treaty Agreement," *Lakeland Times*, October 3, 1989, p. 1). Like the Mole Lake band, members of the Lac du Flambeau reservation turned down the offer ("No Deal, Indians Say: Chippewa Vote No on Pact," *Wisconsin State Journal*, October 26, 1989, p. A1).

The court's affirmation of Indian treaty rights and the exercise of those rights by various Chippewa bands elicited strong cries of foul in some corners. Critics charged that: (1) the treaties are relevant to a different historical period and should carry no legal force today; (2) through intermarriage Indians are now a very heterogeneous population, making designation of who is entitled to exercise treaty rights somewhat arbitrary; (3) Indians gave up their tribal citizenship when the 1924 Indian Citizenship Act was passed; (4) the Chippewa should be able to harvest resources only with tools available at the time of the treaties instead of with modern methods; (5) the exercise of Indian treaty rights will do damage to the underlying natural resources and thereby hurt businesses dependent on tourism; and, crucially, (6) treaty provisions establish privileged and disprivileged groups when everyone should instead be treated equally.

In response to these accusations, the Chippewa and their supporters reminded critics that the United States is, above all else, a nation of laws. As such, valid contracts, especially as reinforced by court rulings, are legally binding and must be respected. In response to the specific criticisms, they argued that: (1) agreements between governments or individuals are not invalidated by age; (2) only the tribe, as a sovereign self-regulating government, has the authority to determine tribal membership (determining tribal membership is not an arbitrary process: only persons who are recognized by the tribe through such methods as blood quantum, birthright, and enrollment in tribal rosters may exercise tribally owned treaty rights); (3) the United States recognized American Indians as having "dual citizenship" and thus is obligated to respect those dual rights, because Indians were not required to forfeit tribal membership when they were granted citizenship; (4) critics are employing double standards by insisting that the Chippewa use only harvesting methods in practice at the time of the treaties while non-Indian developers of the land are able to use whatever technical advances are available to extract coal, timber, minerals, and other resources; (5) the Chippewa, far from draining all the natural resources in the area, are responsible for taking only a small fraction of the fish and game harvest in comparison with recreational fishermen and hunters; (6) the Chippewa are not the recipients of "special" rights but rather are exercising their legal property rights: "Retaining rights to minerals on land when it is sold, or as in some states retaining the right to frail for pecans or a right to the air space after the land is sold, are all of a similar nature. Property rights such as these are enjoyed by us all and are not a special right of Indian people" (Great Lakes Indian Fish and Wildlife Commission [GLIFWC] 1990).

Indian tribes in Wisconsin, in cooperation with the State Department of Natural Resources (DNR), currently regulate how much hunting and fishing Indians do. Despite treaty provisions allowing longer seasons and the use of different methods than non-Indian sportsmen use, the Indian take in deer and fish is small compared with that of non-Indian sportsmen. Even during the earliest stages of the treaty rights controversy, when white alarm was at its height, figures for 1983 showed a registered deer kill of 644 for Indians out of a total of 225,000 ("Tribal Rights," *Milwaukee Journal*, October 14–17, 1984). Tribal figures placed the number of walleye taken in 1989 by Indian fishers at 16,394. Figures from the DNR showed that non-Indian fishers took 672,000 walleye ("Danger of Fishing Disputed," *Wisconsin State Journal*, March 4, 1990, p. 15A). However, regardless of the growing availability of statistics on the negligible effects the Chippewa had on the fish and game supply, the subject of treaty rights became a hot-button issue.

THE ANTI-TREATY PROTEST MOVEMENT

Relations between the Chippewa and local Wisconsin residents have never been entirely amicable (U.S. Commission on Civil Rights 1989). Since the advent of the reservation system, the Chippewa have largely been regarded as an indolent group who live off of the federal-government dole at the white taxpayers' expense. After the reaffirmation of Chippewa treaty rights in 1983, however, tensions between Indians and non-Indians reached a new level. A sampling of newspaper headlines conveys the heated pitch of the controversy that erupted after the 1983 LCO ruling:

- "North Woods Steaming with Racial Hostility" (*Milwaukee Journal*, October 14, 1984, n.p.)
- "Indian Spearfishing Ends with Ceremony, Race Insults" (*Wisconsin State Journal*, May 1, 1987, p. 3)

- "Indian Spearfishing Dispute Poised to Boil Over" (*Wisconsin State Journal,* February 7, 1988, p. 3)
- "Report Targets Racism as Basis for Indian Treaty Rights Tension" (*Capital Times,* January 17, 1990, p. 1)
- "Legal Expert: Spearfishing Fight Racial, Not Treaty Issue" (*Capital Times,* April 20, 1990, n.p.)
- "2,000 Treaty Rights Foes Stage Protest" (*Wisconsin State Journal,* April 16, 1989, p. B6).

Tensions resulting from discrimination, harassment, physical threats, and actual violence against the Chippewa became such a concern that the Wisconsin Advisory Committee to the U.S. Commission on Civil Rights called for a community forum in 1984 and again in 1989 to discuss the issue of Indian-white conflict in northern Wisconsin. Tensions were particularly high during the 1988 and 1989 spearfishing seasons. Throughout the years of controversy, concerns were repeatedly voiced over the seemingly imminent prospect that violence would lead to the deaths of either Chippewa Indians or their supporters. Incredibly, however, no killings occurred during the dispute.

In this period of open hostility, several treaty protest groups emerged, including Protect America's Rights and Resources (PARR), Stop Treaty Abuse (STA), Equal Rights for Everyone (ERFE), and Wisconsin Alliance for Rights and Resources (WARR). While the groups varied in terms of size and longevity, all decried the "unjustness" of the Voigt decision, claiming that the ruling gave the Chippewa "special" rights that were denied the average (that is, white) citizen. The collective goal of these groups was the abrogation of Indian treaty rights and the complete dissolution of the reservation system (GLIFWC 1994). At the height of the hysteria, treaty opponents painted a scenario in which the Chippewa would eventually decimate the fish and game populations in the area with their "unsportsmanlike" and "inhumane" fishing and hunting practices. As a result of this assumed decimation, they argued, the tourism industry in northern Wisconsin would be ruined.

The emergence of these groups added a new dimension to the hostility between Indians and non-Indians. Organized disruptions of activity at boat landings, anti-treaty demonstrations, public rallies, and political lobbying for the abrogation of treaties, as well as efforts to recall politicians perceived as sympathetic to the Chippewa cause, were some of the actions spearheaded by the groups. While not officially encouraged, protesters also threw rocks and beer bottles, swamped Indians' boats (flooded them by creating large wakes with their own boats), used physical intimidation, and even planted pipe bombs (GLIFWC 1994; "Spearing Harasser Gets Year in Prison," *Capital Times*, January 6, 1990, p. 19; "We'll Be There: Treaty-Rights Foes Pledge Resistance to the 'Injustice' of Chippewa Spearfishing," *Isthmus*, March 30, 1990, p. 1).

Treaty protesters gained particular notoriety for their raucous presence at boat landings. The following news article relates what became a familiar chain of events with the coming of each spring:

> The ice is beginning to give way on the lakes of northern Wisconsin, and soon the Chippewa will renew a ritual as old as their ancestors' memories. They will take to the water in boats to spear the fat walleye that come to spawn each spring in the cold shallows.
>
> But among the small towns and lakeside resorts in this part of the state, the Indians' annual spearfishing has become the occasion for an uglier seasonal rite. On spring nights, for the last two years, hundreds of whites have gathered at boat landings to hurl taunts, racial slurs and sometimes stones at Indian fishermen.
>
> With the spearfishing season expected to begin soon, state, local, Federal and tribal officials are girding for another round of protests in which whites will accuse Indians of exploiting tribal fishing rights to strip some lakes of valuable sporting fish. (*New York Times*, April 8, 1990, p. 14)

The Chippewa would normally give notice of the number of boats that would be on the water on a given night during their spearfishing season. On learning which lakes the Chippewa intended to fish, protest groups would spread the word to as many members as possible and encourage their presence at the boat landings. Most protesters' activity took the form of sign carrying, shouting, and otherwise making their presence known to the spearfishers and the news media. Protesters with more threatening thoughts in mind, however, took to the water to harass and disrupt spearfishers directly, by dragging anchors to cloud the water, shining bright lights to temporarily blind the fishers, and pounding on boat bottoms to scare the fish away ("Spearing Harvest Up Despite Cold, Harassment," *Vilas County News-Review*, April 27, 1988, p. 1). Law enforcement officials, however, successfully cut down on such activities as old and new laws forbidding protesters from interfering with spearfishers were enforced.

A tamer method by which treaty opponents—both those affiliated with organized groups and individual protesters—expressed their views was through writing letters to various newspapers. Consider the following letters sent to the *Vilas County News-Review* and the *Lakeland Times,* two papers published in strongholds of treaty opposition:

To Editor:

Please explain why a defeated nation imposes all these demands. Haven't we already paid 10 times over for the freedoms we fought for? This land no more belongs to them than to us [if] we fail to defend it. Where is their obligation for the defense of this country now? Are they of the opinion all these freedoms are free? Isn't it time they change their life-styles, worked for a living and paid their taxes like the rest of us? [No buy out.] No! No! No! (L. Mehrens, taxpayer and veteran, *Lakeland Times,* October 20, 1984, p. 7)

To Editor:

. . . As for their [the Indians'] livelihood, there is not one family that needs spearing for this purpose. We, the taxpayers, feed them, build their houses, pay for their education, and medical. I just read where 50 percent of Wisconsin tax goes to support the Indians. And you say they need spearing for their livelihood. (Stella Caskey, *Vilas County News-Review,* April 4, 1988, p. 14)

While leaders of treaty protest groups have been adamant that their activities were about protecting natural resources and were therefore an "exercise of rights, not of racism" (Loew 1990), numerous academic and civil rights reports, as well as press accounts, have charged that racism and anti-Indian bigotry were largely responsible for fueling the treaty rights controversy. Such claims are difficult to discount in light of such evidence as these letters voicing popular negative Indian stereotypes, as well as bumper stickers urging citizens to "Spear an Indian, Save a Muskie," and "Shoot an Indian, Save 25 Deer."

By the early 1990s the treaty protest movement had lost much of its momentum. Repeated charges of racism and hostile encounters at boat landings cast an increasingly ugly shadow over such organizations as PARR and STA, leading some members to drop out of the groups and discouraging others from joining. By 1991 newspaper accounts were reporting a notable decrease in the number of treaty protesters at boat landings and were even expressing hopeful optimism that peace and normalcy were returning to the northern part of the state:

- "Year of Change Calms Waters in Spearing-Rights Dispute" (*Janesville Gazette*, April 14, 1991)
- "All Quiet on Spearing Front" (*Superior Evening Telegram*, April 20, 1991, p. 1)
- "Spearing Finds Acceptance" (*Wisconsin State Journal*, April 14, 1991)
- "Spearfishing No Longer Town's Hottest Topic" (*Wausau Daily Herald*, April 21, 1991, p. 1)
- "A Blessedly Silent Spring" (*Milwaukee Journal*, May 10, 1992).

The change in sentiment was apparent even to STA leader Dean Crist, who left the issue of whether to terminate the organization's protest activities to a membership vote ("Crist Calls for Vote on Ending Protests," *Milwaukee Journal*, April 19, 1991). While members did vote to continue with their protest activities, and a few days later even mustered an estimated 250 people to protest at a boat landing ("Spearing Tension Remains High after Near-Riot," *Milwaukee Sentinel*, April 22, 1991), the organization never regained the force and popularity it had enjoyed throughout the 1980s.

Several factors contributed to the decline in anti-treaty sentiment. First, there was the growing perception among the general population that the Chippewa were doing their part to cooperate with state conservationists and sportfishermen by voluntarily restocking lakes with fish from their own hatcheries and reducing their spearing quotas ("Lac du Flambeau to Donate Walleye for Restocking Lakes," *Milwaukee Sentinel*, April 20, 1991; "State, Indian Agencies Agree to Work Together," *Capital Times*, May 23, 1990, p. 8A; "Indians, Business Work Together on Walleye Population," *Wisconsin State Journal*, July 1, 1990, p. 6H). Second was the dissemination of more accurate information regarding the environmental impact of spearfishing. A $300,000 federally funded study on the fish population reported that spearfishing accounted for no more than 4 percent of the nearly 625,000 walleye taken annually by sportfishermen. Third, new legal rulings imposed penalties for impeding or obstructing legal hunting, fishing, and trapping ("New Law Targets Those Who Try to Impede Fishermen," *Capital Times*, April 10, 1990, p. 3A). STA, for example, was eventually barred from boat landings because its protests were seen as racially motivated. Fourth, negative publicity was casting treaty opponents as "redneck" racists—a portrayal that was, in turn, instrumental in swaying protest leaders, such as PARR chairman Larry Peterson, to recast the movement's image and to employ less confrontational tactics. Peterson went to great lengths to stress that PARR's grievance was with "the politicians, not the Indian people" ("Peaceful Protest," *Edgar Record Review,* April 29, 1992, p. 4). And a fifth factor was Judge Crabb's ruling, in LCO VII, that the Chippewa were entitled to only 50 percent of the available annual harvest, which contributed greatly to calming fears about resource depletion.

Today, white and Indian residents of the North Woods have come a long way toward rebuilding relations since the violent confrontations of the late 1980s. Each side, while wary, seems resigned to the fact that the other side is not going to go away. Nevertheless, treaty rights remain a hot-button issue, always threatening to crack the fragile veneer of peace. In 1996, for example, when the Lac du Flambeau Indians announced their intention to spear 100 percent of their share of walleye (which meant zero fish for regular-season fishermen), the response from the surrounding white community was immediate: there was talk of reviving landing protests, a boycott of the Lac du Flambeau casino was called, and T-shirts appeared showing a spear stuck through a stack of gaming chips and emblazoned with the words, "Spear This!" ("Once Again, Angry Voices Are Echoing in the North Woods," *Wisconsin State Journal,* April 24, 1996). While official accounts suggest that residents of the North Woods have ended their fight, deeper healing between the two sides remains elusive.

Meanwhile, treaty rights battles involving other tribes and white communities continue to be waged across the nation. Recent controversies include: tribal gambling rights in California, Connecticut, and New Jersey ("On the Horizon, the Specter of a Casino," *New York Times,* July 27, 1993; "Economies Coming to Life on Indian Reservations," *New York Times,* July 3, 1994); hunting rights in South Dakota, where the 1999 big game hunting season was canceled owing to shortages of deer, turkey, elk, and antelope, and fliers and an ad in a local newspaper appeared proclaiming open "Indian hunting season" on Sioux reservations and describing regulations for where and in what manner Indians could be killed ("Campbell Asks Reno to Investigate Anti-Indian Fliers," Associated Press, November 4, 1999); spearfishing rights in Minnesota and Michigan, where the fight was eerily similar to what was experienced in Wisconsin ("Minnesota Prepares for Walleye Spearing—They're Hoping to Avoid Conflict on the Lakes," *Wis-*

consin State Journal, April 6, 1997; "Michigan Pact Resolves Battle over Limits on Indian Fishing," *New York Times,* August 8, 2000); whaling rights in the state of Washington, where global protests ensued after the Makah tribe resumed its ancient practice of hunting gray whales ("Reviving Tradition, Tribe Kills a Whale," *New York Times,* May 18, 1999); and tribal sovereignty issues in Montana concerning the taxation of non-native businesses located on the Crow reservation ("Backlash Growing as Indians Make a Stand for Sovereignty," *New York Times,* March 9, 1998). This cursory glance across the nation reveals that one thing is clear: treaty rights and tribal sovereignty issues are not going to go away any time soon.

CONCLUSIONS

Our purpose in this chapter has been to lay the historical foundation needed for an examination of public opinion in the Wisconsin treaty rights controversy. As even this brief recounting makes clear, Indian-white relations have a very long, complicated, and troubled history. Unfortunately, it is beyond the scope of our mission to grapple with this varied and rich history in detail. Instead, we have tried to identify core epochs in Indian-white relations, as well as the content and influence of whites' stereotypes of Native Americans. All of this, of course, bears in both distal and more immediate ways on the emergence of the Wisconsin treaty rights controversy.

This history is offered not as mere context setting, but also for its constitutive place in the theoretical ideas we advance concerning the enduring power of ethno-racial divisions and theoretical leverage in understanding such divisions provided by group position theory. Among the continuities echoing from the past and reverberating in the present are the influence and the remarkable adaptive capacity of anti-Indian prejudice. As our review suggests, those who came to be labeled "Indians" were categorized and seen as different, other, and essentially inferior. The content and valence of the stereotypes about Native Americans have moved in near lockstep with the needs and interests of significant segments of white America.

Chapter 3

BETWEEN PREJUDICE AND SELF-INTEREST:
TREATY RIGHTS SALIENCE AND PUBLIC OPPOSITION

It's been a long time since Custer. They should fit into the melting pot, and if they can't, they should have no more rights than we do.

Anti–treaty rights CITRS respondent

A contract is a contract and treaties cannot be abrogated without shame.

Pro–treaty rights CITRS respondent

In late 1989 and throughout 1990 the treaty rights dispute was very much a live issue in Wisconsin. The governor and the state attorney general were trying to pressure the Chippewa into accepting a financial "buy-out" of their rights. Litigation continued as well. Judge Crabb issued rulings on whether the Chippewa could seek financial damages for past abridgement of their rights and the scope of their right to hunt deer. Protests at the boat landings remained intense occasions. News media throughout the state provided regular and in-depth coverage of the hostilities surrounding the Chippewa's exercising of their treaty rights. In January, for instance, a major report was published that pointed to racism as a cause of the treaty controversy ("Report Targets Racism as Basis for Indian Treaty Rights Tension," *Capital Times*, January 17, 1990). The spring fishing season raised anew the specter of open conflict ("Spearfishing Site Quiet, But Signs are Ominous," *Capital Times*, April 13, 1990). There was also a noticeable increase in headlines emphasizing cooperation between the two sides, as well as articles (most notably a "Cultures in Conflict" series published in the *Wisconsin State Journal*) designed to promote greater cross-cultural understanding ("Spearing Season Winds to a Quiet End," *Capital Times*, May 5, 1990; "State, Indian Agencies Agree to Work Together," *Capital Times*, May 23, 1990; "Spearing Conflict Has Come a Long Way," *Wisconsin State Jour-*

nal, May 6, 1990). It was in this context that our survey was conducted and we attempted to gauge public opinion on the treaty rights issue.

In this chapter we address three aspects of the conflict. First, we examine whether there was in fact a substantial "public" engaged with the treaty rights dispute. If there were not, it would be impossible to speak of sociologically meaningful public opinion on the treaty rights of the Chippewa Indians. The question is not a trivial one, given both prior research on public opinion and the nature of the treaty rights issue itself. Many studies show the U.S. public generally has little detailed knowledge about politics and public affairs. As a result, posing and even receiving answers to questions on matters of politics in surveys is no guarantee that the opinions offered are well grounded and substantial (Converse 1964; Kinder 1998; Zaller 1992).[1] This risk of little public engagement was particularly great in our case because the treaty rights dispute was focused in the North Woods, the upper third of Wisconsin, an area that is home to well under a third of the state's population. The results we report below establish that by 1990 the treaty rights dispute had become a topic of broad public salience and engagement. There was, in the sociologically relevant and portentous sense, a genuine public opinion taking shape.

Second, we assess the distribution of opinion regarding the assertion by members of the Chippewa tribe of their rights to fish, hunt, and log according to their traditions. Although off-reservation spearfishing was the most acute point of conflict, we found that each of the specific off-reservation rights was broadly unpopular among white Wisconsin residents. This was clearly a case of the courts' protecting the rights of a minority group against widespread and often intense disagreement among the majority population. Indeed, this feature of the dispute makes the treaty rights controversy directly relevant to other issues in American racial politics, such as the once bitter disputes over school busing for desegregation, the ongoing debates about affirmative action, and various efforts to curtail the rights and social benefits made available to immigrants. The legally and constitutionally protected right of a minority was upheld or enforced against the popular will of the majority.

Third, we pose the classic theoretical and political question of whether opposition to the treaty rights derived from ignorance and anti-Chippewa prejudice or from a more realistic clash of interests and instrumental contingencies. Was this a controversy driven mainly by emotions and irrational animus, or one driven by reason and the material stakes posed by the issue? Our results point to important effects of both prejudice and self-interest on public opinion regarding the treaty rights. Those searching for a "simple and sovereign" account in either prejudice alone or vested interests alone will be disappointed by these results. However, as we argued earlier, most instances of racial politics simultaneously and unavoidably mobilize intergroup attitudes as well as those interests woven into the fabric of group relations—precisely as our theory of group position maintains. That both prejudice and vested interests matter is perfectly sensible under group position theory. The problem this result poses for some, we suspect, lies in the penchant in the social sciences for framing research and theoretical tests in terms of mutually exclusive critical tests, when our research tools (theories included) and the underlying social phenomena are frequently ill-suited to such unicausal models.

TREATY DISPUTE SALIENCE

We sought to gauge the salience of the treaty rights issue by asking all respondents, early in the questionnaire and prior to any other explicit reference to the dispute, "Have you heard or read anything about the controversy over Indian treaty rights?" Results for this question are shown in Figure 3.1. The vast majority of respondents statewide, 84 percent, answered in the affirmative. In a follow-up question asked only of those who said "yes" to the previous item, we asked respondents whether, in the six to nine months prior to the survey, they had "seen any newspaper articles or stories that dealt with Indian treaty rights?" Again, an overwhelming majority responded in the affirmative.

One way to put these results in perspective is to compare the responses with a measure of general interest in politics. Table 3.1 displays responses to a question in the survey on general interest in politics and shows how this item relates to the salience of the treaty rights issue. Nearly one-third of our respondents expressed little regular interest in politics (responses of "slightly" or "not at all interested"), and a small minority, fewer than one in five (16.7 percent), described themselves as "very interested" in politics. To be sure, there is a clear relationship between the salience of the treaty rights dispute and an individual's general level of interest in politics. Those with greater general involvement in tracking political affairs were more likely to attend to the treaty dispute as well. More important from the vantage point of establishing broad public engagement with the issue, how-

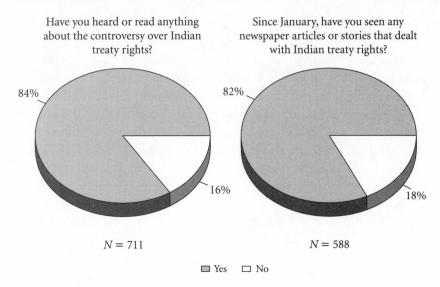

Have you heard or read anything
about the controversy over Indian
treaty rights?

Since January, have you seen any
newspaper articles or stories that dealt
with Indian treaty rights?

84%

82%

16%

18%

$N = 711$

$N = 588$

☐ Yes   ☐ No

FIGURE 3.1 Salience of the treaty rights dispute.
Source: Chippewa Indian Treaty Rights Survey, 1990.

ever, is that nearly two-thirds of the respondents who said they are "not at all interested in politics" had nonetheless paid some attention to the treaty rights dispute.

We also examined the salience of the treaty rights issue in relation to two other measures of potential general involvement with politics: level of education and strength of ideological leaning. Level of education is typically found be a consistent influence on levels of political knowledge and sophistication (Delli Carpini and Keeter 1996; Zaller 1992). All else being equal, individuals who declare themselves to be "extremely liberal" or "extremely conservative" in outlook have tended to claim substantially politicized social identities. Table 3.2 displays how these alternative measures of general engagement with politics related to treaty salience. There is a clear and monotonic association between level of education and the salience of the treaty rights issue, with virtually all college-educated respondents having had at least some exposure to the issue. More important from our point of view is that fully 73 percent of those who did not finish high school also reported this basic level of treaty rights salience. Differences by education were less pronounced for the exposure to newspaper coverage.

Only a small fraction of the sample declared themselves to be strong po-

TABLE 3.1   Interest in politics and treaty salience

	Very interested	Interested	Slightly interested	Not at all interested
Overall	16.7%	48.7%	27.9%	6.6%
Informed about treaty rights				
Yes	89.8	86.0	82.5	65.2
No	10.2	14.0	17.5	34.8
(N)	*(118)*	*(344)*	*(194)*	*(46)*
Chi-squared				16.69***
Seen newspaper coverage				
Yes	91.5	83.9	75.2	61.3
No	8.5	16.1	24.8	38.7
(N)	*(106)*	*(292)*	*(157)*	*(31)*
Chi-squared				20.94***

$*p < .05$ $**p < .01$ $***p < .001$

Source: Chippewa Indian Treaty Rights Survey, 1990.

litical ideologues, and this variable does not clearly differentiate among respondents in basic treaty rights salience. However, given some attentiveness to the treaty rights issue, strong ideologues were significantly more likely than both those with more moderate identifications and "middle of the roaders" to report having consumed news coverage on the issue. But again, even here, a high fraction of those without strong ideological inclinations reported both basic attentiveness to the treaty rights issue and exposure to newspaper coverage.

The salience of the treaty rights dispute for those who otherwise are modestly or weakly engaged with politics should not be read as implying that the issue achieved overarching public importance. Early in the questionnaire and, again, prior to any explicit reference to the treaty dispute, we asked the standard open-ended question, "What do you think are the most important problems facing the State of Wisconsin?" The treaty rights dispute was the first mention among only 5.3 percent of our respondents, falling well behind a concern with taxes (34.7 percent), environmental issues (10.1 percent), and welfare policy (8.0 percent). Indeed, mention of the treaty dispute was seventh on the list of problems spontaneously mentioned.[2]

TABLE 3.2 Education, ideological extremity, and treaty salience

	Education			
	BA degree or more	Some college	High school diploma	Less than high school diploma
Overall	23%	28%	39%	10%
Informed about treaty rights				
Yes	93	86	80	73
No	7	14	20	27
(N)	(163)	(201)	(273)	(70)
Chi-squared				19.08***
Seen newspaper coverage				
Yes	85	82	82	74
No	15	18	18	27
(N)	(151)	(172)	(214)	(49)
Chi-squared				3.19 ns

	Ideological extremity		
	Strong ideologues	Ideologues/ Weak leaners	Middle of the road
Overall	3%	57%	40%
Informed about treaty rights			
Yes	71	86	82
No	29	14	18
(N)	(17)	(405)	(282)
Chi-squared			4.63 ns
Seen newspaper coverage			
Yes	100	85	77
No		15	23
(N)	(12)	(347)	(225)
Chi-squared			8.81**

*p < .05   **p < .01   ***p < .001

Source: Chippewa Indian Treaty Rights Survey, 1990.

Note: Not all columns sum to 100 due to rounding.

In sum, the adult population of the state was aware of and attuned to the treaty rights dispute, though the issue was not of all-consuming prominence. More than four out of five of our respondents were aware of the issue, and an equally large fraction of those respondents had actually seen newspaper articles on the topic. The salience of the issue reached deep into even those segments of the population otherwise poorly educated or quite disinterested in politics. The treaty rights dispute was not merely a conflict in the North Woods among an engaged few; it was a matter of substantially engaged public opinion statewide.

TREATY RIGHTS ISSUE ATTITUDES

Of those respondents who reported to us that they had "heard or read about the controversy," we asked a series of questions about substantive opinions on the off-reservation rights of the Chippewa Indian tribe. Three questions in the survey dealt, respectively, with off-reservation hunting, off-reservation spearfishing, and off-reservation logging, to assess the core issue attitude of interest to us. Off-reservation spearfishing, of course, was the preeminent source of overt controversy and conflict. Off-reservation hunting and the potential for off-reservation logging were also matters of litigation and major court rulings, and they constituted the other significant resource access and use issues raised by affirmation of the treaty rights. The distribution of responses is shown in Table 3.3. Each treaty-reserved and court-affirmed right was opposed by a solid majority of Wisconsin residents at a point some six years after the Voigt decision. Thus 59 percent (combining "somewhat" and "strongly oppose" responses) opposed off-reservation hunting, 70 percent opposed off-reservation fishing, and 64 percent opposed off-reservation logging. Support for the treaty rights of the Chippewa was never voiced by more than one in three of our respondents. To wit, the Chippewa's rights were contested not only by a highly mobilized few at the boat landings but also statewide at the bar of white public opinion.

Although providing a clear indication of the tilt of public sentiment, these individual survey items cannot of themselves convey the full complexity of public thinking and discourse on the treaty rights dispute. What frames of reference do individuals bring to the issue? What ideas and arguments for and against the treaty are average individuals invoking? Is there a dominant thread to discourse on treaty rights? Do people speak in terms

TABLE 3.3   Attitudes toward off-reservation treaty rights

	Off-reservation hunting	Off-reservation fishing	Off-reservation logging
Strongly favor	4.1%	3.4%	1.6%
Somewhat favor	28.0	21.1	18.5
No opinion	8.6	5.4	15.8
Somewhat oppose	35.0	40.1	35.9
Strongly oppose	24.4	30.0	28.1
(N)	(567)	(582)	(581)

Source: Chippewa Indian Treaty Rights Survey, 1990.

Note: Not all columns sum to 100 due to rounding.

of practical contingencies and personal concerns, or in terms of antagonistic groups and "us versus them"? We knew we could gain much deeper insight into public opinion by allowing respondents to explain why they took certain positions on the treaty rights issue. Following the question on spearfishing—easily the most visible and divisive aspect of the treaty controversy—we asked our respondents to explain in their own words why they favored or opposed off-reservation spearfishing. Table 3.4 presents the distribution of open-ended responses as categorized according to a number of basic themes. There is a sense in which treaty supporters and treaty opponents draw from different frames of reference when called on to explain their attitudes.

Below we consider in detail the three most frequent explanations offered by supporters and opponents of treaty rights. We chose to emphasize the top three categories in each camp for several reasons. Doing so covers a large portion of the sample (nearly 60 percent), it allows us to consider in some detail important variants and subthemes within major categories, and it captures central ideas in the controversy as depicted in much of the media coverage.

TREATY OPPONENTS

More than two-thirds of our sample opposed off-reservation spearfishing. When asked to explain why, the most common explanation given was some variant of "equal rights for everyone." This type of response was given by 23 percent of those opposed to spearfishing (and by just under two in ten respondents overall). At the core of this theme was a sense that

TABLE 3.4 Open-ended explanations of reasons for treaty rights attitudes

	Statewide	Percentage of total sample
Reasons for favoring		
Contract, legal right, valid contract	38%	10%
Indians have as much right as anyone else	13	4
Indians were here first	21	6
We owe debt to Indians	13	4
Doesn't hurt natural resources	4	1
Hold Indians accountable	1	2
OK with limits or quotas	4	3
Other/don't know	6	See below
(N)	(142)	
Reasons for opposing		
OK with limits or quotas	3	3
Unnecessary, plenty of fish on reservation	5	4
Indians should stay on reservation	15	12
Will hurt supply of fish	11	8
Treaty outdated	8	6
Everyone should have equal rights	23	17
Using modern equipment	4	3
Taking advantage	4	3
Abuse rights	6	5
Other/don't know	21	9
(N)	(407)	(549)

Source: The Chippewa Indian Treaty Rights Survey, 1990.

Note: Not all columns sum to 100 due to rounding. "See below" indicates a category that was the same in both panels; these entries were combined to show statewide percentage.

the treaty rights were unfair, indeed that they were tantamount to a plainly "un-American" failure to treat people equally. Within this theme of unfairness, however, four quite distinct variations emerged. First, for some respondents the unfairness at stake was clearly a violation of an important principle:

[If] they want to be a part of the country, [then] why can't they follow the rules?
—*Sixty-four-year-old male, registered nurse, some post–high school education*

I think that that's being prejudiced against everyone else.

> —*Twenty-nine-year-old female, sales promoter, some post–high school education*

I don't know. My husband and I have discussed this a lot. Because to me that doesn't seem fair. I think that everyone is equal. I don't think the color of a person's skin should give them rights or deny them rights.

> —*Twenty-six-year-old female, animal caretaker, some post–high school education*

I feel that the rights of American citizens should be equal and I do understand that they've been mistreated in the past and a treaty was made. But in this day and age equal rights is an important issue.

> —*Thirty-five-year-old female, secretary, high school graduate*

These respondents felt that an important societal value—equal treatment of individuals by the government—was being violated.

A second and more frequent variant of the unfairness theme stressed, in effect, that "people like me" are shortchanged or disadvantaged by the preservation of Indian treaty rights:

I think they are American citizens, and we all pay taxes, and why should they have any more benefits than anyone else?

> —*Thirty-nine-year-old male, mechanic, some post–high school education*

We are all American citizens and we all have to abide by the same Constitution. They shouldn't have more rights than the rest of us. I can't help it that they got a treaty from years ago. They wanted to be citizens and they are.

> —*Forty-five-year-old female, records clerk, some post–high school education*

I just don't feel that after all these years it is right. They are governed by the same government that we are, and they should abide by the same rules we do.

> —*Forty-one-year-old female, therapist, some post–high school education*

We can't do it, so why should they do it off the reservation?

> —*Twenty-six-year-old male, sales supervisor, college graduate*

It's been a long time since Custer. They should fit into the melting pot, and if they can't, they should have no more rights than we do.
— *Forty-nine-year-old female, kitchen worker, high school graduate*

A third, more pragmatic variant expressed by some respondents extended the "people like me are shortchanged" argument. For those respondents involved in sportfishing, the treaty rights were a special injustice:

I'm a fisherman myself and I gotta pay so much for my license, and they go and take whatever they want [and] we get punished for it. Every year I get less fish.
— *Thirty-six-year-old male, plumbing supervisor, some post–high school education*

We have people that buy licenses for fishing, and if the Indians are allowed to take all the fish that they want, that's not fair.
— *Sixty-seven-year-old female, farmer, high school graduate*

Because I can't do the same thing they're doing. When they are off the reservation they should fish with [a] license like everyone else.
— *Twenty-nine-year-old male, engine repairman, some post–high school education*

The fourth variant on the general unfairness of not treating everyone equally was more explicitly racial in nature. Some respondents saw whites as a group suffering under the imposition of treaty rights:

Because I think that the white person is now a minority. I think that what is good for one race is good for them all.
— *Fifty-eight-year-old male, welder, high school graduate*

Because they should have the same rights as white people.
— *Forty-four-year-old male, wholesaler, non–high school graduate*

Well, I just think that they are making the white people the minority by giving them something that we do not have. And I think that it is going to come to a big fight.
— *Seventy-nine-year-old female, retired high school teacher, college graduate*

It is worth noting that fewer than one in five of those respondents who offered this type of explanation had graduated from college. Many had, however, completed high school and gone on to some vocational training.

The second most common of the explanations for opposing off-reservation spearfishing, offered by 15 percent of treaty rights opponents and about 12 of the overall sample, emphasized that the Indians had special entitlement on the reservation only. This view has much in common with the unfairness of unequal treatment theme, but it is mainly concerned with where traditional tribal fishing methods are practiced, rather than whether any differences should be permitted:

> Well, I figure they have their territory there and I don't feel they should go off of it.
> —*Seventy-nine-year-old female, paint machine operator, non–high school graduate*

> On the reservation, let them spearfish there. Off the reservation, it's equal rights for everyone.
> —*Fifty-one-year-old male, cashier, high school graduate*

> I think that what they do on the reservation is fine. But off it, they should abide by the laws everyone else does. Now they use more modern equipment, too, than they did in the past.
> —*Forty-one-year-old male, police officer, college graduate*

As some of these remarks imply, the theme of restricting spearfishing to the reservation included a sense of competition and loss for non-Indians:

> Because they have fish on the lakes out on the reservation and now they are coming to take our fish.
> —*Forty-eight-year-old male, mechanic, high school graduate*

> Because they have their area to fish in and that's where they should be. And if they make whites stay off their land, then they should stay put.
> —*Thirty-eight-year-old female, sales supervisor, high school graduate*

> Because off-reservation they are in direct competition with the sports fisherman.
> —*Thirty-nine-year-old male, mechanic, college graduate*

The third major theme among treaty rights opponents asserted that off-reservation spearfishing was damaging to the supply of fish. This type of response came from 11 percent of treaty rights opponents, representing slightly fewer than one in ten of our overall sample. Respondents who offered this explanation seemed the most emotional about the issue and were the most likely to state several grievances against Native Americans as a group. In particular, many offered the angry claim that the Indians were overfishing:

They're taking all the fish.
—*Nineteen-year-old male, timber cutter, high school graduate*

They're going to kill all the god-damned fish if they keep going at this rate. It's bullshit and they make a profit off all the fish they take; they sell it.
—*Twenty-seven-year-old male, truck driver, high school graduate*

They're using up all our natural resources and [they] take advantage of [the] situation and want a free ride.
—*Fifty-four-year-old female, secretary, high school graduate*

'Cause they are cleaning out our lakes 'til there is nothing, and they don't need it. They all get welfare and everything free.
—*Thirty-eight-year-old female, bookkeeper, some post–high school education*

Well, I believe that they're wrecking our natural resources and they're not eating what they take. They're doing it just to spite the white people.
—*Forty-two-year-old female, bookkeeper, some post–high school education*

Some of the responses were more reasoned in tone:

When these treaties were set up, that was fine and dandy, but in the present time, they're doing a lot of damage to [the] environment and supply of fish. They should be severely governed over [or] limited. [I'm] not against the Indian[s].
—*Thirty-four-year-old male, firefighter, some post–high school education*

No one else is allowed to fish during spawning season, and for every fish they kill, they kill that many little fingerlings.
—*Sixty-three-year-old female, machine operator, high school graduate*

And some of those concerned with damage to the fish supply spoke explicitly of reducing the take for other fishers or of the impact on tourism:

Because I'm a fisherman, and it has caused the size and bag limits to go up [down] and it has hurt tourism and the size of muskies and other fish in this area.
    —*Thirty-four-year-old male, laborer, high school graduate*

Well, they take a lot of fish and that ruins the tourist business up here.
    —*Eighteen-year-old male, machine operator, high school graduate*

I think that they are taking away from the fish for everyone else. I am a fisherman and I know.
    —*Forty-four-year-old male, carpenter, high school graduate*

It is perhaps ironic but also theoretically consequential that among the most common themes of opposition, the remarks in the "damage the supply of fish" category come the closest to reflecting open bigotry. An important element of prejudice is suggested by the multiple and easily generalized abuses credited to Indians. It is worth emphasizing again that the actual take in fish by the Chippewa bands amounts to a small fraction of the total harvest.[3] The respondents' insensitivity to the actual facts of the case, the frequency of broad stereotyping, and the raw emotional quality of many of the responses suggests that the complaint of damage to the fish supply is often a part of or tied to a bundle of ideas better understood as a form of prejudice rather than a legitimate, practical grievance (a point we elaborate on in Chapter 4).

Other reasons respondents gave for opposing the treaty rights included assertions that the Chippewa abuse their rights or take advantage of the situation; that they use modern fishing equipment instead of following their ancient traditions; and that off-reservation fishing is just unnecessary, given the fish available on the reservation. Some respondents simply said the treaties were outdated. Only 4 percent of spearfishing opponents literally said "don't know" when asked to explain their opinion, but many others just reiterated their opposition without giving a clear substantive rationale, or they gave a highly idiosyncratic response.

TREATY PROPONENTS

Among those who favored off-reservation spearfishing, the most common theme in their open-ended accounts concerned the validity of a contract between the U.S. government and the Chippewa Indians. Almost two out of five treaty rights supporters offered this kind of explanation (10 percent of the overall sample). Some of these respondents simply asserted that the treaty rights were part of a valid contract.

The broad theme of a legal contract, however, also had four noteworthy variations. First, to some respondents the Indians had a claim to certain rights:

> It just seems right. They seem to have old rights that they should be able to keep.
> —*Twenty-seven-year-old female, service-worker supervisor, college graduate*

> I think we made an agreement and signed it. It is their land and is part of their rights.
> —*Fifty-nine-year-old male, clergyman, college graduate*

Second, other respondents apparently took the court rulings upholding the treaty rights as an authoritative statement of the law:

> Simply because it is legal for them to do so. If it were ruled illegal, I would be against it.
> —*Forty-three-year-old female, administrator, high school graduate*

> Because the court said that they could do it. I don't feel my personal opinion goes over their legal rights.
> —*Fifty-year-old female, lawyer, postgraduate education*

Third, for some respondents the emphasis on the law included a closely related belief that no harm was done by the Chippewa's use of their court-affirmed treaty rights:

> I think that we should abide by the treaties, and I don't feel the number speared interferes with the number for sports fishermen.
> —*Thirty-seven-year-old female, health teacher, college graduate*

> It's a legal settlement. They are not abusing [the] resource.
> —*Thirty-year-old male, physicist, postgraduate education*

And fourth, a number of comments indicated a sense of moral outrage at the possibility of violating a legally valid treaty:

> Because they have the right by treaty, and a treaty signed by the American government should be valid.
> —*Sixty-four-year-old female, high school teacher, college graduate*

A contract is a contract, and treaties cannot be abrogated without shame.
   —*Thirty-six-year-old female, physician, postgraduate education*

An essential point about the legal-contract theme should be noted. This was the preferred justification for supporting the treaty rights among the well-educated respondents. Fully 60 percent of those who offered this justification were college graduates, and many held advanced professional degrees. This figure well exceeds the 23 percent of the sample as a whole who graduated from college and even the 36 percent of college-educated respondents who favored off-reservation spearfishing. The importance of upholding the law stands out as the distinctive motif in explanations offered by well-educated respondents.

The second most common theme expressed by those who favored the treaty rights was the idea that the United States has a historical and moral obligation to Native Americans. Many of these respondents, particularly men, put the nature of this obligation very simply:

They have their rights because they were here first.
   —*Twenty-six-year-old male, welder, high school graduate*

Well, it was their land before it was ours and I think they're entitled to their laws and we're entitled to ours.
   —*Fifty-one-year-old female, maid, non–high school graduate*

A number of respondents added to this theme of debt and obligation a concern with protecting American Indian heritage and atoning for how the U.S. government dealt with Indian peoples in the past:

It's kind of like their way of life and their heritage, and it's kind of hard for us to take it away from them.
   —*Twenty-two-year-old female, registered nurse, some post–high school education*

They were here before I was, and I feel like they were treated pretty shabbily. Their traditions should continue.
   —*Thirty-four-year-old female, nurse's aide, college graduate*

An important element seeming to underlie most of the remarks concerning a debt owed to the "first of this land" is the notion of proper claim to the land and its resources. This idea of debt tied for third place among the most common reason offered for supporting the treaty rights.

The other third-place response involved the assertion that "Indians have as much right as anyone else." For some respondents, this idea is closely related to the legal contract theme, but perhaps because of limited vocabulary or level of education, the idea was not articulated so directly as to warrant placement in that category. A number of these respondents, however, did not have full information about the treaty rights issue. They said they favored treaty rights but evidently were unaware that this involved a departure from the fishing privileges available to others. Some respondents interpreted the question to mean merely allowing the Chippewa to fish off-reservation just as everyone else does.

Smaller proportions of those favoring the treaty rights spoke mainly about the lack of harm to natural resources, and the need to limit and regulate the fishing take and to hold the Chippewa accountable. Several other types of responses were given by fewer than 2 percent of the sample or were so idiosyncratic as to only fit in the category of "other." Those responses were grouped with the small number of treaty proponents (fewer than 1 percent) who said "don't know" when asked to explain their view.

The open-ended responses do much to put the traditional attitude-question responses into fuller perspective—a perspective better informed by the ideas, terms, and substance of discourse on the treaty rights dispute. Certainly the open-ended responses increase our confidence that most respondents not only understood our questions but also gave frank and thoughtful answers. Rather than offering putatively safe or publicly acceptable opinions and platitudes, most individuals appear to have spoken their mind. We have no way to gauge the absolute level of "socially desirable" responding that may have taken place, and surely some did occur. It is difficult, however, to come away from reviewing the explanations offered by our respondents, in their own words, without feeling that most people told us precisely how they felt.

In addition, the open-ended responses cast a different and more sharply illuminating light on attitudes expressed about treaty rights. The reasons that lead people to express similar positions can differ widely. For some, grounds for favoring treaty rights rest on a principle of legally valid contracts, and for others, on the historical debt the U.S. government is seen as owing to all Native Americans. Even similar core themes can embrace quite distinctive subthemes or elements. Thus many respondents oppose the

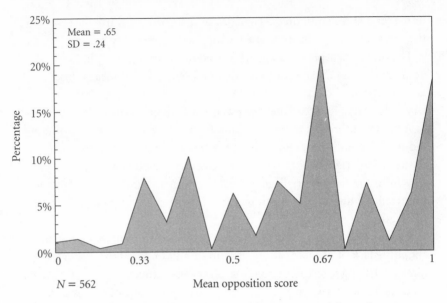

FIGURE 3.2 Distribution of the opposition-to-treaty-rights scale.
Source: Chippewa Indian Treaty Rights Survey, 1990.

treaty rights because they see them as unfair special treatment, a sort of treatment that violates traditional American notions of equality. But some respondents express this objection more as a principle, whereas for others it carries an explicit element of group or fraternal deprivation, and for some fraction of both, it appears to be an emotion-arousing concern. Those speaking of a feeling of group deprivation suggest, in effect, that "we," "us," "everyone else," or "people like me" are at a disadvantage relative to Chippewa Indians. Indeed some of those who view the treaty rights as unfair actually see the issue as further proof of the increasing powerlessness of whites in the face of minority-group demands and gains.

As all serious students of public opinion know, a simple distribution of opinion in response to a single attitude or opinion question does not capture the full dimensionality of public thinking on complex social and political issues (Kinder 1998; Sheatsley 1983). The limitations of single items, despite the repeated claims of many anti-quantitative ideologues (Esposito and Murphy 1999), need not limit entire social surveys and, even less so, the extensive literature that is based on them (Bobo 1997; Krysan 2000; Sears et al. 2000). It is possible to capture much of both the central tendencies and the terms of popular discourse about a critical social issue, such as the treaty rights dispute, via social surveys (a point that will become even clearer in Chapter 4).

Having established the general salience of the treaty dispute and the basic distribution of opinion on key dimensions of the issue, and having tapped into the actual terms of discourse about the issue, our concern is to focus on a better, theoretically grounded, and systematic understanding of the factors that shaped opinion on the treaty rights. For this part of the analysis, the three treaty-rights issue attitudes form our main indicator of public opinion on the treaties and our primary dependent variable. Responses to the questions are quite highly intercorrelated. The average Pearson's correlation is .68 and a simple additive scale, scored to run from a low of 0, reflecting support for the treaty rights, to a high of 1.0, reflecting consistent opposition to the treaty rights, is highly reliable (Cronbach's alpha = .86). The distribution on the opposition-to-treaty-rights scale is depicted graphically in Figure 3.2, which shows the clear overall—but not massively skewed—tilt toward treaty opposition.

IS IT PREJUDICE?

Many believed that the reserved rights of the Chippewa Indians became a subject of widespread opposition, controversy, and social protest because of prejudice and racism. Proponents of this view did not need to look very far to find support for their view. News media frequently ran stories emphasizing the role of racism and intolerance in fueling the treaty controversy, as a number of headlines suggest:

- "Candidate Says He's Finding Support for Pro-White Platform" (*Capital Times,* January 17, 1990)
- "Fighting Freeloading Stereotype" (*Wisconsin State Journal,* February 25, 1990)
- "Schools Fight Racism" (*Wisconsin State Journal,* February 18, 1990)
- "Inouye Riding to Rescue State from Its Rednecks" (*Wisconsin State Journal,* March 8, 1990)

The charge of racism angered many residents of the North Woods, who felt misjudged by reporters from "down state." Some residents maintained an active campaign of letter writing in defense of their views, emphasizing that the issue was not about race but about rights ("Racism La-

bel Overdone—Again," *Vilas County News-Review,* April 28, 1988; "A Word
on Racism," *Vilas County News-Review,* April 19, 1989; "Spearing Is Issue,
Not Racism," *Capital Times,* March 12, 1990). Nevertheless, charges of racism were hard to dismiss, given how candid many protesters were in sharing their views with the press, as in the following examples:

> Just up the road from the Pelican Lake landing, at Bruce and Betty's Bar,
> the talk was all of spearfishing, and it was not friendly. "Just don't write
> how we're bigots up here," said one patron after spotting [on] a reporter
> the special badge required to cover the boat landings. On the wall behind
> the bar a flyer was prominently displayed, headed, "First Annual Indian
> Shoot." It described the rules for shooting Indians for sport and gain.
> "That's just a joke," explained Bruce, who was trying to organize friends
> to protest at the landing. Betty added, "I grew up with the coloreds in
> Chicago. I'm no bigot. I went to school with niggers." ("Spearfishing Site
> Quiet, But Signs Are Ominous," *Capital Times,* April 13, 1990)

> As for their [the Indians'] livelihood, there is not one family that
> needs spearing for this purpose. We, the taxpayers, feed them, build their
> houses, pay for their education, and medical. I just read where 50 percent
> of Wisconsin tax goes to support the Indians. And you say they need
> spearing for their livelihood. (Letter to the editor by Stella Caskey, *Vilas
> County News-Review,* April 2, 1988)

In Gordon Allport's formulation of classical sociocultural theory, prejudice is said to have many of its roots in ignorance. Intergroup contact—
to address the lack of direct exposure to and experience with members of
a minority group—is hypothesized to reduce prejudice. As Allport explained: "Contacts that bring knowledge and acquaintance are likely to en-
gender sounder beliefs concerning minority groups, and for this reason
contribute to the reduction of prejudice" (1954, p. 268). Generally higher
levels of knowledge and cognitive sophistication have, likewise, been an
element in accounting for the often-observed positive relation between
level of education and tolerance (Bobo and Licari 1989; Hyman, Wright,
and Reed 1975; Schuman et al. 1997; Stouffer 1955). For example, Stephan
and Stephan (1984) argued that ignorance and intolerance resulted from a
lack of meaningful, positive contact between members of different social
groups. They showed that if intergroup contact improved levels of cultural
knowledge about members of another group, attitudes toward members

of that group improved correspondingly. As they explained: "Ignorance causes prejudice because ignorance creates anxiety about out-groups, because out-groups are presumed to be dissimilar from the in-group, and because the information void regarding out-groups is filled with negative stereotypes" (Stephan and Stephan 1984, p. 249). Prejudice is most directly expressed in the form of negative stereotypes and negative feelings or affect. To test the classical prejudice theory, our Chippewa Indian Treaty Rights Survey measured relevant knowledge as well as stereotypes and affect. We will now consider each of these in turn and how they may relate to opinions on the treaty rights themselves.

KNOWLEDGE AND EDUCATION

It is often argued that minority-rights issues become controversial because some fraction of the dominant group holds inaccurate beliefs and information about the minority group and its rights. This produces or exacerbates unwarranted fears and assumptions about the group. Thus proponents of school busing frequently found themselves trying to rebut claims that educational outcomes for white students would be harmed by integration. Similarly, advocates for immigrant rights are compelled to insist that immigrants do pay taxes, make a net positive contribution to the economy, and are generally law abiding. Disagreements over "the facts" of the case and attempts to rebut erroneous claims were very much a part of the Wisconsin treaty dispute as well. Indeed the question of the public's level of knowledge was particularly relevant for our survey because both the scope and the practical effects of the treaty rights were often exaggerated ("Towns Start Legal Maneuvering to Confront Issue of Year Around Hunting and Fishing by Indians," *Vilas County News-Review*, March 9, 1983; "Ruling Allows Chippewa Indians Off Reservation Hunting Anytime," *Vilas County News-Review*, February 3, 1983).

We decided to focus the knowledge questions on what was a key point of contention: did the Chippewa's use of their reserved treaty rights pose a genuine resource threat, specifically to the supply of fish? In particular, we posed factual questions about aspects of the treaty issue that, if broadly understood, should have encouraged a more favorable response to the treaty rights. First, we asked whether the Chippewa bands cooperate with the state in monitoring the fishing and deer hunting of tribal members. As Table 3.5 shows, 50 percent gave the correct answer of yes. Second, we

TABLE 3.5   Treaty knowledge questions

	Do Chippewa monitor hunting and fishing?	Do Chippewa have fish-rearing programs?	Are Chippewa allowed unlimited fishing?
Yes	50.3%*	28.3%*	52.0%
No	31.6	32.7	34.5*
Don't know	18.0	39.0	13.5
(N)	(592)	(596)	(591)

Source: Chippewa Indian Treaty Rights Survey, 1990.
Note: Not all columns sum to 100 due to rounding. Asterisk indicates correct response.

asked whether the Chippewa maintain their own fish-rearing and stocking programs. In this case, only 28 percent gave the correct answer (yes). And third, we asked whether the Chippewa are allowed an unlimited number of fish. Even though the court decision allowing the Chippewa only half of the officially designated safe harvest had been widely publicized, only 35 percent gave the correct answer of no.

The generally low level of knowledge about the treaty rights is summarized in Figure 3.3. Nearly a third of our respondents answered all three questions incorrectly. Another third answered only one of the questions correctly. And barely one in ten gave correct answers to all three questions. On this basis there is ample reason to suppose that ignorance about the nature of the treaty rights, and about how the Chippewa act to preserve the underlying resources, constituted a major source of opposition to the treaty rights. This is in fact born out by the simple correlation between the knowledge index and the opposition-to-treaty-rights scale, which is $-.21$ ($p < .001$). As levels of knowledge increase, opposition to the treaty rights tends to decrease.[4]

Given that specific treaty-related knowledge is important, does level of education matter? Many studies have found a negative association between level of education and a variety of indicators of prejudice (Duckitt 1992; Hyman, Wright, and Reed 1975; Schuman et al. 1997). Although the argument that education leads to deeper genuine tolerance and greater commitment to equality (McClosky and Brill 1983; Prothro and Grigg 1960) has been debated and vigorously challenged (Jackman 1994; Jackman and Muha 1984), there is less dispute over whether education is likely to increase levels of information. As Figure 3.4 shows, in our results there is a strong monotonic relationship between level of education and overall knowledge about the treaties ($F = 5.20$, $df = 3$, $p < .001$). Although none

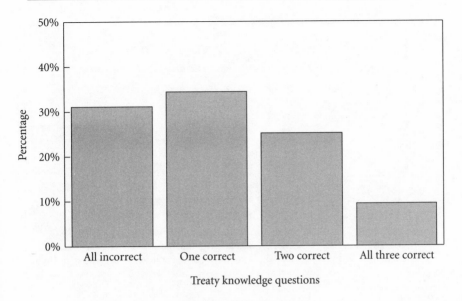

FIGURE 3.3 Treaty knowledge.
Source: Chippewa Indian Treaty Rights Survey, 1990.

of the education levels is particularly well informed, there is a clear-cut difference between, for example, those who did not complete high school and those with a college education or more.

Education does not, however, have the same straightforward impact on attitudes toward the treaties, an indication that something much more than information was shaping opinions on the treaty rights. To be sure, as Figure 3.5 shows, those with the highest level of education were indeed the least likely to oppose the treaty rights. But high school graduates were the most likely to oppose the treaties, and those with some college were about as hostile to the treaties as those who did not finish high school. In addition, even the separation between the college educated and the high school graduates is not very large. Level of education certainly influences information levels, but it has a less pronounced, nonmonotonic effect on opposition to treaty rights.[5]

STEREOTYPES AND AFFECT

A lack of information or a low level of education are only indirect indicators of whether racial prejudice might be relevant to opposition to treaty rights. Establishing a stronger direct role for prejudice would require

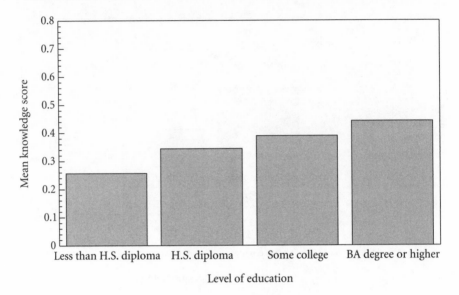

FIGURE 3.4 Treaty knowledge by education.
Source: Chippewa Indian Treaty Rights Survey, 1990.

showing that negative beliefs and feelings toward the Chippewa were also a part of the political environment in which the treaty rights were debated. To be sure, some have argued that prejudice is likely to have its most potent influence on policy views among the poorly educated (Sniderman and Piazza 1993). There is strong evidence that, although hostility to racial minorities may be lower in some absolute sense among the highly educated, those highly educated individuals who are prejudiced are especially likely to translate that prejudice into a rejection of policies beneficial to minorities (Sidanius, Pratto, and Bobo 1996). It remains an open empirical question, then, whether more direct indicators of prejudice will influence views on a matter like the treaty rights. That is, inaccurate or low levels of information do not automatically mean that stereotypes and negative intergroup feelings will carry a political punch in this context.

We measured stereotypes with a series of questions that called for respondents to rank each of three groups—whites, Indians, and blacks—on a series of 1-to-7-point bipolar trait-rating scales. We included questions on blacks as a way of gauging generalized prejudice versus particular-group and context-specific dynamics (a matter explored in more detail below). The trait scales posed in the questions were: rich (1) to poor (7),

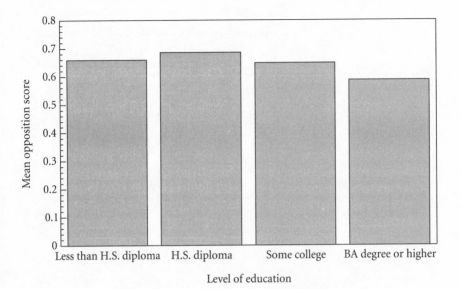

FIGURE 3.5 Treaty opposition by education.
Source: Chippewa Indian Treaty Rights Survey, 1990.

hardworking (1) to lazy (7), prefer to be self-supporting (1) to prefer to live off welfare (7), and respect nature (1) to do not respect nature (7). This set of traits thus includes a basic assessment of group economic success (rich or poor), commitment to the core American values of the work ethic (laziness and welfare dependency), and a trait of special relevance to Native Americans in general and the treaty rights dispute in particular (respect for nature). We have rescored each trait rating to range from a low score of 0, indicating the most favorable stereotype images, to a high score of 1, indicating the most unfavorable stereotype image. Mean scores are shown in Table 3.6, as is the proportion of respondents giving a negative rating (above the midpoint on the scale). We also show a "balance" score, which is the difference between the proportion positive and the proportion negative on each trait (Bobo and Kluegel 1997).

The first thing to note is that, with only one exception, white respondents gave their own group the lowest (most favorable) rating on each trait. The one exception is the respect for nature dimension, where, on average, our white respondents actually rated Indians more favorably than members of their own group. The general pattern of in-group favoritism is quite consistent with the finding that members of dominant social groups

TABLE 3.6 Stereotype distributions

	Mean	Proportion negative ratings	Balance	N
Rich/poor				
Whites tend to be poor	.452	14%	23	703
Indians tend to be poor	.692	70	−56	700
Blacks tend to be poor	.649	64	−28	702
Tend to be lazy				
Whites tend to be lazy	.414	14	28	688
Indians tend to be lazy	.584	41	−28	681
Blacks tend to be lazy	.572	42	−28	681
Prefer welfare				
Whites prefer welfare	.354	11	50	690
Indians prefer welfare	.552	40	−17	685
Blacks prefer welfare	.572	46	−26	690
Do not respect nature				
Whites do not respect nature	.451	25	13	701
Indians do not respect nature	.399	22	31	700
Blacks do not respect nature	.564	40	−24	697
Absolute stereotype rating scale				
Whites	.406	17	48	678
Indians	.513	41	−1	672
Blacks	.570	59	−38	675
Difference score scale				
White–Indian	.108	57	−33	669
White–black	.163	70	−61	673
Negative affect toward Indians	.564	19	23	583
Oppose intermarriage with Indians	.440			703
Oppose intermarriage with blacks	.578			704

Source: Chippewa Indian Treaty Rights Survey, 1990.

routinely credit themselves with favorable qualities in comparison to minority group members (Sachdev and Bourhis 1991; Sidanius and Pratto 1999).

Second, the respondents plainly see Indians as economically disadvantaged. Indeed, by a slight margin Indians were rated closer to the poor end of the continuum than blacks. Third, there was a clear tendency to rate Indians most unfavorably on the laziness and welfare-dependency dimensions. Fourth, there is a slight tendency for the overall stereotype trait rating—a simple average of the three personality trait items (laziness, welfare dependency, and no respect for nature)—for blacks to be more negative than that for Indians (.570 versus .513).

These results, despite the common assertion that people will not say unflattering things about minority group members in response to survey questions, show that many respondents attributed negative qualities to blacks and to Indians. Figure 3.6 depicts the average percent of negative stereotype ratings for Indians and blacks. Nearly 60 percent of the sample gave blacks an overall negative stereotype rating, as did 41 percent of respondents when rating Indians. Some 40 percent rated Indians unfavorably on each of the three trait measures, and 73 percent did so when we look at only the laziness and welfare-dependency measures. Hence it is clear that respondents did not offer slavish, "politically correct," positive ratings. Differences in the overall ratings of groups and on particular traits within a target group did occur. Notwithstanding some degree of socially desirable responding, the stereotype trait ratings seem to be a reasonably sensitive way of gauging stereotype perceptions.

The potential for prejudice, at least in the form of negative stereotypes, to influence the politics of treaty rights is quite plain. Many whites hold quite unflattering stereotypes about American Indians. This pattern of beliefs could easily provide a basis for opposing the treaty rights. The key question now becomes how these stereotypes relate to attitudes on treaty rights. We computed a simple Indian stereotype scale based on responses to the three trait-related items on laziness, welfare dependency, and respect for nature. The items share an average inter-item correlation of $+.34$ and a Cronbach's alpha of .59. For purposes of comparison, we also computed a black stereotype scale (average inter-item correlation, .36; Cronbach's alpha, .62). As expected, the Indian stereotype scale is positively correlated with the opposition-to-treaty-rights scale ($r = +.38$, $p < .001$). As stereo-

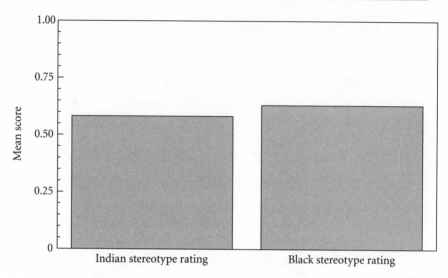

FIGURE 3.6 Stereotype rating of Indians and blacks.
Source: Chippewa Indian Treaty Rights Survey, 1990.

type beliefs about Indians become more negative, opposition to the treaty rights increases.

A stronger test of a prejudice-based argument about the treaties, however, would involve finding an effect of antiblack stereotypes on opposition to treaty rights. One way of understanding prejudice is to view it as a general irrational tendency to denigrate out-groups (Altemeyer 1988). Two of the foundational works in the social psychology of prejudice adopted this view of prejudice. William Graham Sumner's pioneering discussion of ethnocentrism defined it as a tendency to downgrade all other out-groups and cultures in relation to the in-group (1906). Likewise, Theodor Adorno and colleagues' work on authoritarianism depicted prejudice as a general syndrome of hostility to out-groups (Adorno et al. 1950). Exactly this view of prejudice motivated Sniderman and Piazza (1993, especially pp. 52–55) to treat anti-Semitism as a key indicator of the extent to which prejudice drives opposition to social policies targeted to benefit African-Americans. Our data show that although there is a correlation between opposition to treaty rights and negative black stereotypes, this correlation is much weaker than for either the knowledge index or the Indian-stereotype scale. The correlation between the black-stereotype scale and opposition to treaty rights is only +.17 ($p < .001$).

We should be clear that, in other respects, the Indian-stereotype and black-stereotype scales function exactly as expected in relation to some other types of intergroup attitudes. For example, the CITRS included a question on openness to racial intermarriage with blacks and one on openness to racial intermarriage with Indians. Responses to the black intermarriage question are significantly correlated with the black-stereotype scale ($r = -.20$, $p < .001$) such that as stereotypes about blacks become more negative, openness to racial intermarriage with blacks declines. The same pattern is observed in the relation between Indian stereotypes and the Indian intermarriage item ($r = -.24$, $p < .001$).[6] The weaker correlation of black stereotypes with treaty opposition is therefore not a result of the black stereotype items' tapping something other than prejudice.

We also included a direct measure of affective reaction to Indians. Affect was measured with a single item asking respondents whether their basic feelings toward Indians were strongly positive (6 percent), somewhat positive (36 percent), neither positive nor negative or don't know (39 percent), somewhat negative (16 percent), or strongly negative (4 percent). This measure is clearly related to both the Indian stereotype scale ($r = +.29$, $p < .001$) and to the Indian intermarriage item ($r = -.31$). The single, global, negative-affect item is also related to treaty opposition ($r = +.31$, $p < .001$): the more negative a respondent's basic affective reaction to Indians, the more likely he or she was to oppose the treaty rights.

To this point we have shown that knowledge about the treaty rights was low and that level of knowledge has a small but statistically discernible bivariate relation to opposition to the treaty rights. What is more, we have shown that negative stereotypes of Indians are relatively common, and that these perceptions exhibit an even stronger relation to opposition to the treaty rights than does level of knowledge. Similarly, the general negative-affect measure also has a clear association with opposition to the treaty rights. Yet none of these patterns has the potential to explain the large amount of overall variation in treaty rights attitudes. Furthermore, the most conservative test of an irrational-animus argument—an effect for black stereotypes on opposition to treaty rights—yields very weak results at best. Thus prejudice is certainly a plausible contributor to opposition to the treaty rights, but at this juncture it does not exhaust all explanations that may matter. Considerable room remains for other factors to play a role in treaty rights attitudes.

IS IT SELF-INTEREST?

In our development of group position theory we stressed the importance of a person's stake or interest in an issue. With respect to public opinion on an issue like the treaty rights, the populace tends to be divided between a more spectator-like mass public and those segments of the populace that have a more immediate concern or interest. As Herbert Blumer put it: "The issue which creates the public is usually set by contesting interest groups. These interest groups have an immediate private concern in the way the issue is met and, therefore, they endeavor to win to their position the support and allegiance of the outside disinterested group. This puts the disinterested group, as Lippman has pointed out, in the position of arbiter and judge" (Blumer 1946, p. 192). With respect to matters of race relations, Blumer called for paying close attention to significant lines of division in the population marking off those with interests engaged in a particular situation from those lacking such immediate involvement. As he explained:

> Thus, a deeper and more realistic analysis of the "situation" would move along the line of isolating the structure of interests and the structure of control in the situation. Studies of the structure of interests would seek to identify the relevant people of the racial groups who have interests in the situation, and in learning what these interests are—which individuals, associations, and institutions have interests in maintaining the relationship, which are indifferent to it, and which have interests which incline them towards a change in the relationship—where such individuals, associations, and institutions are placed in relation to each other; and what their respective positions of power or strategic advantages are. (Blumer 1958b, p. 437)

The argument from self-interest is, in a sense, even stronger in general theories of political behavior, where the rational pursuit of material ends through politics has long been assumed. In his classic statement on politics, Anthony Downs, in fashioning his "economic theory of democracy," argued that "we borrow from traditional economic theory the idea of the rational consumer. Corresponding to the infamous *homo economicus* which Veblen and others have excoriated, our *homo politicus* is the 'average man' in the electorate, the 'rational citizen' of our model democracy" (Downs 1957, p. 7, emphasis in original). Although himself a critic of the self-interest hypothesis, political psychologist David Sears has characterized the self-interest hypothesis as the bedrock of Enlightenment theorizing about political motivation: "The notion that human behavior is governed at least in part by selfish urges is a part of virtually every psychology and moral philosophy in Western thought" (Sears and Funk 1990, p. 2).

In developing the symbolic politics and symbolic racism theories, Sears and colleagues argued that, to become a scientifically testable and falsifiable hypothesis, the potency of self-interest is best gauged by individual and objective vulnerability to a social or policy change. We find this view largely persuasive.

With respect to the treaty rights dispute, two lines of interest demarcate the population. First and foremost, the Chippewa treaty rights have legal force only in roughly the upper third of Wisconsin, in those areas that are traditional Chippewa territory. For this reason, when the survey was designed we oversampled individuals living in those counties in the state covered by the treaties. We use a simple indicator of residence in treaty versus nontreaty counties as one of our main self-interest measures. Second, the critical resource at stake was access to natural resources via fishing (especially) and also hunting. We thus asked all respondents whether they themselves or anyone in their household took part in fishing or hunting. A substantial fraction of the total sample meet at least one of these conditions, with 61 percent of the sample reporting that someone in the household was involved in fishing and/or hunting. The two forms of self-interest in the issue are related and thus mutually validating. That is, fully 81 percent of treaty-county residents lived in households where someone was involved in fishing or hunting activities, as compared with only 58 percent of nontreaty-county residents.

Both forms of self-interest are related to opposition to the treaty rights. As Figure 3.7 shows, residents of the treaty counties were significantly more likely to oppose the treaties than those living in the remainder of the state. Likewise, those involved in fishing or hunting were significantly more likely to oppose the treaties than those who do not engage in such outdoors activities. This is our first clear indication that broad public opinion on the treaty rights was shaped by whether the issue had some material and personal relevance to individuals.

One possibility, of course, is that the relation of self-interest to treaty rights attitudes is mainly a function of prejudice. That is, individuals involved in fishing and hunting, or who reside in the treaty counties, may suffer from greater ignorance about the treaties and may also harbor

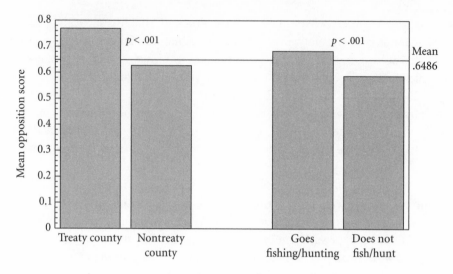

FIGURE 3.7 Treaty opposition by self-interest.
Source: Chippewa Indian Treaty Rights Survey, 1990.

deeper feelings of prejudice. To assess this possibility, we estimated a series of ordinary least squares (OLS) regression models with knowledge, affect, and stereotypes, separately, as dependent variables. Each self-interest variable was included in the models. In addition, we included measures of age, sex, education, income, and political ideology.

Our multivariate models include several respondent-background characteristics that we have not discussed prior to this point. Everything else being equal, older persons often express greater prejudice and hostility to the political aspirations of racial minorities (Schuman et al. 1997). We understand age effects to mainly reflect cohort differences in the degree of exposure to more tolerant times and outlooks during critical stages of political socialization (not as an effect of aging per se). Men often express greater hostility to racial minorities, and greater resistance to social change that appears to benefit minorities, than women do (Sidanius, Pratto, and Bobo 1994). Prior evidence on the effects of income are more mixed, but holding level of education constant, respondents with higher levels of income are sometimes found to express more negative intergroup attitudes. This presumably reflects a desire to preserve status inequalities of wealth and privilege (Schuman et al. 1997; Sidanius and Pratto 1999). The OLS models also include political ideology based on self-identification on a

TABLE 3.7 Multivariate models of prejudice measures

	Knowledge of treaty rights	Negative affect toward Indians	Indian stereotype rating		Black stereotype rating
			Model 1	Model 2	
Constant	.512***	.407***	.507***	.291***	.371***
	(.071)	(.060)	(.039)	(.048)	(.041)
Age	−.001	−.000	.001	.000	.001
	(.001)	(.001)	(.001)	(.000)	(.000)
Female	−.102***	−.011	−.018	−.009	−.006
	(.001)	(.020)	(.014)	(.013)	(.012)
Income	.001	.015**	.006	.001	−.003***
	(.008)	(.006)	(.004)	(.004)	(.004)
No H.S. diploma	−.046	.006	−.037	−.033	−.022
	(.049)	(.036)	(.026)	(.025)	(.022)
Some college	.035	−.033	−.018	−.012	.001
	(.032)	(.024)	(.018)	(.017)	(.015)
BA degree or more	.127***	−.074**	−.106***	−.088***	−.047**
	(.036)	(.027)	(.020)	(.019)	(.016)
Treaty county	.062*	.118***	.081***	.053***	−.004
	(.027)	(.020)	(.015)	(.014)	(.012)
Goes fishing/hunting	.042	.042	.026	.016	−.014
	(.031)	(.023)	(.017)	(.016)	(.014)
Conservative		−.032		.130***	.071*
		(.050)		(.034)	(.030)
Blacks tend to be poor					.262***
					(.029)
Indians tend to be poor				.087**	
				(.029)	
Negative affect toward Indians				.230***	
				(.029)	
Adjusted *R*-squared	.06	.08	.12	.23	.15
N	573	570	545	545	556

*p < .05   **p < .01   ***p < .001

Source: Chippewa Indian Treaty Rights Survey, 1990.

scale ranging from political liberal, at one extreme, to political conservative at the other. Ideological liberals typically express less negative stereotypes toward racial minorities and, all else equal, are more likely to support social policies beneficial to minority groups than are political conservatives. The results of these analyses are shown in Table 3.7.

In general, we found that level of education and treaty-county residence were the most consistent influences on the range of measures of ignorance and prejudice. The better educated respondents, particularly those who graduated from college, were more knowledgeable and expressed less hostility to minorities, whether gauged by negative affect or stereotyping measures. With respect to knowledge, only three variables influenced levels of knowledge about the treaty rights: sex, education, and county of residence. Men had higher levels of knowledge about the treaty rights than women did. Those who completed college were significantly more knowledgeable than those with only a high school education. And residents of the treaty-affected counties were more knowledgeable than those in the remainder of the state.

The substantively most pregnant finding is that residence in treaty counties increased negative stereotyping of Indians but did not influence negative stereotyping of blacks. This result confirms, as we argued above, that the treaty county measure is an issue-specific measure of meaningful contextual self-interest. It does not delineate segments of the population that are generally more hostile to racial minorities. Instead, it sharply delineates those with a focused hostility to Native Americans.[7]

MULTIVARIATE MODELS OF TREATY OPPOSITION

To this point we have entertained two broad classes of explanations for opposition to the treaty rights: racial prejudice and material self-interest. The evidence suggests that each of the indicators of racial prejudice—bad information, negative stereotypes, and hostile feelings—is a contributor to opposition to treaty rights. The evidence also suggests that each of the indicators of being materially touched by the issue—living where the treaties have legal force, engaging in fishing and hunting—contributes to opposition to the treaty rights. Does one set of influences, or variable, matter more than the others?

Figure 3.8 provides an initial comparison of the relative strengths of the several prejudice measures. It shows the correlation between opposition to

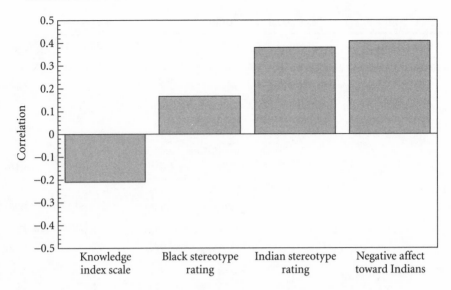

FIGURE 3.8 Correlation of prejudice measures with treaty opposition.
Source: Chippewa Indian Treaty Rights Survey, 1990.

treaty rights and the knowledge index, the black stereotype scale, the Indian stereotype scale, and the negative-affect-toward-Indians item. The
weakest correlation among these variables is that for the black stereotype
rating.

We estimated four models of treaty opposition, results for which are
shown in Table 3.8. The first model includes only the demographic background characteristics, as a baseline for comparison. We should note that
the linear effects of age, sex, income, and education account for approximately 6 percent of the variation in attitudes on the treaty rights. Income
has no effect; however, age, sex, and education do influence opposition to
the treaty rights. Older respondents, men, and high school graduates were
typically more likely to oppose the treaty rights.

Our central question is, how much leverage do the theoretical arguments based on prejudice and on self-interest give us in accounting for
treaty rights opinion? Model 2 begins to answer this question by introducing the measures of treaty-county residence and involvement in fishing or
hunting. Both self-interest variables have highly significant effects on opposition to the treaty rights.

The third model incorporates all of the social-psychological measures of

TABLE 3.8 Multivariate models of treaty opposition

	Model 1	Model 2	Model 3	Model 4
Constant	.791***	.645***	.440***	.424***
	(.050)	(.052)	(.070)	(.070)
Age	.002*	.002**	.002*	.002**
	(.001)	(.001)	(.001)	(.001)
Female	−.068***	−.067***	−.070***	−.070***
	(.020)	(.019)	(.018)	(.018)
Income	−.005	−.003	−.007	−.007
	(.006)	(.006)	(.005)	(.006)
No H.S. diploma	−.084*	−.078*	−.006	−.058
	(.038)	(.036)	(.033)	(.033)
Some college	−.032	−.022	−.007	−.004
	(.025)	(.024)	(.022)	(.022)
BA degree or more	−.117***	−.087***	−.027	−.028
	(.028)	(.027)	(.025)	(.025)
Treaty county		.112***	.067***	.066***
		(.020)	(.020)	(.019)
Goes fishing/hunting		.087***	.073***	.073***
		(.023)	(.021)	(.021)
Knowledge of treaty rights			−.094**	−.090**
			(.030)	(.030)
Conservative			.087	.094*
			(.045)	(.046)
Stereotypes of Indians			.214***	.229***
			(.065)	(.055)
Stereotypes of blacks			.042	
			(.073)	
Blacks tend to be poor			−.005	
			(.056)	
Indians tend to be poor			−.015	
			(.047)	
Negative affect toward Indians			.242***	.244***
			(.041)	(.040)

TABLE 3.8 (continued)

	Model 1	Model 2	Model 3	Model 4
Not satisfied with economic situation				.026
				(.028)
Finances worsened		(.038)		−.029
				(.026)
Adjusted R-squared	.06	.16	.30	.30
N	524	524	524	524

$^*p < .05$ $^{**}p < .01$ $^{***}p < .001$

Source: Chippewa Indian Treaty Rights Survey, 1990.

prejudice: the knowledge index, Indian stereotype scale, black stereotype scale, and Indian affect. Model 3 also includes the perceived economic status of Indians and of blacks. Collectively, the prejudice indicators do explain substantially more of the variation in opinions on the treaty rights as compared with Model 2, which includes just the demographic variables and self-interest measures.

Three key factors stand out in the results for Model 3. First, the prejudice measures of most overt relevance to the treaty dispute—knowledge, Indian stereotyping, and Indian affect—all have significant effects in the expected directions. Net of all other variables in the model, the more knowledge a person had about the treaty rights, the less likely he or she was to oppose them. Net of all other variables in the model, individuals with negative stereotypes of Indians or who expressed general negative affect toward Indians were more likely to oppose the treaty rights. In short, prejudice appears to matter. Second, however, the black stereotypes measure is not related to treaty opposition. Opposition to the treaty rights was not, therefore, driven by some generalized anti–out-group animus. Third, both measures of self-interest continue to bear highly significant net relations to treaty opposition, even after taking all of the prejudice measures into account. It is also worth noting that inclusion of the knowledge, stereotyping, and affect measures appears to account for the direct education effect on treaty rights attitudes. One immediate implication of these results is that if racial prejudice matters in this context, it is not of a highly generalized, ethnocentric type. If it were, we would have found important effects of antiblack stereotypes on treaty rights opposition. It would seem that something more directly linked to the relations between whites and Native Americans is at issue in the dispute over the rights of Chippewa Indians.

ECONOMIC VULNERABILITY AND PREJUDICE COMBINED?

Many commentators on the treaty rights dispute argue that the conflict sprang from a combination of economic stagnation in upper Wisconsin and scapegoating based in economic frustration—that, in effect, the Chippewa became an easy target for resentment among those who were most economically vulnerable and marginal. And, they argue, without that economic marginality and the willingness of some activists to play on attendant feelings of frustration, the issue would never have been such a source of controversy and conflict. As legal scholars Rennard Strickland and colleagues put it: "The economic distress of northern Wisconsin provides a fertile bed for the exploitation of fear and frustration. The leadership vacuum created by state inaction has been filled by several groups, among them PARR, ERFE, and STA. All of these groups focus their attention on the exercise of treaty rights, but use racist literature, hate-group organizing techniques and propaganda to convince non-Indians that their livelihood is threatened by Chippewa treaties" (Strickland, Herzberg, and Owens 1990, pp. 15–16).

There is some immediate plausibility to the hypothesis that economic stagnation fed hostility to the treaties. Upper Wisconsin is economically very dependent on tourism, much of which is based on sportfishing. With the Department of Natural Resources reducing bag limits for non-Indian fishermen wherever the Chippewa announced they would be spearfishing, and amid the general turmoil over the issue, it is certainly possible that some of the most economically fragile individuals would have been most threatened by the treaty rights. Also, residents of the upper third of the state tend to be less well educated and less affluent than those in the remainder of the state. Specifically, as our sample confirms, residents of treaty counties have lower levels of education than those from nontreaty counties (12.7 versus 13.3 years, $p < .001$). There is an even larger gap in annual income between residents of treaty and nontreaty counties, favoring the latter (in 1990, approximately \$20,654 versus \$26,325, $p < .001$).

We followed three strategies to assess the effect of the economy on treaty opposition. First, we reestimated the third model shown in Table 3.8 to specify and include interactions between treaty-county residence and edu-

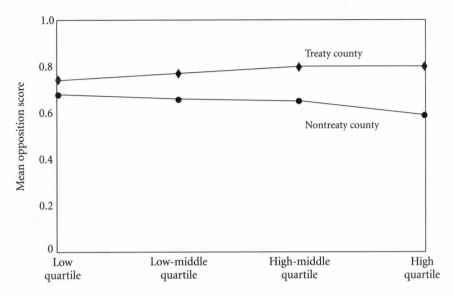

FIGURE 3.9 Interaction of income and treaty rights opposition.
Source: Chippewa Indian Treaty Rights Survey, 1990.

cation, and between treaty-county residence and income. That is, we expressly tested for the possibility that poorly educated and lower-income respondents who also lived in treaty counties would be particularly likely to oppose the treaties. With respect to education, the results do not support this hypothesis at all. We did find evidence of a significant interaction with income, but the direction of the effect was not in line with the economic vulnerability hypothesis. As displayed in Figure 3.9, there is a very slight tendency for treaty opposition to rise with increasing income among treaty-county residents, but it decreases as income increases in nontreaty counties. This pattern may be better interpreted as meaning that those individuals who were likely to be the inn and lodge proprietors, the restaurant and bar owners, and other relatively high-income people in the North Woods were the ones most hostile to the treaty rights.

Our second strategy in seeking support for the economic-vulnerability hypothesis was to restrict the analysis to treaty-county residents only and to test for stronger effects of prejudice on treaty opposition among economically marginal individuals (again, as indicated by income and level of education). These tests also failed (see Table 3.9). We found no statistically discernible evidence that stereotypes or negative affect had a larger impact

TABLE 3.9 Treaty opposition and perceived economic well-being (treaty counties only)

	Model 1	Model 2	Model 3
Constant	.614***	.573***	.626**
	(.103)	(.135)	(.116)
Age	.000	.000	.000
	(.001)	(.001)	(.001)
Female	−.037	−.036	−.037
	(.025)	(.025)	(.025)
Family income			
Low quartile	−.032	−.053	−.037
	(.034)	(.116)	(.034)
Low-middle quartile	−.035	.027	−.041
	(.034)	(.135)	(.034)
High-middle quartile	−.037	.035	−.030
	(.037)	(.139)	(.038)
Education			
No H.S. diploma	−.070	−.067	−.105
	(.042)	(.043)	(.154)
Some college	−.031	−.023	−.075
	(.030)	(.030)	(.104)
BA degree or more	−.010**	−.088*	−.345**
	(.036)	(.037)	(.126)
Hunt or fish	.077*	.077*	.085**
	(.034)	(.034)	(.034)
Knowledge	−.069	−.071	−.063
	(.042)	(.042)	(.042)
Conservative	.026	.027	−.000
	(.061)	(.063)	(.062)
Indian stereotype scale	.147*	.356*	.180
	(.073)	(.169)	(.095)
Indian rich/poor	.038	.050	.058
	(.052)	(.054)	(.053)
Negative affect	.203***	.017	.137
	(.053)	(.120)	(.078)
No H.S. diploma*negative affect			.319
			(.172)

TABLE 3.9 (continued)

	Model 1	Model 2	Model 3
Some college*negative affect			.074
			(.133)
BA degree*negative affect			.107
			(.147)
No H.S. diploma*stereotype			−.225
			(.263)
Some college*stereotype			−.255
			(.168)
BA degree*stereotype			.355
			(.218)
Low quartile*negative affect		.264	
		(.147)	
Low-middle quartile*negative affect		.195	
		(.159)	
High-middle quartile*negative affect		.212	
		(.177)	
Low quartile*stereotype		−.202	
		(.200)	
Low-middle quartile*stereotype		−.281	
		(.237)	
High-middle quartile*stereotype		−.613	
		(.227)	
Adjusted *R*-squared	.18	.18	.20
N	254	254	254

*$p < .05$ **$p < .01$ ***$p < .001$

Source: Chippewa Indian Treaty Rights Survey, 1990.

on treaty opposition among lower income or poorly educated respondents, even when the analysis was constrained to residents of the North Woods.

As a third strategy, we examined the subjective or perceived well-being of treaty-county and nontreaty-county respondents. Our survey contained two measures of subjective economic well-being: one question that asked about satisfaction with family finances and another that asked whether things had been getting better or worse. The questions were worded as follows:

> We are interested in how people are getting along financially these days. So far as you and your family are concerned, would you say that you are pretty well satisfied with your present financial situation, more or less satisfied, or not satisfied at all?
>
> During the last few years, has your financial situation been getting better, getting worse, or has it stayed the same?

As might be expected, both questions are significantly correlated with education and with income. As education or income increased, financial satisfaction ($r = .14$, $p < .001$ for education; $r = .31$, $p < .001$ for income) rose and individuals reported feeling better about their financial situation ($r = .17$, $p < .001$ for education; $r = .21$, $p < .001$ for income). In addition, treaty-county residents reported significantly lower satisfaction and were significantly more likely to report feeling worse about their financial circumstances than were nontreaty-county residents. Yet the questions have only quite weak correlations with opposition to treaty rights, .07 (not significant) in the case of "financial satisfaction" and .10 ($p < .05$) in the case of the "better or worse" item.[8]

With Model 4 of Table 3.8, we tested the importance of these assessments of economic well-being in predicting opposition to the treaty rights. Neither measure had a significant impact on opposition to treaty rights, and the two together did not bring a significant improvement in fit compared with Model 3. As a consequence, we do not believe that the economic-class variant of the self-interest argument has much bearing in accounting for expressed opposition to the treaty rights.

We wish to emphasize four points in summarizing the results discussed in this chapter. First, on the whole the results provide strong support for taking the treaty rights issue as a topic on which mass public opinion really did take shape. People were exposed to the controversy. Most of our respondents had at least read newspaper articles dealing with the issue (and had almost certainly watched television news coverage as well). People typically articulated the bases of their views in ways that were substantive and that mirrored in important respects elite discourse and the larger public debate over the treaty rights. In the light of the open-ended accounts of opinion, it seems reasonable to infer that the subject was indeed a matter of discussion among family members and friends. Moreover, the open-ended remarks reassure us that respondents felt at ease enough to candidly disclose their views, rather than feeling they could say only what seemed safe, expected, or "politically correct." The treaty rights issue, though not, to be sure, of intense personal importance to all of our respondents (a matter we examine in more detail in Chapter 5) was plainly of broad salience. Indeed, it was salient to a degree and substantially cut across lines of education and general engagement with political affairs. Furthermore, views on the several resource issues—spearfishing, hunting, and logging—raised by the treaty rights form a highly coherent attitude. In sum, we believe that there was a sociologically grounded and meaningful public opinion on the treaty rights dispute.

Of course, we cannot say with any precision how typical the treaty rights dispute is in terms of matters of political controversy, nor even how typical it is of matters racial politics. There are good reasons to suppose, however, that the salience and coherence of opinions that we observe here occur more often than not with topics of racial politics. If true, this would be important for two reasons. It would undercut the commonplace assertion that surveys measure sociologically meaningless mass opinion (Blumer 1948). Just the opposite is likely to be the case where race issues are concerned. Also, it would say something larger still about matters of race politics, at least, if not about politics more generally: to wit, that group cleavages bear enormous importance for public opinion, especially those cleavages along long-standing, visible, and salient racial lines (Conover 1988; Dawson 1994, 2000; Kinder 1998). Such divisions involve substantial identities and conditions in society about which people care and that they often readily monitor.

Second, we want to emphasize that each of the major forms of off-reservation treaty rights was opposed by a majority of Wisconsin residents. The tilt of opinion was clear. The struggle over the Chippewa treaty rights thus reflects the classic conflict in American race politics during the post–World War II period: a minority group right or claim or policy initiative meeting with open hostility from the white majority. Again, some fraction of our respondents was clearly very emotionally aroused by the issue, and this was true whether they strongly favored or strongly opposed the treaty rights.

Some spoke of the "shame" involved with failing to live up to a treaty agreement. Others spoke with bitterness of having their access to natural resources compromised and diminished.

Third, prejudice in its most classic senses matters in the treaty rights dispute. Levels of ignorance about the real effects of the Chippewa's exercising of their rights was high. Nearly a third of the sample answered all of the knowledge questions incorrectly and barely one in ten answered all three correctly, despite frequent and intensive media discussion of the treaty rights issue. It is fair to say that the knowledge vacuum was to some degree filled by anti-Indian stereotypes and negative affective orientations. In our multivariate models, levels of knowledge, negative stereotypes, and negative affect toward Indians all made significant net contributions to opposition to the treaty rights.

Fourth, those with the greatest likelihood of having a personal stake in the issue were also among those most likely to oppose the treaty rights. People who live in the areas where the treaties have legal force and those who come from households that include fishermen or hunters tended to oppose the treaty rights. In short, self-interest matters for public opinion. This is a case in which those with more of an objective, personal stake in a matter of race politics are among those most vehemently opposed to the assertion or protection of minority group rights.

Despite many speculations that the treaty dispute was rooted principally in the combination of economic hard times and scapegoating in the North Woods, we do not find much evidence consistent with this claim. To be sure, residents of the treaty counties are less well educated, have lower incomes, and worry more about their economic circumstances than do residents of the nontreaty counties. However, these economic characteristics do not strongly predict opposition to the treaty rights. Neither do they exert any greater influence on treaty attitudes in the treaty counties than they do elsewhere. And there is no sign that the economically vulnerable were any more likely than otherwise similar treaty-county residents to translate prejudice into hostile attitudes toward the treaty rights.

On several levels these results leave us with a puzzle that requires further scrutiny. Anti-Indian prejudice and self-interest are related. Individuals living in the treaty counties were not only more hostile to the treaty rights, they also were the most hostile to Native Americans generally. It is telling, and contrary to the expectation of Sniderman and Piazza (1993), that this pattern was not a result of higher general ethnocentrism or a broad syndrome of prejudice in the treaty counties. Specifically, treaty-county residents were no more likely to express hostility to blacks than those living in the remainder of the state of Wisconsin, and attitudes toward blacks do not figure directly in opposition to the treaty rights.

Beyond this puzzle, the open-ended comments point to a number of reasons for opposition to the treaty rights that are not well evaluated by general measures of prejudice or by our self-interest measures, whether those measures are used alone or in tandem. That is, the feelings of fraternal deprivation and *group* loss so frequently expressed are not elements of the standard prejudice formulation, nor can they be coming from narrow notions of private self-interest. The collective or sociological basis to treaty rights opposition is not captured in the classical prejudice approach. Likewise the many claims voiced by respondents (and in the rhetoric of many anti-treaty activists) about the practical harms done by the Chippewa's exercising of their treaty rights are not well indexed by traditional notions of prejudice or self-interest. To account for more of the spread of public opinion on the treaty rights, and to better understand the role played by feelings of group deprivation and claims of practical harms, we will have to assess more direct measures of those factors.

Chapter 4

DISENTANGLING RACIALIZED POLITICS:
GROUP POSITION, INJUSTICE, AND SYMBOLIC RACISM

> Well, I am not prejudiced against anyone for the color of their
> skin and I don't think all of them are like this. But I know some of
> them, because of the color of their skin, feel they should get things
> other people don't.
>
> CITRS respondent explaining answer to a symbolic racism question

> They seem to get all these handouts that we can't get, and we pay
> for them.
>
> CITRS respondent explaining answer to a symbolic racism question

> They get all these state grants. Us white people are trying to make
> it too. And it's unfair to the American families just trying to get
> along.
>
> CITRS respondent explaining answer to a group competition question

> I don't see how people think this way. And I have all types of
> friends. They are just trying to survive like anyone else.
>
> CITRS respondent explaining answer to a group competition question

Politics, it is often said, is fundamentally about who gets what. And the role
of government, following on the above, is to carry out the authoritative allocation of scarce resources. A decision about who has access to natural resources and under what conditions is, therefore, an eminently political
question, and it is one on which the courts spoke decisively with respect to
the treaty rights of the Chippewa. That decision effectively charged the
state of Wisconsin with compliance with and the effective administration
of those rights. And yet the issue certainly was no arid bureaucratic matter.
Instead, the decision provoked a heated political controversy that pivoted

on deeply felt claims about who was *justly* entitled to what rights and privileges from the government.

Indeed, a list of the movement groups formed by treaty rights opponents reads like a principled invocation of core American values and beliefs—values and beliefs capable of evoking powerful emotions and containing deep-rooted presumptions of right and entitlement: Protect America's Rights and Resources, Equal Rights for Everyone, Stop Treaty Abuse. These groups were not self-proclaimed "white citizens' councils" or, worse yet, offshoots of the Ku Klux Klan. These anti-treaty groups and much of the rhetoric they adopted did not stress an openly anti-Indian posture.[1] Instead, they positioned themselves as representatives of a justly aggrieved citizenry. They attempted to portray the assertion of the treaty-reserved, and now court-affirmed, off-reservation rights of the Chippewa as an irrational circumstance, subject to abuse, transparently unfair, and harmful to the natural resources and to the ideal of equality before the law. These were people who, in their own eyes and words, had been dealt a grave injustice.

Such a framing of opposition to the treaty rights stands in contradistinction to a view of treaty rights opponents as motivated either by coarse racial prejudice or simply by the stuff of self-interested politics. Indeed, one would be hard-pressed to extract a sense of racial group struggle from this type of rhetoric. Yet the protests at the boat landings were often thoroughly peppered with racial epithets and symbols. These protests were the very incarnation of racial tension. As the opening paragraph of a story in the *Milwaukee Journal* put it in October 1984: "Hostility is poisoning the tranquil waters of Northern Wisconsin. Tension crackles through its forests, where your race determines when and where you can shoot deer" ("North Woods Steaming with Racial Hostility," *Milwaukee Journal,* October 14, 1984, p. 1).

With regard to public opinion, then, we are led to ask, was the treaty dispute a fight over who was perceived as morally deserving of government attention and special privilege? Or was it strictly about the hard-headed politics of resource allocation and use? Or is this very way of posing the issue too simple, inasmuch as the question of who is entitled to enjoy particular resources raises as many normative issues of ought and should—of fairness and unfairness—as it does pragmatic questions of how much, when, and to whom a resource gets allocated. All of these issues are complicated even further when the "who" involved are not just disparate individuals or formal organizations, but are members of socially defined racial groups: that is, matters become much more roiled when a political decision about who gets what falls along a long-standing line between "us versus them."

Our general purpose in this chapter is to assess the merits of the three major hypotheses in the social sciences about the sources of whites' resistance to racial change. One interpretation, which we term the injustice-frame hypothesis, hews closely to an account of treaty opposition that many leaders of the anti-treaty protests might well embrace. A second view of the rejection of the treaty rights, and the one we have stressed from the outset, is that it comes out of a form of prejudice that involves the protection of group position in response to a sense of competition, threat, and lost privilege. A third view, based in the theory of symbolic racism, contends that a new form of politicized racial animus is the main source of opposition to initiatives that protect or advance the claims of racial minorities. It is prejudice, to be sure, according to this theory, but this form of prejudice is not simply traditional stereotyping and negative affect, and it is certainly not tied to any personal or group-based stake in the issue. Rather, from a foundation of negative beliefs and feelings about racial minority group members, a politically potent and unreasoned racial resentment develops—a resentment that is then vented when the rights of the minority group are made salient.

We will show that, in the final analysis, the injustice frame and symbolic racism models are better understood as subsumed elements, or minor tributaries, of the larger flow of the great river that is the struggle for group position. In broad outlines, this chapter will show that the treaty rights dispute, at its core, was a struggle for group position. In Chapter 3 we found *both* racial prejudice and self-interest to strongly predict opposition to treaty rights. Just as the group position theory predicts, a bedrock of negative stereotypes and feelings among whites, particularly those with the greatest stake or vested interest in the dispute, was mobilized by perceptions of competition and threat.

Our analysis proceeds in several steps. We first address an effort to develop multiple item measures of the core concepts invoked by each theory. Do any appreciable fraction of our respondents embrace the ideas advanced in each of these theories? Our results show, at first blush, that considerable segments of the populace agree with ideas based in the injustice-frame, group-position, and symbolic-racism perspectives. On its face, each approach has at least initial validity as an account of public opinion on the treaty dispute.

We next attempt to determine how deep is the empirical basis for maintaining clear distinctions between feelings of injustice, perceptions of competition and threat, and symbolic racism. Do we need such theoretical pluralism and complexity in order to characterize the nature of public opinion on the treaty rights dispute? We conclude that the answer to this question is no. The data strongly favor the group position formulation. This stage of our empirical analysis draws, in part, on detailed open-ended responses to one of the group competition items and one of the symbolic racism items. We also explore a detailed analysis of the correlates and determinants of each construct, in a search for the unique contribution of the concepts invoked across the full set of theories. We conclude that a substantially simplified conceptual structure is possible, as opposed to one drawing on the full array of concepts from traditional prejudice theories, the injustice frame, group position, and symbolic racism. As the group position model maintains, group affect and stereotyping provide a foundation for racial prejudice but fall short of what makes prejudice an active and politically significant social force. Feelings of group competition and perceived threat constitute the razor's edge of political dispute and contention.

In the final section of this chapter we turn to a full formal model of opposition to the treaty rights. Do the concepts in these theories add to our understanding of opposition to the treaty rights? Specifically, do these ideas contribute something to our understanding not captured by the effects of racial prejudice and self-interest that we have already seen? And, in particular, does our simplified array of concepts give us greater leverage in explaining opposition to the treaty rights? As expected under the group position model, group competition and perceived threat have the strongest direct effects on opposition to the treaty rights. But, as we also found in Chapter 3, self-interest exerts a powerful organizing influence on all of the key social-psychological components of treaty rights opposition.

THE INJUSTICE FRAME MODEL

According to the injustice frame, minority group rights, claims, and policies are rejected by the majority of whites on sensible, reasoned, and concrete grounds. If emotion is involved, it is mainly embroidery resulting from a perception that a wrong-headed social policy has been foisted upon the populace. We believe it is particularly important for scholars to take this line of argument seriously. The injustice frame is often the visible

"presenting" face in the public rhetoric of those contesting progressive racial change (see Taylor 1986 on the antibusing movement and Rieder 1985
on opposition to community desegregation) or actively advancing conservative policy change (as in former California governor Pete Wilson's brief
for Proposition 187, an anti-immigration ballot initiative). A full and fair
test of the competing explanations must, therefore, assess the empirical
merits of this posture.

Finding strong evidence to support the injustice frame hypothesis would
require several mutually reinforcing empirical patterns. First, many people
would have to accept or affirm beliefs consistent with this perspective. If
few people accepted that the off-reservation treaty rights had harmful effects, the injustice frame approach would likely offer little help in explaining opposition to the treaty rights. Second, the beliefs would have to form a
coherent, interrelated, and reliable cluster of beliefs that would define a
perspective of some depth and robustness. Third, while adherence to this
perspective might flow to some degree from self-interest, it should have little or nothing to do with racial prejudice, particularly in its more overt
manifestations, such as stereotypes and negative affect. The pure form of
the injustice frame stresses the reasoned and at least superficially race-neutral basis of such beliefs. Fourth and finally, injustice frame beliefs would
have to provide the core of opposition to the treaty rights.

To presage our results a bit, the injustice frame cup is at best half full.
Many people do accept aspects of the injustice frame, and the views do
form a coherent set of ideas. However, prejudice and self-interest play a
very large part in the formation of these beliefs, and there are strong
grounds to doubt that a race-neutral set of practical grievances is, in the
final analysis, a substantial element of the animosity to treaty rights.

A range of specific claims against the treaty rights was voiced by opponents. The CITRS recorded four main types of complaints: that the treaties
created two classes of citizens, that the supply of fish would be hurt, that
tourism would be hurt, and that the treaties were anachronistic. We expressly tried to avoid using charged language (no sweeping qualifiers, such
as *all* or *most*, were used in the question wording), and no obviously partisan catchphrases or symbols were invoked (the questions did not contain
such phrases as "equal rights for everyone," "America's resources," or "pre-
serving Native American heritage"). So far as possible, the items sought to
gauge dispassionate, race-neutral, and reasoned grievances.

A great many of our respondents endorsed elements of the injustice

TABLE 4.1 Injustice frame questions

	Creates two classes	Hurts fish supply	Hurts tourism	Treaties are needed
Strongly agree	18%	40%	32%	22%
Somewhat agree	37	27	28	26
No opinion/neutral	16	8	9	3
Somewhat disagree	20	16	18	20
Strongly disagree	9	10	14	30
(N)	(587)	(588)	(586)	(586)

Source: Chippewa Indian Treaty Rights Survey, 1990.
Note: Not all columns sum to 100 due to rounding.

frame argument against Chippewa off-reservation treaty rights. As Table 4.1 shows, more than half of our sample agreed that affirmation of the treaty rights created two classes of citizens (combining "strongly agree" and "somewhat agree" responses). Even more lopsided fractions endorsed claims that the exercise of off-reservation treaty rights hurt the supply of fish and hurt tourism. Fully 40 percent strongly agreed with the hurt-the-supply-of-fish claim and another 27 percent answered "somewhat agree." And 50 percent rejected the idea that the treaties are still needed today (combining "strongly disagree" and "somewhat disagree" responses). In short, most elements of the injustice frame were endorsed by Wisconsin's white residents.

In addition, the beliefs appear to constitute a coherent perspective on the treaty rights. The items are all positively intercorrelated, sharing an average correlation of .30. A simple additive scale based on an average across the four items is reasonably reliable (Cronbach's alpha = .63).

Although it might have been ideal to include at least one open-ended question to gauge respondents' frame of reference in their own terms, we did not do so in this case. Based on our pre-test results, we decided not to include a separate open-ended follow-up question to any of the standard injustice frame items. Our pre-test results suggested that this would have appeared highly redundant to many respondents, who frequently invoked injustice frame–type arguments in explaining their opposition to the treaty rights. Recall that, in Chapter 3, the results showed that many respondents did rely on elements of the injustice frame in explaining why they opposed the treaty rights. However, as noted earlier, we hesitate to interpret these statements as unambiguous validation of the injustice frame hypothesis. Recall also that many of the comments carried an overtone of prejudice. In some instances, remarks embraced factually incorrect ideas (such as harm to the supply of fish); more often, they also occasioned a litany of derogatory comments about Native Americans.

A virtue of the traditional survey items on beliefs about the effects of the treaty rights is that we can now formally test for whether these beliefs are "cool," dispassionately held perceptions or "hot," ideology- and prejudice-infused positions. We use the injustice frame scale to assess more formally how such beliefs may relate to levels of knowledge about the treaty rights and levels of overt prejudice. Figure 4.1 shows the correlation between the injustice frame scale and our measures of political ideology, treaty knowledge, negative stereotypes, and negative affect toward Indians. The injustice frame scale is significantly correlated with each of these measures, but clearly the strongest correlation obtains for the two racial prejudice measures. In particular, the purest of the prejudice indicators—negative affect—has the strongest correlation with adherence to the injustice frame beliefs ($r = .37, p < .001$).

But more than prejudice is involved with adherence to the injustice frame perspective. As Figure 4.1B shows, the injustice frame scale is significantly related to each of the self-interest measures as well. In particular, there is a substantial difference between treaty-county residents and those in nontreaty counties. Residents of treaty counties are more likely to believe that harms result from the exercising of off-reservation treaty rights. By the same token those involved in fishing and hunting activities are more likely than those not involved in such activities to endorse the injustice frame perspective.

To the extent that it constitutes a coherent point of view, the injustice frame perspective appears to have multiple roots. Acceptance of such views rests in part on conservative ideology. Somewhat more so, the beliefs flow from inaccurate knowledge about the treaty rights. And much more substantially still, these beliefs stem from racial prejudice and the level of vested interest or stake one has in the treaty dispute, with more prejudiced and self-interested individuals exhibiting the greatest endorsement of the injustice frame perspective. At a minimum, these patterns undermine the view of injustice frame proponents that these are "cool," reasoned, dispassionate orientations to matters of race politics. These are views rooted in

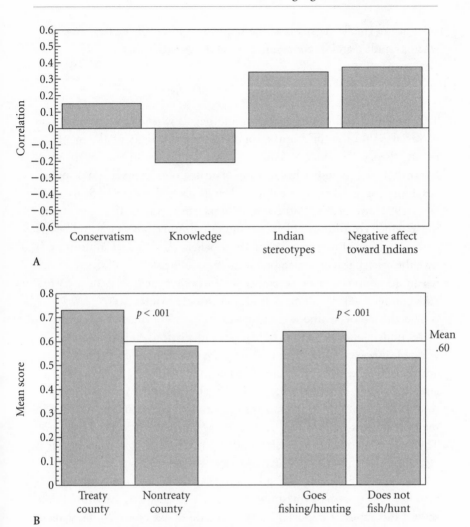

FIGURE 4.1 Relation of the injustice frame to psychological measures
(A) and self-interest measures (B).
Source: Chippewa Indian Treaty Rights Survey, 1990.

what are normally regarded as the hot points of racial politics, especially when prejudice and interests join and reinforce each other.

THE SYMBOLIC RACISM MODEL

That prejudice is thoroughly woven into beliefs when it comes to matters of racial politics is, in many respects, the core insight of the symbolic racism theory. The theory maintains that, while traditional, overt, anti-minority racial prejudice has lost much of its political force, a new politicized form of racial resentment has taken its place (Kinder and Sears 1981; Sears 1988). According to the symbolic racism theorists, this new resentment, which constitutes a blend of traditional American values and beliefs and early-learned negative feelings and beliefs about racial minorities, is now the crucial way in which prejudice manifests itself in politics. The values in question center on reverence for such cherished ideals as the work ethic, individualism, and other tradition-oriented views.

The theory of symbolic racism was initially formulated as a way to better understand the politics of black-white relations. Since it was first developed, however, its applications have expanded to address many other groups and issues. For example, it has been applied broadly to matters of language policy, immigration, and the larger question of multiculturalism. And the concept has been applied or found useful by scholars working in many countries besides the United States (Brown 1995; Duckitt 1992). Thus it is a reasonable extension and test of the theory to see whether it also applies in the case of Native American–white relations.

Our survey contained four questions designed to tap into symbolic racism. Responses to these questions are shown in Table 4.2. We should note several theoretically important features of these questions. None of them makes explicit racial group comparisons. Each item contains strong or clearly evaluative language, such as "less attention than they deserve" or "take unfair advantage." And none of the items refers to concrete, material resources; instead they speak in vague terms of "government attention," "influence," and "special privileges." In short, the items aim to draw out the sort of emotion-infused, vague resentment against minority groups that is specified in the symbolic racism theory.

Although seldom as widely endorsed as the injustice frame beliefs, the elements of symbolic racism were indeed endorsed by a substantial number of our respondents. Forty-eight percent said they agree ("strongly"

TABLE 4.2 Symbolic racism questions

	Indians take unfair advantage	Indians get less government attention	Indians have too little influence	Indians work hard like everyone else
Strongly agree	24%	12%	12%	16%
Somewhat agree	24	19	25	27
No opinion/neutral	16	12	18	19
Somewhat disagree	26	30	32	19
Strongly disagree	11	27	13	20
(N)	(587)	(583)	(581)	(583)

Source: Chippewa Indian Treaty Rights Survey, 1990.
Note: Not all columns sum to 100 due to rounding.

combined with "somewhat") that Indians take unfair advantage of special privileges given them by the government. Just under 60 percent rejected the idea that Indians get less attention from government than they deserve (combining "strongly disagree" and "somewhat disagree" responses), and 45 percent similarly rejected the idea that Indians have too little influence. Nearly two out of five (almost 40 percent) rejected the idea that Indians are hardworking. Thus we find that a substantial fraction of white Wisconsin residents endorse the elements of symbolic racism where Native Americans are concerned.[2]

Furthermore, the symbolic racism questions do reveal a coherent perspective or attitude. All of the items share a positive intercorrelation, ranging from a low of .24 to a high of .49, with an overall average correlation of .38. A simple additive scale of the four items is very reliable (Cronbach's alpha = .71).[3] There indeed appears to be a coherent set of ideas at work among the respondents.

Is symbolic racism related to ideology, to levels of knowledge, and to the traditional prejudice measures? Unlike the injustice frame hypothesis, the theory of symbolic racism would expect to find significant relationships between each of these factors and the attitude of symbolic racism. Figure 4.2A shows quite clearly that these expectations are borne out. Both more conservative people and people with less knowledge about the treaties are more likely to adopt symbolic racism attitudes toward Native Americans than are those of a liberal leaning or with greater knowledge about the treaties. Even more strongly are negative stereotypes and negative affect

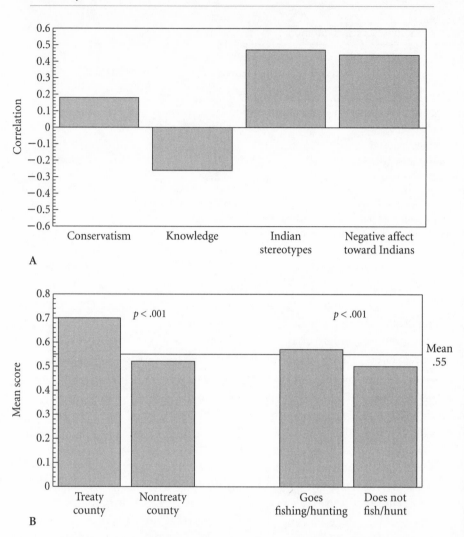

FIGURE 4.2 Relation of symbolic racism to psychological measures (A)
and self-interest measures (B).
Source: Chippewa Indian Treaty Rights Survey, 1990.

implicated in symbolic racism. Indeed, the correlation of stereotypes and
symbolic racism is quite substantial at +.47 (*p* < .001). Those with a traditional outlook and those exhibiting racial prejudice, as gauged by inaccurate issue knowledge, openly biased beliefs, and negative feelings, are the
most likely to express symbolic racism, just as the symbolic racism theory
predicts.

Although the above patterns for psychological measures are consistent with symbolic racism theory, the picture quickly becomes more complex. The results reported in Figure 4.2B strongly contradict the expectations of symbolic theory. Here we see clear and highly significant effects of both of our self-interest measures on symbolic racism. The impact of treaty-county residence is particularly large, as a full two-tenths of a point (on a 0 to 1 scale) separates treaty-county and nontreaty-county respondents. Here we should emphasize that none of the survey items in question directly referred to Chippewa Indians, none referred to court rulings or treaties, and none referred to the use or consumption of environmental resources. Save for making reference to Indians or Native Americans, nothing about the wording of these items was tailored to the specific features or history of the Chippewa treaty rights dispute. In fact, just the opposite was the case, as each item was directly modeled on symbolic racism items used in the context of black-white relations in previous studies. As a consequence, these data provide strong evidence that even symbolic racism can be shaped by the *configuration of interests* at stake in a matter of racial politics.

In this case, the survey did follow the "take unfair advantage" symbolic racism item with an open-ended question asking respondents to explain why they felt the way they did (whether they agreed or disagreed with the question). These results are especially important in light of the strong effects of self-interest on symbolic racism. What is more, the open-ended comments do much to validate our findings and to shed light on the fact that both racial prejudice and self-interest shape symbolic racism. Table 4.3 shows responses to the open-ended follow-up question. Because the types of responses do differ in important ways, we present the data separately for those who agreed with the question and those who disagreed, as well as showing the overall percentage that offered a particular response.

Although specific details in the open-ended responses to the "special privileges" item vary, many of the comments constitute little more than vague resentment or, when more elaborate, highly unsympathetic stereotypes, a finding that is consistent with the expectations of symbolic racism theory. The single most common response among those who agreed that Indians take unfair advantage of "special privileges" suggested that Indians are "given one thing and then demand another." The following examples epitomize the vague resentment characteristic of these reactions:

They just seem to want it all.
  —*Thirty-one-year-old female, short-order cook, high school graduate*

TABLE 4.3 Open-ended responses for attitudes about Indians taking unfair advantage of privileges given to them by the government

	Statewide	Percentage of total sample
Reasons for agreeing that Indians take unfair advantage		
Given one thing, demand another	25.0%	12.2%
Take advantage of assistance	16.6	8.5
Irresponsible	16.2	8.1
Can't generalize	2.4	9.0
Pushing rights too far	10.8	5.2
No ambition/lazy	5.2	2.6
Only some cause problems	4.1	9.8
Should be treated equally	3.4	1.7
Treaty rights outdated	3.0	1.5
Other/don't know	13.3	See below
(N)	(276)	
Reasons for disagreeing that Indians take unfair advantage		
They don't take advantage	19.7	8.9
Just a few cause problems	17.2	See above
Doing what others would do	15.0	7.0
Indians treated unfairly	10.2	5.2
Can't generalize	14.8	See above
Take advantage of assistance	1.6	See above
Irresponsible	1.2	See above
Given one thing, demand another	1.2	See above
Other/don't know	19.1	20.3
(N)	(259)	(591)

Source: Chippewa Indian Treaty Rights Survey, 1990.

Note: "See below" and "See above" indicate categories that were the same in both panels; these entries were combined to show statewide percentages.

Well, it just seems that you give them an inch and they take a mile.
    —*Thirty-four-year-old male, pest control worker, college graduate*

I don't know how to say it. I just feel they ask a lot.
    —*Seventy-nine-year-old female, food preparer, some post–high school education*

I hear stories about them taking advantage.
   —*Thirty-one-year-old female, manager, some post–high school education*

Not all of the responses in the "given one thing and then demand another" category were so vague, however. Indeed some remarks contained what was arguably an explicit sense of group or fraternal deprivation. For example:

When we give them an inch, they take a mile is a good way of putting it.
   —*Twenty-year-old female, waitress, some post–high school education*

They get a lot of privileges. I just feel they get a lot more privileges than a lot of American people get out there.
   —*Twenty-eight-year-old female, stock and inventory clerk, high school graduate*

Both sets of comments invoke a line between us and them, though neither uses very direct racial language or terminology. As the dominant racial group whose entitlement and privilege are ordinarily taken for granted, whites typically need not invoke race explicitly to secure their position. They need only appeal to a status quo ante and mark off "the other." As Tuan has explained: "Most whites do not consciously consider how their racial status informs the world they see and experience. As the racial norm, the standard by which other groups are judged and deemed to deviate from, they have the social, political, and economic privilege to ignore their racialization" (1999a, p. 22). With respect to the open-ended questions in our survey, although emphasizing the theme "given one thing, they demand another," the comments from white respondents who agreed with our key symbolic racism question contain at least an implicit sense of loss and in-group/out-group comparison.

The second most common response among those who gave "agree" responses to the "take advantage" question stressed specifically that Native Americans exploited assistance given to them by the government. For instance:

They can have almost anything they want. They get aid and everything else. All you have to do is be an Indian and you get all that stuff, you know.
   —*Sixty-two-year-old male, bus driver, high school graduate*

Because they're getting everything free, with no taxes. And they can do everything they want without licenses.
—*Forty-three-year-old female, supervisor of building service workers, high school graduate*

In these examples, the group comparison and sense of loss are arguably implied, although plainly they are not an explicit element of the responses.

More than a few of the explanations involve an explicit sense of a resource transfer or loss, an in-group versus out-group comparison, or both. Consider these four examples:

I shouldn't say this. I work in a bank. So, if they want to live on a reservation, then they shouldn't get paid by white man's taxes.
—*Fifty-three-year-old female, office clerk, high school graduate*

They want our tax dollars for their support money, and they don't have to pay taxes.
—*Sixty-four-year-old male, heavy-truck driver, high school graduate*

Well, it seems that the government backs them up on everything and they seem to get away with everything. And now they go in and get a lumber harvest and we are paying for it. It seems we are always paying for everything.
—*Forty-year-old male, machine operator, high school graduate*

Because of what's been happening. They get to fish wherever they want to, and they get money from the government. If we have to pay to get licenses, we should get money from the government too.
—*Ninety-nine-year-old male, retired, non–high school graduate*

Each of these remarks conveys an underlying belief that hardworking people who dutifully pay their taxes must nonetheless watch as their money and a set of "special privileges" flow to members of a racial minority group.

A number of respondents directly voiced coarse, even virulent racial stereotypes of Native Americans. However, much of the bitterness attached to these stereotypes seemed to result from the perceived and emotionally loaded issue of resource loss or transfer of resources between groups. Consider these examples:

Well, they sit on their lazy butts and do nothing and they get their welfare checks and go sit in bars all night.
—*Twenty-three-year-old female, waitress, high school graduate*

Well, I think that they feel they're owed this, and I don't think it's fair. It's the same people who are on AFDC and keep collecting and don't bother to do anything to get out of it.
—*Forty-year-old female, bookkeeper, some post–high school education*

Because all they do is sit around and collect welfare. I have not seen an Indian who works.
—*Thirty-two-year-old female, sales supervisor, high school graduate*

I figure that they're, to me, they're more or less wards of the state. I don't know if they're taking advantage of it or not. In my opinion Indians are the only race that can retire the day they're born. They're just whores, you know.
—*Fifty-eight-year-old male, welder/cutter, high school graduate*

And in some cases the racial comparison was quite explicit:

Umm, because they seem to get all these handouts that we can't get, and we pay for them.
—*Thirty-six-year-old female, sewing machine operator, high school graduate*

Because whites don't get their share of stuff and it's not fair to us. They don't pay no rent.
—*Thirty-four-year-old female, carpet installer, non–high school graduate*

A good number of respondents gave disagreeing responses to the statement that Indians take unfair advantage of privileges. It is important to consider, albeit more briefly, the tenor of these open-ended accounts as well. The most common explanations for "disagree" responses involved the ideas that "they don't take advantage" (19.7 percent), "just a few cause problems" (17.2 percent), and they're just "doing what others would do" (15.0 percent; see Table 4.3). Some of the remarks in these categories emphasized the legal status of the treaties:

As long as they've got the right by court rulings, they're staying within the bounds of that. I just disagreed with what the rulings are.
—*Thirty-four-year-old male, laborer, high school graduate*

Well, I think when it's been ruled that it's their right, you can't accuse them of taking advantage.
—*Forty-three-year-old female, manager, high school graduate*

Other respondents stressed simply that privileges were not abused. For example:

> I don't think they . . . no. The implication I got was that they would overuse their privileges, and I don't see that here.
>> —*Forty-one-year-old female, elementary school teacher, college graduate*

> I do not think that they are abusing their rights to fish there. They have been fishing there for hundreds of years. They need the food.
>> —*Twenty-year-old male, interviewer, some post–high school education*

A number of respondents dealt directly with the underlying stereotype embedded in the symbolic racism question: namely, that Indians are deficient compared with whites, particularly with regard to the work ethic. Consider these explanations:

> Indians are people like everybody else.
>> —*Forty-three-year-old male, personnel and labor relations manager, college graduate*

> They're working hard, and people are against them because they're a minority.
>> —*Twenty-five-year-old female, administrative support worker, college graduate*

> I don't think they're in any way trying to take advantage, any more than someone would try to take advantage of a student loan. You can equate it to blacks in America and black oppression. Now it's Indians. If you offer it to them, they take it.
>> —*Thirty-five-year-old male, photographer, college graduate*

Thus, as was true of those who gave agreeing responses, individuals were making group comparisons. In addition, as these comments suggest, respondents were thinking about concrete, material aspects of how individuals make a living, not engaging the question in the abstract or taking it as an opportunity to vent feelings of tolerance or intolerance.

On the one hand, these results provide the most direct evidence available that the symbolic racism questions activated a concern with the Protestant work ethic. The open-ended comments include repeated references to ambition, hard work (or the lack thereof), freeloading, self-sufficiency, and playing by the rules. Without any overt prompting, respondents often mentioned welfare dependency, squandered tax dollars, and other abuses of government largesse. It would be hard to imagine how to tap into a clearer fusion of traditional moral values and anti-Indian affect than is revealed by these open-ended remarks. To this extent, the symbolic racism theory does pinpoint a core element of white racial ideology.

On the other hand, on several levels the respondents' comments raise deep and serious questions about the symbolic racism theory. First, many of the comments could easily come out of racial prejudice as classically understood, vitiating the case for a completely new theoretical model. As we argued some years ago in questioning the need for symbolic racism as a fundamentally new type of prejudice, "theories of prejudice have been routinely concerned with intergroup affect and stereotyping, that is, with feelings and beliefs about the traits of group members" (Bobo 1988b, p. 105). It is not clear that we need a new theory or set of concepts to anticipate or to understand these types of sentiments. Certainly nothing in these data would contradict this original line of criticism of symbolic racism.

Second, contrary to the claims of symbolic racism theory, the comments frequently include group comparisons: that is, they are not simply a venting of antiminority sentiment. The open-ended responses strongly suggest that the respondents' underlying frames of reference involve social comparisons in more collective and often explicit "us versus them" terms. The zero-sum character of the responses—and how many, many respondents perceived the dispute—is captured well in a cartoon that appeared in the *Wausau Daily Herald* during the 1991 spearfishing season (Figure 4.3).

Third, and most telling (and a finding completely at odds with the symbolic racism theory), many respondents spoke of a resource transfer from themselves or similar others to members of a minority group, or of facing a social system that expects and demands more of them than it does of members of the minority group. These are not just emotional and abstract resentments focused on a stigmatized target. The comments reflect group-level grievances rooted in a belief that "people like me" are losing ground relative to "them," now that the social context has been reconfigured in important ways (by court affirmation of the treaty rights). In effect, we believe the symbolic racism measures have much in common with Pettigrew's notions of group or fraternal deprivation (Pettigrew 2002) and with what we have labeled zero-sum or group competition (Bobo

FIGURE 4.3 Group competition as the "Wisconsin dilemma."
Source: Wausau Daily Herald, April 22, 1991.

and Hutchings 1996; Bobo and Johnson 2000). We elaborate on this point below.

By way of summary, at least two features of responses to the symbolic racism items stand out. First, the items clearly tap into what have traditionally been understood as racial stereotypes. Many of our respondents see whites as exhibiting a clearer commitment to the work ethic than do Native Americans (compare Campbell 1967). This is stereotyping as it is classically understood. It involves a social comparison along a trait dimension of high importance to the majority group. Second and more important, however, our respondents are also invoking ideas about legitimate and illegitimate sources of social inequality. That is to say, the symbolic racism items elicit, in part, what sociologists would classify as normative stratification beliefs (Bobo and Kluegel 1993; Huber and Form 1973;

Kluegel and Smith 1986). These are ideas, precisely as the theory of group position predicts, about who is *rightly entitled* to what. To reiterate, Blumer argued in describing the sense of group position that "it stands for 'what ought to be' rather than for 'what is.' It is a sense of where two racial groups belong. . . . In its own way, the sense of group position is a norm and imperative—indeed a very powerful one" (1958a, p. 5).

THE GROUP POSITION MODEL

Perhaps the politics of the treaty rights dispute is indeed better understood as a struggle over group position. At least this seems to be the reasonable implication of the open-ended responses to the symbolic racism question and the quite potent effects of self-interest on the symbolic racism scale. These patterns suggest that aspects of racial prejudice and group conflict merge or blend in the treaty rights dispute. A pattern of this kind is, plain enough, what the group position theory predicts should happen.

If the group position argument is valid, however, we must find more than an association between self-interest and various indicators of prejudice, whether the focus is on traditional measures of stereotyping and negative affect (Chapter 3) or on symbolic racism. According to group position theory, prejudice translates into an active, adaptive, political force via a sense of proper entitlement or prior rights to enjoy certain resources and a sense of threat or challenge to those entitlements from a subordinate group. That is, members of the dominant group must understand themselves as at risk of or as actually experiencing a competitive loss of power, status, or privilege to a subordinate group, and regard the sources or principle agents of that encroachment—the activists who pressured for the change—as negative, hostile, and threatening influences. Such perceptions of group competition and threat are the most proximate psychological roots of a personal rejection of change in the political environment that favors or advances the interests of a racial minority group.

Did any number of our white respondents see themselves, as a group, as losing (or at risk of losing) important power, wealth, status, or other resources to Native Americans? Did the whites see themselves and Native Americans as pursuing intrinsically conflicting aims? Certainly a number of the open-ended remarks reviewed in Chapter 3 in regard to opposition to spearfishing and in accounting for opinions on a symbolic racism item are strongly suggestive that this was in fact the case. To assess this possibil-

TABLE 4.4 Group competition questions

	Protecting rights of Indians hurts whites	Whites and Indians have same goals	Indians get ahead at expense of whites
Strongly agree	12%	21%	12%
Somewhat agree	34	51	20
No opinion/neutral	10	10	22
Somewhat disagree	33	12	32
Strongly disagree	11	6	14
(N)	(586)	(586)	(583)

Source: Chippewa Indian Treaty Rights Survey, 1990.

ity more directly, we developed three new questions to draw out perceptions of group competition (and three questions on perceived threat as well, to be discussed below). Table 4.4 shows the distribution of responses to each item. First and foremost, these questions explicitly invoke group comparisons. Second, they stipulate either a zero-sum conflict or complete harmony of interests between whites and Native Americans. Third, they generally avoid highly charged terms. In these questions we eschewed terms such as *fair* and *unfair*, and likewise avoided additional emphasis on the "special" character of any possible risk of loss or source of conflict. To be sure, the questions speak to a potential zero-sum character in Native American–white relations, but the language was kept as neutral as possible. The items were thus aimed to reverse many of the features of the symbolic racism measures (overt group comparison, neutral language, and realistic stakes or contingencies). We regard these measures as conceptually appropriate but also as a narrow and quite conservative strategy for assessing this element of the group position theory.[4]

A noteworthy number of our respondents, but always fewer than 50 percent, embraced a perception of zero-sum group competition. For instance, 46 percent agreed that protecting the rights of Indians hurts the rights of whites (combining "strongly" and "somewhat agree" responses). A substantial majority, 72 percent, rejected the idea that whites and Indians have basically different values and goals. But roughly one in three agreed with the idea that Indians are getting ahead economically at the expense of non-Indians. While the perception of zero-sum threat is not a solid majority opinion, a sizable fraction of the white population accepts some aspect of the group competition perspective.

As we observed with the injustice frame and symbolic racism questions, the group competition responses constitute a reasonably coherent attitude. All of the items are positively intercorrelated, with an average interitem correlation of .32. A simple additive scale of the items is reasonably reliable (Cronbach's alpha = .60).[5]

Perceptions of group competition are connected to a person's political ideology, level of knowledge about the treaty rights, stereotypes, and affective reactions to Indians (see Figure 4.4A). However, consistent with our measurement intentions and expectations, the group competition items have a stronger cognitive foundation than they do an affective foundation. This is indicated by the strength of the correlation with the knowledge index and the stereotyping scale, both of which are stronger than that observed for either measure with the injustice frame or the symbolic racism items. It is also indicated by the comparatively weak correlation of group competition with the affect item. This pattern suggests that, in posing questions that made explicit group comparisons, spoke to real-world contingencies, and used largely neutral language, we were successful in tapping a heavily cognitive belief about the structure of white–Native American relations. This point becomes important later when we assess how these group competition items relate to injustice frame and symbolic racism measures as well as to the larger matter of opinion on the treaty rights themselves.

Consistent with group position theory, both of the self-interest measures are also significantly related to perceptions of group competition (see Figure 4.4B). There is a sharper difference between treaty-county residents and nontreaty-county residents than there is between individuals in fishing or hunting households and those not in such households. This makes sense inasmuch as none of the group competition items refers specifically to aspects of the treaty rights controversy or to the Chippewa per se. The group competition items refer to the general structure of white–Native American relations, and therefore the quite specific, issue-relevant stake of involvement in fishing and hunting is significant, but less central to identifying those with a vested interest. Here it is useful to compare the injustice frame items, where involvement in these specific outdoor activities has a much stronger influence. The items in the injustice frame scale speak directly to the treaty controversy and the specific resources at stake in the case. As a consequence, the very concrete matter of involvement in fishing or hunting looms larger in shaping responses to these items than it does for the more generic group competition measures. But,

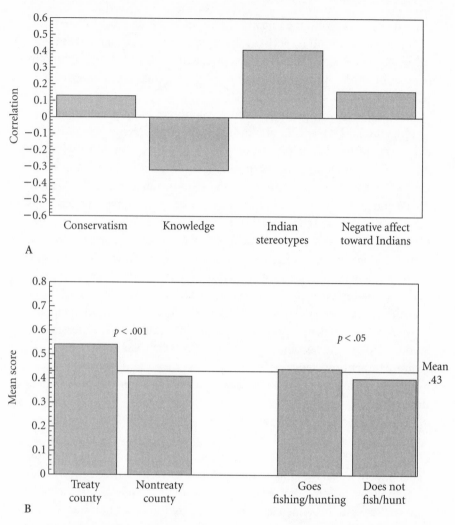

FIGURE 4.4 Relation of group competition to psychological measures (A)
and self-interest measures (B).
Source: Chippewa Indian Treaty Rights Survey, 1990.

importantly, across the board we find significant effects of the self-interest
measures.

As we did for the symbolic racism model, we decided to include an
open-ended follow-up question to one of the group competition questions, to assess the types of ideas and frames of reference that respondents

TABLE 4.5 Open-ended responses for attitudes about Indians getting ahead at whites' expense

	Statewide	Percentage of total sample
Reasons for agreeing that Indians get ahead at whites' expense		
Anyone would take advantage	5.0%	6.8%
Indians don't want to work	12.5	5.9
Wait for welfare; supported by taxpayers	17.8	6.3
Indians exploit rights for money	12.6	4.2
Special privileges just for Indians	7.2	2.3
Fishing rights per se	4.1	1.3
Personal experience	10.8	4.1
Other/don't know	30.0	See below
(N)	(187)	
Reasons for disagreeing that Indians get ahead at whites' expense		
Anyone would take advantage	9.5	See above
Indians don't want to work	3.6	See above
Wait for welfare; supported by taxpayers	1.3	See above
Everyone is trying to get ahead	35.0	19.9
Indians haven't had opportunities	4.0	2.2
Indians face unemployment; poverty	6.5	3.7
Can't generalize	5.4	3.3
Indians are nice people	12.1	6.5
Other/don't know	22.6	33.7
(N)	(316)	(589)

Source: Chippewa Indian Treaty Rights Survey, 1990.

Note: Not all columns sum to 100 due to rounding. "See below" and "See above" indicate categories that were the same in both panels; these entries were combined to show statewide percentages.

brought to the question. Table 4.5 shows the distribution of open-ended responses to the group competition question. Once again we show the responses separately for those who agreed and those who disagreed with the item, and we also show the overall or statewide percentage of respondents who offered a particular type of response. Were respondents really thinking in terms of whether white and Native American relationships have a zero-sum character? Were they thinking about reasonably concrete, material, and real-world contingencies? Or were our respondents just venting another antiminority resentment? We posed the follow-up question after the question on whether Indians were getting ahead economically at the expense of non-Indians. In general, the responses are reassuring that people engaged the matter in terms of group-level competition over real resources.

The three most commonly offered reasons for agreeing that "Indians are getting ahead at the expense" of others—Indians don't want to work (12.5 percent); they wait for welfare or are supported by taxpayers (17.8 percent); they exploit their rights for money (12.6 percent)—all touch on reliance on the state, especially through welfare dependency, but they also invoke other claims. It was perhaps put most simply by a respondent who declared, "They want something for nothing" (forty-year-old male, drafting technician). But many of the comments were more concrete than that. For example:

> They take advantage of us who are working. We have to pitch in to pay for their welfare.
> —*Fifty-two-year-old female, truck driver, non–high school graduate*

> If they are getting food stamps and welfare coming out of our taxes, I'm paying for them living without working. I'm working for them.
> —*Fifty-seven-year-old male, heavy-truck driver, non–high school graduate*

> The government does give them lots of aid which is at non-Indian taxpayer expense.
> —*Thirty-two-year-old female, secretary, some post–high school education*

> Because they're getting more welfare and housing than the whites that need it. They make out like bandits, then throw it away.
> —*Thirty-eight-year-old female, sales supervisor, high school graduate*

As is clear, many respondents personalized a situation they interpreted as involving a transfer of resources via taxation and various social welfare policies.

As an aspect of or variation on these complaints, some respondents emphasized exploitation of the off-reservation fishing rights. Consider these examples:

Well, I've heard that they've been selling the fish that they catch.
—*Twenty-six-year-old female, librarian, high school graduate*

Well, they are spearing our fish then selling them. That's not legal.
—*Twenty-three-year-old female, waitress, high school graduate*

The spearfishing issue. They aren't using fish for their own use. They're selling them. There are less fish to catch because of this. The economy has been hurt by this.
—*Seventy-two-year-old male, manager, high school graduate*

Some of the respondents objected to the existence of casinos, gambling, and other money-making ventures on Indian reservations:

The things that they can do, like having a smokeshop, bingo, gambling, comes from non-Indians. They keep poor records, and no one is really tracking them, and at least a portion of that should go back to non-Indians.
—*Forty-four-year-old male, wholesale/retail buyer, non–high school graduate*

They're allowed the gambling casinos on reservation now, and they get money and housing from the government.
—*Thirty-one-year-old female, manager, some post–high school education*

For some respondents, the racial antagonism contained in their comments about agreeing that the "Indians are getting ahead at the expense of non-Indians" was quite explicit. For instance:

They are asking too much from the government. Niggers don't get all that. This was their land a long time ago, but that is past.
—*Sixty-six-year-old female, occupational therapist, non–high school graduate*

They are screaming that they are minorities, and now white people become a minority.
—*Thirty-one-year-old female, construction inspector, high school graduate*

They get all these state grants. Us white people are trying to make it too, and it's unfair to the American families just trying to get along.
   —*Twenty-eight-year-old female, stock and inventory clerk, high school graduate*

They get to set up their free bingo hall down here. Are they gonna let the blacks set up one too?
   —*Fifty-three-year-old male, sales supervisor, high school graduate*

The question seems to have been quite successful, in short, in eliciting feelings of fraternal deprivation.

Many respondents disagreed with the assertion that Indians were getting ahead at the expense of non-Indians. The great bulk of those who disagreed explained themselves by pointing out that "everyone is trying to get ahead" (35 percent; see Table 4.5). The flavor of these accounts is suggested by the following examples:

They have a right to try to get ahead just as much as we do.
   —*Seventy-year-old female, occupational therapist, high school graduate*

I don't think they do. They try to do the best they can with the resources that they have. I don't think they try to take advantage of white people. There are not a lot of jobs, but I think a lot of Indians want to work.
   —*Forty-five-year-old female, records clerk, some post–high school education*

Only in the fact that the taxpayer foots [the bill for] federal help. But it doesn't really hurt individuals financially.
   —*Fifty-two-year-old male, construction worker, high school graduate*

They don't offer any competition right now to any other groups in the state.
   —*Forty-year-old male, computer science teacher, college graduate*

As these responses indicate, respondents made group comparisons, sometimes invoked race explicitly, and thought in terms of resource transfers via taxes, even while in the main denying that any significant injury to non-Indians was actually occurring.

The concepts important to group position theory do not end with perceptions of group competition over valued outcomes. The sources or

TABLE 4.6 Political threat questions

	Rating of Chippewa leaders	Rating of Chippewa spearfishers	Rating of protesters who support treaty
Strongly positive	3%	6%	6%
Somewhat positive	23	24	21
No opinion/neutral	46	27	20
Somewhat negative	19	28	39
Strongly negative	8	16	14
(N)	(578)	(581)	(586)

Source: Chippewa Indian Treaty Rights Survey, 1990.

Note: Not all columns sum to 100 due to rounding.

agents of pressure for change become a focal point of attention in the struggle for group position. The leaders, activists, and other publicly visible segments of groups are the agents likely to put forth the message and create the social pressure for change beneficial to a racial minority group. As a consequence, evaluations of these activist segments of groups provide the most focused and direct evidence of socially perceived threat.

In developing group position theory, we stressed the importance of public acts, elite public discussion, and declarations by significant social actors in the struggle over group position. Along these same lines, Blumer argued:

> The definition of these events is chiefly responsible for the development of a racial image and of the sense of group position. When this public discussion takes the form of a denunciation of the subordinate racial group, signifying that it is unfit and a threat, the discussion becomes particularly potent in shaping the sense of social position.
>
> ... The major influence in public discussion is exercised by individuals and groups who have the public ear and who are felt to have standing, prestige, authority, and power. Intellectual and social elites, public figures of prominence, and leaders of powerful organizations are likely to be the key figures in the formation of the sense of group position and in the characterization of the subordinate group. (Blumer 1958a, p. 6)

We focused our measures of perceived threat on those publicly salient figures advancing the cause of Chippewa treaty rights: Chippewa tribal leaders, Chippewa spearfishers, and those who went out to the boat landings to

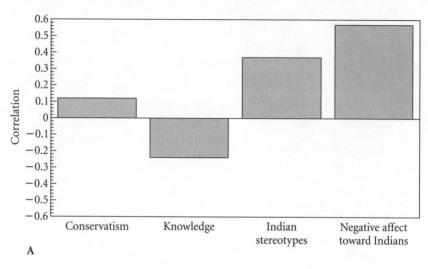

A

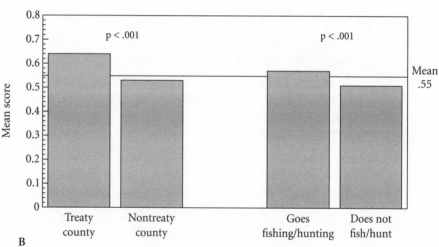

B

FIGURE 4.5 Relation of political threat to psychological measures (A)
and self-interest measures (B).
Source: Chippewa Indian Treaty Rights Survey, 1990.

show support for the Chippewa. The distributions for these items are
shown in Table 4.6.

Comparatively few white Wisconsinites gave favorable ratings to Chippewa leaders, to spearfishers, or to those who protested in support of the
Chippewa treaty activists. Some 44 percent gave either "somewhat" or

"strongly" negative evaluations of the spearfishers, and 53 percent gave comparable ratings to the sympathetic protesters. Here it is important to note, however, that a large fraction expressed an effectively neutral opinion of Chippewa leaders; many fewer offered neutral assessments of the spearfishers and the sympathy protesters. This is broadly consistent with the infrequent coverage of Chippewa leaders in the broader media and with the group position model's theoretical expectations. According to the model, threat should be perceived as greatest from those segments of a group most vigorously pressing for or actively engaged in a realized change in group status positions. Again the items constitute a reasonably coherent set, with an average correlation of .35 and an alpha of .61 for a scale composed of the three items.

Figure 4.5A examines the correlation of the political threat scale with conservatism, knowledge, stereotypes of Indians, and negative affect toward Indians, and Figure 4.5B looks at its correlation with the two self-interest measures. Political threat, like the previous measures, is clearly related to the core prejudice indicators, particularly negative stereotypes and negative affect. It is also the case that treaty-county residents and those involved in fishing and hunting activities expressed higher levels of threat than those residing in the remainder of the state and respondents not involved in those outdoor activities.

THE CASE FOR SIMPLIFICATION

Concepts invoked by each theory have some substantial degree of resonance in the population, and each set of measures exhibits reasonable internal coherence. The patterns of correlation with the other prejudice measures and the relation to the self-interest measures suggest great similarity across constructs. Furthermore, there is much overlap in the substance of the open-ended comments.

To get a more definitive assessment of the determinants, respectively, of the injustice frame, symbolic racism, and the two group position models (group competition and political threat), we estimated a series of multivariate models. For each scale we estimated two models, a baseline model that includes age, education, sex, income, and the two self-interest measures as predictors, and a second model that adds the other relevant social-psychological variables: political ideology, negative affect towards Indians, stereotypes, and treaty rights knowledge. If the injustice frame, symbolic

TABLE 4.7   OLS models of the determinants of injustice frame, symbolic racism, group competition, and political threat scales

	Injustice frame		Symbolic racism		Group competition		Political threat	
	Model 1	Model 2	Model 1	Model 2	Model 1	Model 2	Model 1	Model 2
Constant	.507*** (.052)	.357*** (.065)	.458*** (.051)	.186** (.060)	.507*** (.051)	.308*** (.060)	.426*** (.044)	.243*** (.049)
Age	.002*** (.001)	.002*** (.001)	.002* (.001)	.001 (.001)	-.001 (.001)	-.001* (.001)	.002*** (.001)	.002*** (.000)
No HS diploma	-.096** (.036)	-.086** (.034)	-.039 (.035)	-.017 (.031)	.001 (.035)	.013 (.031)	-.043 (.030)	-.032 (.026)
Some college	-.002 (.024)	.012 (.022)	-.020 (.024)	-.001 (.021)	-.092*** (.023)	-.074*** (.020)	.000 (.020)	.018 (.017)
B.A. degree or more	-.093*** (.027)	-.038 (.026)	-.122*** (.026)	-.045 (.024)	-.163*** (.026)	-.094*** (.024)	-.054* (.022)	-.001 (.020)
Female	-.051** (.019)	-.055** (.018)	-.011 (.019)	-.009 (.017)	-.020 (.019)	-.024 (.017)	-.007 (.016)	-.008 (.014)
Income	.007 (.006)	.003 (.006)	.006 (.006)	-.000 (.005)	.011 (.006)	.005 (.005)	.003 (.005)	-.003 (.004)
Treaty county	.141*** (.020)	.107*** (.020)	.151*** (.020)	.099*** (.019)	.106*** (.020)	.058** (.018)	.082*** (.017)	.028 (.015)

Goes fishing/hunting	.092*** (.023)	.080*** (.021)	.062** (.022)	.044* (.020)	.026 (.022)	.009 (.020)	.064*** (.019)	.045** (.016)
Conservative		.067 (.047)		.102* (.044)		.057 (.043)		.006 (.036)
Negative affect toward Indians		.201*** (.042)		.214*** (.039)		.279*** (.039)		.361*** (.032)
Stereotypes of Indians		.187*** (.058)		.372*** (.054)		.248*** (.053)		.156*** (.044)
Knowledge		-.109*** (.030)		-.099*** (.028)		-.121*** (.028)		-.064** (.023)
Adjusted R-squared	.18	.29	.18	.37	.14	.33	.11	.37
N	533	533	527	527	534	534	531	531

*$p < .05$ **$p < .01$ ***$p < .001$

Source: Chippewa Indian Treaty Rights Survey, 1990.

racism, group competition, and political threat are each tapping unique aspects of the attitudes and beliefs held during the treaty rights dispute, they should exhibit distinct patterns of relation to respondents' demographic characteristics and, especially, to the theoretically important factors of self-interest and traditional racial prejudice in accord with theoretical predictions. The results for our four models are reported in Table 4.7.

The single most important point we wish to emphasize about Table 4.7 is the overwhelming similarity of results for each major attitude scale. At least one, and usually both, of the self-interest variables is significantly related to injustice frame, symbolic racism, group competition, and political threat. What is more, negative affect, negative stereotypes, and treaty knowledge are all significantly related, and in the same direction, to each of the major attitude-scale dependent variables. None of the seemingly unique patterns—the impact of gender on injustice frame beliefs, the impact of ideology on symbolic racism, and the absence of an effect of fishing or hunting on group competition—is sufficiently large or trending in a clearly contradictory direction enough to call into question the basic conclusion of a deeply fundamental similarity in the determinants of the several constructs.

Substantively, those with a self-interested stake in the treaty dispute, particularly and most consistently those who reside in the treaty counties, expressed greater feelings of injustice, greater symbolic racism, and greater feelings of group competition and political threat. We should emphasize that this constitutes strong evidence of self-interest effects. These patterns emerge despite controls for group affect, stereotypes, and treaty specific knowledge. That is, the impact of self-interest clearly survives controls for those other critical cultural beliefs and contextual factors that might well have differentiated treaty-county residents from those living in the remainder of the state.

In addition, the bedrock components of racial prejudice have significant effects on each of the measures. Negative affect toward Indians, negative stereotypes, and lack of knowledge about the treaty rights are among the foundations for injustice beliefs, symbolic racism, group competition, and political threat attitudes. In each case, the effects of the set of prejudice measures are substantial, more than doubling the amount of variance explained by the baseline model.

Yet the full set of results should occasion real intellectual discomfort for advocates of the injustice frame and symbolic racism theories. The former should, as Table 4.7 reveals, have roots in self-interest. But the injustice beliefs should not be strongly dependent on prejudice—and they plainly are. Symbolic racism should, as Table 4.7 reveals, have a solid basis in traditional prejudice indicators of negative affect and beliefs. But it should not be strongly dependent on self-interest—and yet it plainly is.

Group position theory, of course, specifies a role for interests and for affect—for the material contingencies of a dispute and for the identities, attitudes, beliefs, and preferences that lend social conditions their meaning and normative significance—from the very outset. And it does so not as a surface matter of noting contextual conditions or taking stock of necessary social embroidery. Injustice frame theory sees racial animosity and prejudice as a superficial aspect of the real dispute over a set of concrete substantive grievances, and symbolic racism is always mindful that racial disputes occur in social contexts with specific features, but stresses that these potential material contingencies are largely irrelevant to the politics at hand. Group position theory, in contrast, neither displaces the circumstances of group living arrangements and status to the margins of analysis nor marginalizes the ideas and attitudes that constitute constructed social meaning in everyday life. Rather than seeing these two types of factors as competing accounts for racialized political disputes, the group position framework attempts to understand the nature and reasons for the interplay of self-interest and group interests, on the one hand, and negative feelings and beliefs about members of an out-group, on the other hand. The two sets of concerns become linked in the "struggle for group position." And they find their most potent political expression in perceptions of group competition and threat.

In response to these results and theoretical considerations, we are led to remap the set of attitude and belief measures, rather than simply proceeding as though we need six separate constructs to adequately describe the racial attitudes in this domain (affect, stereotypes, injustice frame, symbolic racism, group competition, and political threat). A considerably simplified, though still multidimensional mapping of the key attitudes is in order. Group position theory directs us to emphasize four dimensions: affect, stereotypes, group entitlement and competition, and threat or threatened encroachment. The full set of items can and should be effectively reorganized. Table 4.8 displays the original theoretical specifications and our new remapping of items.

In the first column of Table 4.8, we have the original eighteen items and six-dimension theoretical mapping of constructs. We also show the alpha coefficient for each set of items. Column two specifies the reformulated set

TABLE 4.8 Simplification of racial attitude constructs

Original mapping of constructs	Final mapping of constructs

1. Affect
   Chippewa Indians
	1. Affect
	   Chippewa Indians

2. Stereotypes (alpha = .59)
   Respect nature
   Lazy
   Welfare dependent
	2. New stereotypes (alpha = .74)
	   Respect nature (ST)
	   Lazy (ST)
	   Welfare dependent (ST)
	   Same goals (GC)
	   Work hard (SR)
	   Unfair advantage (SR)

3. Injustice frame (alpha = .63)
   Two classes
   Hurt fish
   Hurt tourism
   Need treaty
	3. New group competition (alpha = .71)
	   Rights hurt (GC)
	   Get ahead (GC)
	   Hurt fish (IF)
	   Hurt tourism (IF)
	   Two classes (IF)

4. Symbolic racism (alpha = .71)
   Unfair advantage
   Government attention
   Indian influence
   Work hard
	4. New political threat (alpha = .72)
	   Chippewa leaders (PT)
	   Chippewa spearfishers (PT)
	   Sympathy protests (PT)
	   Government attention (SR)
	   Indian influence (SR)
	   Need treaty (IF)

5. Group competition (alpha = .59)
   Rights hurt
   Same goal
   Get ahead	

6. Political threat (alpha = .61)
   Chippewa leaders
   Chippewa spearfishers
   Sympathy protests	

Note: GC = group competition; IF = injustice frame; PT = political threat; SR = symbolic racism; ST = stereotypes.

of measures. The new mapping reduces the full set of constructs from six to four. Importantly, neither the injustice frame nor symbolic racism remains a distinct concept in this reformulation. The injustice frame items largely dissolve into the new fraternal deprivation, or group competition, construct or the new political threat construct. The symbolic racism items dissolve into either the new stereotype cluster or the new political threat cluster. We should be clear that one of the symbolic racism items—unfair advantage—is very much at the border of the stereotype and group competition constructs. Yet we believe that, taking into account the full set of correlations, open-ended comments, and relationships to other variables, it leans a bit more in the direction of a stereotype indicator. It is also worth noting that now each construct has a comparatively strong and roughly equivalent reliability score (ranging from .71 to .74).[6]

The reformulated measures constitute a cleaner fit with the group position theory framework. We also believe they offer the best reflection of the underlying meaning of these questions for respondents, given all that we have considered to this point. We will rely on these simplified and reformulated measures in all analyses from this point forward (see Appendix B for full confirmatory factor modeling results).

MODELING TREATY RIGHTS OPPOSITION

The penultimate task for this chapter is to return to an examination of the determinants of treaty rights opposition. Table 4.9 reports the results of the models of treaty rights opposition using the new racial attitude scales. The models are developed in nested steps, beginning with a baseline model containing no explicit racial attitude measures. This baseline model explains 16 percent of the variation in opposition to treaty rights, with opposition being largely attributable to the self-interest measures, political ideology, education, and sex. Men, conservatives, the poorly educated, and those with a stake in the treaty dispute all tended to express greater levels of opposition to the treaty rights.

Model 2 adds the negative affect toward Indians measures. Doing so substantially increases the amount of variance explained. It also results in a slight weakening in the influence of the self-interest measures and of the education coefficients, indicating that some of the impact on treaty rights opposition of living in the treaty counties, being involved in fishing and hunting, and more schooling is mediated by the extent of negative feelings toward Indians in general.

In the third model we add the reformulated stereotyping measure. Introducing this variable brings a further substantial rise in the amount of variance explained, going from 26 percent in Model 2 to 35 percent in Model 3. The impact of the negative stereotypes measures is quite large, easily the largest influence in the model. The self-interest and education

TABLE 4.9 OLS regression predicting opposition to Indian treaty rights

	Model 1	Model 2	Model 3	Model 4	Model 5
Constant	.57***	.45***	.33***	.23***	.21***
	(.06)	(.06)	(.06)	(.05)	(.05)
Age	.002*	.002**	.001*	.001*	.0002
	(.001)	(.001)	(.001)	(.001)	(.001)
No H.S. diploma	−.07*	−.07*	−.06*	−.05	−.05
	(.04)	(.03)	(.03)	(.03)	(.03)
Some college	−.02	−.01	−.003	−.003	−.01
	(.02)	(.02)	(.02)	(.02)	(.02)
BA degree or more	−.08**	−.06*	−.02	−.01	−.01
	(.03)	(.03)	(.02)	(.02)	(.02)
Female	−.06***	−.06***	−.05**	−.04**	−.05**
	(.02)	(.02)	(.02)	(.02)	(.02)
Income	−.002	−.001	−.01	−.01	−.01
	(.01)	(.01)	(.01)	(.01)	(.01)
Treaty county	.11***	.07***	.04*	.03	−.001
	(.02)	(.02)	(.02)	(.02)	(.02)
Goes fishing/hunting	.09***	.07***	.06**	.05**	.03
	(.02)	(.02)	(.02)	(.02)	(.02)
Conservative	.13**	.14**	.07	.06	.04
	(.05)	(.05)	(.04)	(.04)	(.04)
Negative affect toward Indians		.31***	.17***	.11**	.01
		(.04)	(.04)	(.04)	(.04)
New Indian stereotype scale			.45***	.27***	.19***
			(.06)	(.06)	(.05)
New group competition				.38***	.24***
				(.05)	(.04)
New political threat scale					.48***
					(.05)
Adjusted *R*-squared	.16***	.26***	.35***	.42***	.51***
N	504	504	504	504	504

*p < .05   **p < .01   ***p < .001

Source: Chippewa Indian Treaty Rights Survey, 1990.

coefficients shrink a bit further still. In addition, the impact of the negative affect measure shrinks as well, indicating that much of its influence is indirect, via its contribution to negative stereotypes.

Model 4 introduces the fraternal deprivation, or group competition, measure. Doing so again increases the variance in treaty rights opposition accounted for, this time to 42 percent. The coefficients for a number of the variables, particularly treaty county, negative affect, and stereotyping, are reduced. Indeed, the treaty county self-interest measure is no longer a significant direct effect. This implies that a large part of the treaty county effect is the result of residents' greater sense of entitlement to the surrounding natural resources and the sense of loss due to affirmation of the treaty rights that come from living in a part of the state where the treaties have legal force.

Finally, in Model 5 we introduce the new political threat scale. The impact of political threat is substantial. At 51 percent, the overall amount of variance explained by the model is, likewise, substantial and more than three times that of the original baseline model. Although the impact of stereotyping and group competition are reduced by introducing the political threat measure, both continue to exert substantial and significant direct effects on treaty rights opposition. The effect of negative affect, however, is now insignificant, suggesting that its impact on treaty opposition is entirely indirect, via its contribution to stereotypes, group competition, and political threat beliefs. In this model, neither of the self-interest measures have significant direct effects. Thus, once we have taken group competition and especially political threat into account, we understand fully why those with a stake in the issue object to the treaty rights: they fear that, in the struggle for group position, they are losing to those who have pressed the case for affirmation of off-reservation rights for the Chippewa.[7]

We should stress here that Model 5 shows a large improvement in predictive power over that shown in Chapter 3. When we compare Model 3 of Table 3.8 with Model 5 in Table 4.9, we see that the new model adds a full 20 percentage points to the amount of variation explained in opposition to the treaty rights. The group position formulation greatly increases our leverage in understanding the core issue attitudes in the treaty rights dispute. The most proximate determinants of these political views are the sense of group competition and perceived political threat.

We also took the step of estimating a version of Model 5 separately for treaty-county and nontreaty-county respondents. The results are reassuringly similar in the two parts of the state. In particular, political threat is the strongest direct predictor of treaty opposition in both the treaty and nontreaty counties. In the treaty counties, however, the effects of stereotyping and group competition are entirely indirect, via political threat, and involvement in fishing and hunting is such a widespread part of the lifestyle that it does not contribute to treaty rights opposition. Involvement in fishing and hunting is a significant direct predictor of treaty rights opposition among nontreaty-county residents and, consistent with the results in Table 4.9, stereotypes, group competition, and political threat all significantly enhance the likelihood of opposition to the treaty rights.

CONCLUSIONS

In the previous chapter, we presented evidence that many of the claims of pragmatic harms from the exercising of the treaty rights were anything but dispassionate, race-neutral judgments. These claims were often voiced in strong terms and linked with a series of stereotyped complaints against Native Americans. The results of this chapter confirm the earlier suspicion that more than "the facts" of the case lay beneath such claims of a sense of "injustice." Although it would be unfair to reduce all claims of grievance and injustice to manifestations of prejudice, it is clear from the results above that responses to the original injustice frame items are thoroughly infused with negative affect and negative stereotypes, and are fed by inaccurate information.

This is not to gainsay the extent to which there may have been activists who held truly principled complaints against the treaty rights. From the vantage point of broad public opinion, however, we cannot discern a clear and discrete note of grievance. Those scholars who advanced a sort of injustice frame approach to explaining opposition to school busing and desegregation efforts faced much the same dilemma (McClendon 1985; Stinchcombe and Taylor 1980; Taylor 1986). In light of our results, the combination of the open-ended replies to the core treaty-rights opposition question (Chapter 3) and the symbolic racism and group competition items as reviewed in this chapter and the unambiguous dependence of injustice frame views on anti-Indian affect, stereotypes, and lack of knowledge about the treaty rights powerfully vitiates the injustice frame account.

The directness of the racial prejudices brought to the treaty rights dispute was made abundantly clear in many of the open-ended comments from respondents. As a thirty-nine-year-old records clerk put it in responding to a symbolic racism question: "Just . . . well for instance with spearfishing. The Indians come into places with their food stamps and, don't get me wrong, other people do too. But I just get a real negative feeling toward them." The anger and resentment came through no less clearly in responses to one of the group competition items. As a forty-seven-year-old woman who worked as a food preparer said: "Well, I've seen how the Indians live around here and how they try to get everything they can out of the whites." The comments convey a sense of insiders and outsiders, of us versus them, of who is doing right and who is doing wrong, and of who is losing out and who is getting ahead.

But to conclude that prejudice is at work is neither to reduce the matter simply to the orthodox prejudice of negative feelings and beliefs nor to validate, with equal strength, both the symbolic racism and group position theories. To be sure, this chapter yields some of the most powerful evidence we have seen on the extent to which symbolic racism questions tap into sentiments strongly laced with assumptions about the Protestant work ethic. Indeed the evidence from the open-ended replies is a good deal more direct and readily interpretable than that coming from painstaking correlational analyses recently developed by Sears, Henry, and Kosterman (2000) and by Kinder and Mendelberg (2000). It would be wholly insufficient, however, to stop here, because responses to the symbolic racism items involved much more. As the relation to the self-interest measures suggests and many of the open-ended remarks directly articulate, respondents expressed a resentment that is suffused with perceived interests, group comparisons, and feelings of fraternal deprivation. And to an astonishingly frequent degree, respondents actually spoke of a resource transfer when replying to the symbolic racism question. One need not—and we do not—regard these assertions of material loss through paying taxes to support welfare as *realistic* assessments of material loss imposed on the members of one group (whites) by the members of another group (American Indians). There is little doubt that these assertions reflect more exaggeration, stereotype, and animus than they do a tightly reasoned and factual calculus. However, at issue here is not the accuracy of the belief but the meaning to respondents, to the best of our ability to pin it down. Despite the claims and intentions of the theory's originators, symbolic racism is neither just a set of vague resentments nor just the venting of a new politicized hostility to racial minority groups. It also, and perhaps in the main, constitutes a collective grievance about diminished group position and status.

Here it is important to stress that we are not the only analysts to reach this conclusion. In a meticulous analysis of National Election Study data from 1986 and 1992 concerned with black-white relations, sociologist Michael Hughes concluded:

> In short, symbolic racism may, in itself, constitute self-oriented group interest in the sense of status defense. If hard work and self-reliance are symbols that whites use to define their status position and if whites believe blacks can attain similar status (that is, get special favors and benefits) when they do not deserve it, then whites may believe their status has been devalued and express this sense or fear of devaluation as symbolic racism.
>
> Symbolic racism researchers may be correct in arguing that the critical issues are not really busing, affirmative action, welfare, or black political candidates. The critical issue, however, is also not moral resentment and irrational antagonism: The issue represented by symbolic racism is status and power and whites' fear of losing them. (Hughes 1997, p. 74)

An even stronger theoretical conclusion was reached by Eliot Smith in his influential piece on the role of affect in prejudice. He argued that "there is reason to identify symbolic racism with group-based, emotion-linked appraisals" (E. Smith 1993, p. 308) and that such appraisals may flow not from discrete individual exigencies or experiences but rather do very much flow from "perceivers' views of their *group* interests" (p. 309, emphasis in original).

Given the problems our analysis revealed for both the injustice frame model and the symbolic racism model, we conclude that the group position model provides the most complete, internally consistent, and parsimonious accounting of the types of attitudes and beliefs at the heart of the treaty rights dispute. It is useful to recall that group position theory does not declare that group affect and stereotyping are politically irrelevant. Instead, from the perspective of our group position theory, these attitudes form much of the foundation of the outlooks that are more politically proximate: group competition and perceived threat. Likewise, the group position theory does not deny the relevance of self-interest; instead it specifies an organic connection between self-interest and attitudes.

These results, based on a complete elaboration of the group position model, take us further than if we were to rely on classic prejudice theory alone. Affective reactions to Native Americans and stereotyping do matter (as we showed in Chapter 3 and as remains true in the Chapter 4 results). However, Model 5 in Table 4.9 explains a good deal more of the variance in attitudes on the treaty rights than does Model 3 in Table 3.8 (51 percent versus 30 percent).

Having said this, many of the social dynamics of the controversy are still not directly illuminated by even a well-specified social-psychological model of treaty rights opposition. We do not yet know what most white Wisconsin residents made of the overt conflict surrounding the treaty rights, how important the issue became for most people, and how extensively individuals moved from an attitude of opposition to actual involvement in the struggle over the treaty rights. We take up these matters—assessing the protests, issue importance, and actual behavioral involvement—in the next chapter.

Chapter 5

PROTEST, MOBILIZATION, AND MASS COMPLIANCE: MOVING FROM ATTITUDES TO BEHAVIOR

> The spearing season is fast approaching and I for one feel that we native Americans (Polish, French, German, etc.) should change our approach on how to handle this problem. A 3 month old baby does not get its mother's attention at 2:00 in the morning by lying in its crib sucking its thumb. He gets it by screaming at the top of his lungs, and I feel it's about time we started screaming.
>
> Letter to the editor, *Vilas County News-Review*, April 13, 1988

> I will be present at the public landings to exercise my constitutional right to protest. I am not anti-Indian and not a racist. I am against the discriminatory practice of fish spearing. I trust that [Attorney General] Hanaway will see to it that my constitutional right to be at "public landings" will be protected.
>
> Letter to the editor, *Lakeland Times*, June 10, 1988

The 1983 Voigt decision created a sense of alarm in some quarters. On February 2, 1983, immediately following the appeals court ruling that opened the door for the Voigt decision, the front page of the *Vilas County News-Review* carried the headline "Indians Gain Unlimited Fishing, Hunting Rights on Public Lands: Can Hunt, Fish Any Time." The story repeatedly voiced concerns about overfishing, damaging the underlying natural resources, and irresponsible behavior by Indians. Early in the article, reporter Kurt Krueger wrote: "While the federal court's decision stands, Indians will be hunting and fishing in Vilas County, probably day and night, says Gary Scovel, law enforcement supervisor for Vilas, Oneida and Forest Counties. 'For the next few days, they can really kill and harvest anything legally, as long as there is no trespassing,' said Scovel. 'They can shoot deer, any number. They could spear muskies, or any fish. For that matter, they could set a gill net in Eagle River Chair'" (*Vilas County News-Review*,

February 2, 1983, p. 1). The story went on to express optimism that the state would be successful in its effort to win an injunction preventing the Chippewa from exercising their treaty rights.

On the same day, the *Lakeland News* published an open letter to the governor from one of its readers:

> I am writing to voice my concern over the recent ruling on an 1854 treaty agreement with the Chippewa Indians. This antiquated law provides them with the right to ignore hunting and fishing regulations adopted by the state of Wisconsin. I for one am furious about this miscarriage of justice and want you to [be] aware of my feelings. To begin with, both you and I were born on this soil and should be entitled to no more or less than the current generations living on the reservations. I also feel that if this agreement is to be honored, it must further be stated that the pursuit of game must be conducted using the means at hand at the time of the agreement. . . . Heritage, it's true, should be preserved for future generations and that is why we celebrate Octoberfest, St. Patrick's Day and the like, but to include this ancient agreement as part of one's heritage is stupid, to say the least. I intend to do all in my power to revoke this ruling and I implore you to do the same. (*Lakeland Times,* February 3, 1983, p. 5)

Of course, despite these and many other declarations against the treaty rights, the fight to stop the Chippewa from exercising those rights did not succeed.

As we have seen, the ultimate legal validation of the treaty rights ushered in a period of significant protest and social mobilization against the Chippewa's exercising of their treaty rights. The protests were variously loud, boisterous, and often intense situations, generating great concern about the possibility of real violence. A *New York Times* article in April 1988 described the surreal atmosphere surrounding the normally placid lakes of northern Wisconsin: "With white-tailed deer prancing along the forested shores of Big St. Germain Lake under a moonlit sky, this North Woods region seemed posed for a portrait of splendor and tranquility. But a National Guard helicopter whirred overhead. Police officers stood by in riot gear. And an ambulance waited near the shore, just in case" (*New York Times,* April 24, 1988).

By 1991 the state had routinized its crowd-control procedures. The *Wausau Daily Herald* published a major feature story outlining the process, identi-

The season   Status of spearfishing in 1991

Crowd control at a boat landing

This is a typical setup used to maintain crowd control at boat landings.

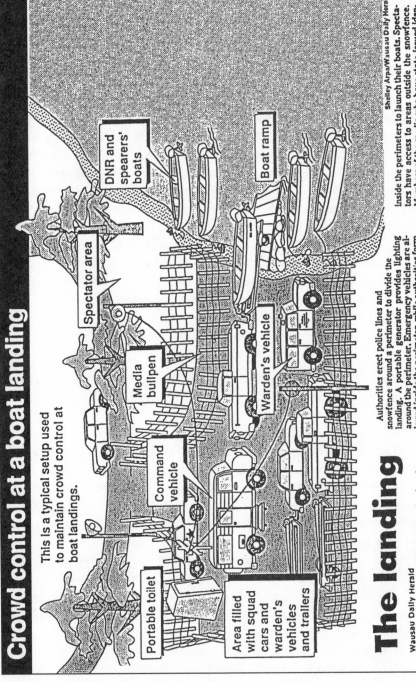

Spectator area

DNR and spearers' boats

Boat ramp

Media bullpen

Warden's vehicle

Command vehicle

Portable toilet

Area filled with squad cars and warden's vehicles and trailers

The landing

Wausau Daily Herald

Law enforcement officials have developed a crowd-control system to maintain order at boat landings.

Authorities erect police lines and snowfence around a perimeter to divide the landing. A portable generator provides lighting around the perimeter. Emergency vehicles are allowed inside the perimeter, while authorities form a barrier by standing along the snowfence. Chippewa spearers or any boaters are allowed

inside the perimeters to launch their boats. Spectators have access to areas outside the snowfence. Members of the media who have state-issued identification have access to a media area — known as the bullpen — inside the landing.

Shelley Arpa/Wausau Daily Herald

fying the placement of command vehicles, the game warden's vehicle, the media bullpen, police lines, fencing, power generators, the boat ramps, and even the portable toilets brought in for the large crowds (see Figure 5.1).

That same year the *Milwaukee Sentinel* published a front-page story under the headline "Spearing Tension Remains High a Day after Near-Riot." It reported that nearly 250 protesters, mostly treaty opponents but with a good number of treaty supporters as well, had shown up at Squirrel Lake in Minocqua and begun a bitter confrontation. Though no violence occurred, the story noted that

> officers had to form a wedge to allow supporters of the Chippewa to get through the crowd of protestors. "This is the worst I've seen in a couple of years," said a state law enforcement official who has been at virtually every significant boat landing demonstration in seven years. "They're young, they're drunk and talk about racist—whew." Spearfishing law enforcement coordinator Alan Shanks blamed both sides for what he said was a near-riot Saturday. "I think it was six of one and half-dozen of another" in terms of blame, Shanks said. "Gasoline and matches don't mix." (*Milwaukee Sentinel*, April 22, 1991, p. 11)

The head of Protect America's Rights and Resources was reported to have carried a mock gallows, with the dummy in a noose representing "Wisconsin Rights, Resources, and Citizens." Anti-treaty protesters took an American flag featuring an Indian face away from pro–treaty rights protesters who had come to show their support for the Chippewa. This flag was doused with gasoline and burned.

The threat of violence had long been attached to the protests at the boat landings. Some groups, like Stop Treaty Abuse, had tried announcing on the radio which lakes the Chippewa were going to fish on, to increase the size of the crowds at the boat landings. They seemed to court a larger show of displeasure—and perhaps disruption. For example, the *Vilas County News-Review* ran a story during the 1988 spearfishing season reporting that

FIGURE 5.1 North Woods boat landings.
Source: Wausau Sunday Herald, April 7, 1991. Drawn by Shelley Arpa.

Dean Crist of Minocqua, president of STA, said, "Let's put this in the simplest terms: If you want to avoid violence during the spearfishing season—stop the spearing."

Crist said violence should be avoided. But he said frustration is building among treaty opponents because of what he called the state's poor management of negotiations with the Chippewa and of poor defense in the federal lawsuit brought by the Chippewa.

Crist said mishandling of the case has led to higher frustration, and that "violence is the last step of frustration." (*Vilas County News-Review,* April 13, 1988, p. 2)

These types of angry assertions by anti–treaty rights activists were part of an effort to mobilize the public, to shape public opinion, and to put pressure on state and federal officials concerned with the issue. Such statements, and the atmosphere they contributed to at the boat landings, prompted state officials, including then Wisconsin governor Tommy Thompson, to issue repeated calls for calm and restraint and to allocate additional funds for greater security measures.

Our purpose in this chapter is to illuminate a series of issues attached to the protest and controversy themselves. Prior to this point we have mainly been concerned with the core issue attitudes of support for or opposition to the treaty rights. Now we shift our focus to (1) how the mass public made sense of the protests; (2) how important or central the dispute became to individuals; (3) how active and involved individuals were with the issue; and (4) how individuals ultimately wanted to see the state government resolve the issue. The fact that there was such sustained and often intense contention and controversy was what made the treaty rights a matter for public opinion. In this chapter, then, we focus on the domain of political action, not merely preferences and beliefs. The vast majority of studies of public opinion, including the most prominent works of the past decade in the area of race and politics, exclusively address issue opinions and related beliefs (Kinder and Sanders 1996; Schuman et al. 1997; Sniderman and Piazza 1993). We wish to greatly broaden the scope of investigation here by taking up assessments of the protests, of issue importance or centrality, and of actual forms and levels of participation in the controversy.

These questions and their answers, aside from bearing directly on the substance of the treaty rights dispute, may be informed by two distinct but related lines of theoretical inquiry. First, the issues are relevant to the liter-

ature on micro-mobilization processes in the study of collective behavior
and social movements. One aim of this chapter is to examine what *meaning* the protest actions around the treaties took on for the public at large.
An older tradition in collective behavior and social-movement research
might well have treated this as a question of whether movement actions
were understood as true social protest or as criminal and deviant behavior (Sears and McConahay 1973; Turner 1969). Under a social-protest interpretation, an action is understood as having roots in "the feeling of
grievance that moves it and in the intent to provoke ameliorative action"
(Turner 1969, p. 816). In somewhat different language, the question is
whether movement actions are seen as having credible and legitimate underlying motivation. Contemporary scholarship in this area would define the issue as an aspect of social-movement framing processes (Benford
and Snow 2000). Protest is thus, in part, a communicative act, an act of
signification, aimed at encouraging particular understandings of the problem, the actors, the antagonists, and specific responses to the situation.

A second, intersecting line of research concerns the social-psychological
literature on the attributes of attitudes, namely whether an attitude is important or central to the individual (for reviews, see Petty, Wegener, and
Fabrigar 1997; Schuman 1995). We are interested not only in the level of
importance or centrality of a topic but also, given the relative paucity of
work in this domain, in what causes an issue to rise to a higher level of personal importance and, likewise, what social-psychological and behavioral
consequences flow from highly central attitudes. In terms of the sources of
attitude centrality, one strong hypothesis identifies self-interest as the key
factor (Citrin and Green 1990). To wit, those with a more tangible stake in
an issue or outcome are more likely to rank it as a matter of high personal
importance (Boniger, Krosnick, and Berent 1995; Young et al. 1987). With
regard to the consequences of attitude centrality, social psychologists suggest that the more important an attitude or issue is, the more likely the
attitude (or issue) is to find expression in significant social behavior and
the more likely it is to figure in the evaluation of related political actors
and issues.

Concerns with protest as a communicative act and with the impact of
varying levels of issue importance across individuals both have a place in
the group position theory of prejudice. It is useful here to recall that a core
feature of the group position dynamic is the public clash between elite segments of groups and communities in contesting one another and advanc-

ing competing understandings of the situation and of appropriate "group positions." Likewise, our group position theory stresses the importance of the underlying configuration of interests in a situation, and also how the circumstances are likely to structure action on an issue. As Blumer explained:

> We also need to perceive the appreciable opportunity that is given to strong interest groups in directing the lines of discussion and setting the interpretations that arise in such discussion. Their self-interests may dictate the kind of position they wish the dominant racial group to enjoy. It may be a position which enables them to retain certain advantages, or even more to gain still greater advantages. Hence, they may be vigorous in seeking to manufacture events to attract public attention and to set lines of issue in such a way as to predetermine interpretations favorable to interests. (1958a, p. 6)

The sense of group position does not inhere in a given set of categories and material circumstances. It is created, negotiated, and constantly defined in what social psychologist Herbert Kelman (1974) once called "the sphere of action." Interests and interest groups play a large part in mobilizing people and in promoting various understandings of social conditions.

These layers of concern with protest behavior and the perceived importance of the treaty rights dispute come together in consequential ways. As we will show, the anti–treaty rights protesters were at best only partially successful in convincing the public they were motivated by legitimate grievances. Our data show that although many accepted the claims of concern about damage to the natural resources or the unfairness of "special" rights and privileges, many others took the view that anti-treaty protesters were motivated to a troubling degree by prejudice, racism, and publicity-seeking. As a consequence, individuals who might have been more concerned about and more fully won over to the treaty opponents' cause were instead put off. Treaty protesters were even less successful in convincing others that the issue was one of high importance. One direct sign of this is that only a small fraction of the population came to regard the treaty dispute as an acutely central and important matter. To be sure, those with a self-interested stake in the treaty dispute were more likely to rate the matter as one of high importance. Yet even among those with a stake in the issue, the fraction who said the issue was of the very highest importance remained low.

A protest movement that faces a deeply mixed view of its legitimacy, a populace that is not moved to rate the issue as intensely important, and a judicial system that has authoritatively ruled against its objectives runs the risk of failing to achieve its core objectives. To the extent that groups such as Protect America's Rights and Resources, Equal Rights for Everyone, and Stop Treaty Abuse had elimination of the treaty rights as their goal, they did indeed fail. But to the extent that they sought to influence the climate of opinion and, as part of that, to affect crucial legal rulings and administrative actions, they were arguably at least modestly successful.[1]

Despite the era of litigation and the social protest over the treaty rights, the phase of intense controversy did eventually pass. The protests waned greatly after 1991, and the once-prominent movement groups disappeared by the mid-1990s. Treaty rights eventually came to be taken for granted. Many of the seeds of that social acceptance were sewn during the period under investigation in our research. We believe the data in this chapter do much to identify why the controversy did not last or escalate into an even more acute, sustained, and destructive social division. Two factors seem critical: first, even among those opposed to the treaty rights, the issue ranked as a matter of the highest personal importance for only a comparatively small fraction of the population; second, the legitimacy of the courts and features of the court rulings themselves severely undercut the rhetoric of the most vociferous treaty opponents and thereby created the basis for popular acceptance of legally affirmed but also delimited off-reservation treaty rights for the Chippewa Indians.

WHY DO THE PROTESTS OCCUR?

The survey included a series of questions aimed at identifying what people understood the motivations of the protesters to be. Social protest has many purposes, and among them is influencing a potentially important third party in any major political dispute: namely, public opinion. The survey posed four questions about protesters' motivations that asked, respectively, whether anti-treaty protesters were motivated by prejudice against Indians, by the belief that spearfishing damaged the supply of fish, by the belief that it was unfair for some to enjoy rights that others did not have, and, finally, by the media, which were blowing things out of proportion. Two of these accounts of the protest should, if endorsed, work against the legitimacy of the protesters: attributing the protest to racial prejudice and attributing it

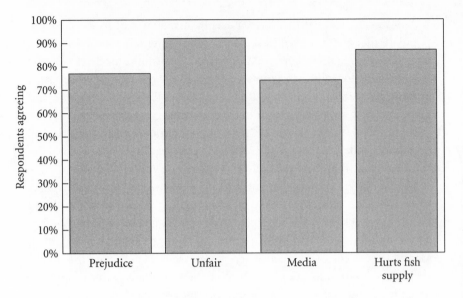

FIGURE 5.2 Perception of what motivates protesters.
Source: Chippewa Indian Treaty Rights Survey, 1990.

to media distortion or sensationalism. And of course the other two attributions embrace the explicit claims offered by many treaty opponents
themselves. Results for these questions are shown in Figure 5.2.

It should be noted that on several grounds the anti-treaty protesters
faced a lower threshold for winning over the public than do many other
protest groups in the domain of U.S. racial politics. Anti-treaty protesters
were members of the more privileged and dominant racial group. The activist groups were not seeking to impose costs on or limit the privileges of
the dominant group and its members. Instead, they pressed the case for returning to a state of affairs in which treatment of the majority and minority groups was equivalent. They accused the courts and agents of the state
of having erred in a way that hurt the majority and its interests. They were
not seeking sweeping or fundamental social reform or resource redistribu-
tion in order to improve the circumstances of a historically disadvantaged
minority.

Nonetheless, our results suggest that the public developed a decidedly mixed assessment of the reasons behind the protests. On the one
hand, the two most frequently endorsed attributions for the protests affirm
key claims of the treaty protesters. Fully 92 percent of the sample accepted

the claim that protesters objected to some people having rights that others did not enjoy. Almost as many, 87 percent, also endorsed the idea that protesters perceived spearfishing as damaging the supply of fish. These patterns are consistent with our earlier findings about acceptance of aspects of the "injustice frame" perspective on the treaty rights. For many respondents, anti-treaty protesters succeeded in communicating that message.

On the other hand, a very high number in the sample, 77 percent, attributed protest involvement to prejudice against Indians. And a nearly equivalent 74 percent attributed protest involvement to media sensationalism. Thus protests at the boat landings in the North Woods not only helped spread the core claims of treaty opponents but also contributed to a view of the conflict as rooted in prejudice and as a reaction to media attention.[2]

If the logic of the self-interest hypothesis is correct, there are good reasons to expect those with a stake in the treaty dispute to adopt more favorable views of the anti-treaty protesters. The results reported in Table 5.1 show some partial support for this logic, but they also identify important complexities. Respondents living in the treaty counties were substantially less likely to believe that protesters were motivated by racial prejudice, and they were significantly more likely than their counterparts throughout the remainder of the state to believe that protesters were motivated by a grievance over unequal rights and damage to the supply of fish. But those in treaty counties were no more or less likely to view media coverage as the reason for the protests than those residing in other parts of the state. Results were much weaker for those involved in fishing and hunting. In this case, those who did not fish and hunt were more likely than those who did to attribute protest participation to racial prejudice.

We also asked our respondents to provide a general summary evaluation of the anti-treaty protesters: did they have "strongly positive feelings," "somewhat positive feelings," "no feeling in either direction," "somewhat negative feelings," or "strongly negative feelings" about the protesters? Combining the "somewhat" and "strongly positive" responses, we found that only 25 percent of the sample expressed a positive view of the protesters. A full 21 percent expressed a "strongly negative" view, and another 37 percent a "somewhat negative" view. Given the results discussed in Chapter 3, that about two-thirds of the population expressed opposition to the treaty rights, it is surprising just how critical many respondents were of the anti-treaty activists.

TABLE 5.1 Why are there protests against the practice of spearfishing?

	Protesters prejudiced against Indians	Protesters believe unfair for some to have rights	Media blows problem out of proportion	Protesters believe spearfishing damages fish supply
Total percentage agreeing	77%	92%	74%	87%
County				
Nontreaty county	80	91	75	86
Treaty county	65	97	71	94
Goes hunting/fishing				
No	88	93	77	86
Yes	72	92	73	88
Opposition to treaty rights				
Low	93	90	71	75
Medium	78	91	83	91
High	61	95	67	96

Source: Chippewa Indian Treaty Rights Survey, 1990.

The reasons for the negative evaluations seem to be largely rooted in the perception of the anti-treaty activists as motivated by prejudice and publicity. Table 5.2 reports the results of an ordinary-least-squares regression model designed to predict scores measuring affect toward anti-treaty protesters (scored from 0 to 1, with 1 indicating strongly negative evaluations). The perceptions that the activists were motivated by prejudice and by media attention both significantly enhanced negative evaluations of the protesters. Those who believed that protesters thought the rights were unfair, however, were less likely to rate the protesters negatively. Since such a high fraction of the sample believed that the protesters were at least in part motivated by a concern over damage to the fish supply, this variable did not contribute to the overall evaluation. Two other patterns are worthy of note and underscore the extent to which the anti-treaty protesters were tarnished as bigoted publicity seekers. There was no impact of political ideology on evaluations of the protesters, and the highly educated respon-

TABLE 5.2 OLS regression predicting negative affect toward protesters

	Model 1	Model 2
Constant	.32***	.26**
	(.08)	(.09)
Age	.002**	.003**
	(.001)	(.001)
No H.S. diploma	−.01	.04
	(.05)	(.05)
Some college	.08**	.05
	(.03)	(.03)
BA degree or more	.11***	.09**
	(.04)	(.03)
Female	.09***	.08***
	(.03)	(.02)
Income	−.01	−.01
	(.01)	(.01)
Treaty county	−.07**	−.05
	(.03)	(.03)
Goes fishing/hunting	−.03	−.001
	(.03)	(.03)
Conservative	.11	.08
	(.07)	(.06)
Protest: Prejudice		.15***
		(.03)
Protest: Rights unfair		−.12**
		(.05)
Protest: Media		.13***
		(.03)
Protest: Damage fish supply		−.03
		(.04)
Adjusted *R*-squared	.07	.17
N	526	526

*p < .05   **p < .01   ***p < .001
Source: Chippewa Indian Treaty Rights Survey, 1990.

dents were substantially more likely to adopt negative views of the protesters than the less well educated. Under other circumstances, one might expect liberals and the better educated to take a more generous view of involvement in protest. Since in this case the movement activists had a conservative bent, we do not find such support forthcoming.

We also examined how interpretations of the protests related to attitudes on the treaty rights (Table 5.1). Strong treaty-rights opponents were less likely to view the protests as rooted in prejudice or as driven by media sensationalism, as compared with treaty-rights supporters. Treaty opponents were more likely to believe that protesters were motivated by a concern with damage to the fish supply than were treaty supporters.

But if we view the anti-treaty protesters as seeking to sway the public in favor of their tactics and larger cause, the results of the protest-motivation questions in relation to the self-interest measures and to attitude on the treaty rights are less than sanguine. For example, nearly two-thirds of treaty-county residents attributed protest participation to prejudice against Indians, as did a similar fraction of strong treaty-rights opponents and an even higher fraction of fishermen and hunters. Moreover, even among those most strongly opposed to the treaty rights, almost half (42 percent) gave the anti-treaty protesters somewhat or strongly negative evaluations. Although much of the public opposed the treaty rights and accepted aspects of the case made by the anti-treaty activists, the activists simply did not enjoy unalloyed approval and legitimacy, even among those who might arguably have been their core constituents.

JUST HOW IMPORTANT IS THE ISSUE?

Even if the protesters were viewed in mixed terms, the open challenge to the use of the treaty rights might well have convinced much of the public that this was a highly important issue requiring involvement and intervention. In Chapter 3 we reviewed in detail the broad public salience of the treaty rights dispute, and concluded that the issue had risen to a fairly high level of general public awareness. That the public was aware of the dispute and had formed some basic opinions on the matter does not mean, however, that the issue was of high or even equal importance to all those aware of it.

We assessed the importance of the treaty rights issue with two questions. In the first one we asked: "Compared with how you feel on other public is-

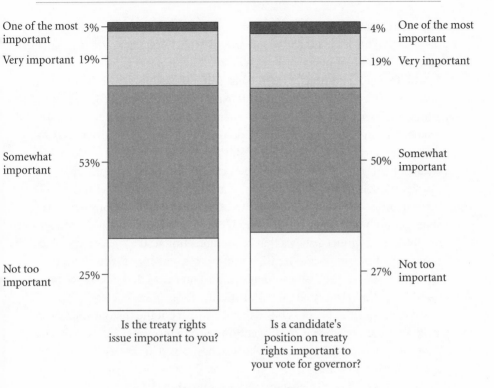

One of the most important 3%

Very important 19%

Somewhat important 53%

Not too important 25%

Is the treaty rights issue important to you?

4% One of the most important

19% Very important

50% Somewhat important

27% Not too important

Is a candidate's position on treaty rights important to your vote for governor?

FIGURE 5.3 Issue centrality.
Source: Chippewa Indian Treaty Rights Survey, 1990.

sues, would you say that Indian treaty rights is one of the *most* important issues to you, a very important issue, a somewhat important issue, or not too important?" The second question focused on the electoral relevance of the treaty rights issue: "How important is a candidate's position on Indian treaty rights when you decide how to vote in the election for governor—is it one of the most important issues you would consider, a very important issue, somewhat important, or not too important?" The basic distribution of responses to each question is shown in Figure 5.3.

Only about one in five respondents said the treaty rights issue was either "very important" or "one of the most important" issues to them, whether asked in reference to other political issues or in terms of gubernatorial voting. Indeed, only a quite small fraction of respondents, fewer than 5 percent for each question, gave the issue the highest possible importance or "centrality" rating. Thus, notwithstanding the general salience of the treaty dispute (Chapter 3), for the great majority of white Wisconsin residents the treaty rights issue ranked as a matter that was only "somewhat important" or "not too important."

Still, two key questions remain concerning the extent to which the dispute was perceived as a highly central issue: does self-interest contribute to attitude importance, and does self-interest enhance the impact on issue importance of a respondent's attitude on the treaty rights? Responses to the two importance questions are highly correlated ($r = .63, p < .001$). We created a simple additive scale of the items and estimated ordinary-least-squares models of the determinants of attitude importance, with the self-interest measures and the issue attitude on treaty rights as our key variables (a number of other control variables were also included in the model; see Table 5.3). Model 4 shows that both opposition to the treaty rights and involvement in fishing and hunting significantly enhance the likelihood of rating the treaty rights issue as highly important (indeed, these are the only variables in the model that exert statistically discernible effects).

We next consider the possibility that the impact of the treaty-rights issue attitude on importance is contingent on self-interest. In effect, we wish to know whether treaty opponents who also have a vested interest in the issue are more likely to translate their attitude on the treaty into a judgment that the issue is of greater importance. The results shown in Model 5 of Table 5.3 strongly suggest that they do. That is, among people who fish or hunt, opposition to the treaty rights is more likely to be translated into a judgment of high issue importance than it is among those not involved in fishing and hunting. Similarly, treaty opponents living in the treaty counties are more likely to translate their attitude into a judgment that the issue is important than are those who do not live in the treaty counties. In short, it is the combination of issue attitude and self-interest that determines an overall judgment about the importance of the issue. People who oppose the treaty and who also have stake in the issue are the most likely to rate it as a highly central problem.

This is a very important set of results. Most of the research on self-interest effects in political psychology suggests that self-interest matters little for public opinion (Citrin and Green 1990; Sears and Funk 1990). The great bulk of these studies, however, have examined only issue attitudes. It is more likely that self-interest becomes a consequential factor in terms of other types of outcomes, like judgments of issue importance or centrality and, of course, actual behavioral involvement in an issue. As was suggested

TABLE 5.3 OLS regression predicting importance of the treaty rights issue

	Model 1	Model 2	Model 3	Model 4	Model 5
Constant	.484***	.452***	.274***	.205***	−.389***
	(.050)	(.053)	(.064)	(.063)	(.079)
Age	−.001	−.001	−.002*	−.001	−.001
	(.001)	(.001)	(.001)	(.001)	(.001)
No H.S. diploma	−.010	−.001	.014	−.011	−.018
	(.038)	(.038)	(.038)	(.037)	(.036)
Some college	.002	.002	.010	.014	.013
	(.025)	(.025)	(.025)	(.024)	(.024)
BA degree or more	−.068*	−.064*	−.041	−.021	−.018
	(.027)	(.028)	(.028)	(.027)	(.027)
Female	−.033	−.031	−.017	−.018	−.019
	(.020)	(.020)	(.020)	(.019)	(.019)
Income	−.001	−.002	−.000	−.002	−.004
	(.006)	(.006)	(.006)	(.006)	(.006)
Interest in politics		.067	.078*	.060	.060
		(.041)	(.040)	(.039)	(.038)
Opposition to treaty rights			.210***	.136**	−.171
			(.043)	(.044)	(.094)
Goes hunting/fishing				.119***	−.039
				(.023)	(.069)
Treaty county				.034	−.148*
				(.021)	(.065)
Hunt/fish*treaty rights					.253**
					(.101)
Treaty county*treaty rights					.252**
					(.087)
Adjusted R-squared	.01	.01	.05***	.11***	.13***
N	539	539	539	539	539

*$p < .05$ **$p < .01$ ***$p < .001$

Source: Chippewa Indian Treaty Rights Survey, 1990.

by Bobo (1983), concerning weak self-interest effects on whites' opposition to school busing: "Objective individual vulnerability should have more to do with behavior than with attitude formation when dealing with a highly salient social issue like busing. People can form an opinion about an ongoing and controversial issue like busing simply by thinking in terms of the interests of 'myself and people like me.' People need not be touched by busing directly . . . it is largely those who are directly affected who become politically active" (Bobo 1983, p. 1208). This logic was later borne out in the work of Taylor (1986), to some degree, and even more convincingly in Green and Cowden (1992).

These results have both substantive import, in terms of how the politics of the treaty rights dispute played out, and theoretical import, for our understanding of how prejudice and group conflict figure into everyday life and politics. Even though the treaty dispute involved a salient ethno-racial divide, even though members of the dominant ethno-racial group lost ground relative to the minority group, and even though anti-treaty activists mobilized, dramatized their grievances, and garnered significant media and public attention, most white Wisconsin residents did not feel an intense personal engagement with the issue. As a result, even though most whites opposed the treaty rights and accepted key claims made by treaty opponents, the issue was not central to a large enough fraction of the population to seriously threaten the legitimacy of the court rulings or, ultimately, to undermine the Chippewa's actual exercising of their court-affirmed rights.

Theoretically, then, one can speak of prejudice and group conflict without the assumption of fundamental and diametrically opposed interests between groups or intensive, across-the-board antagonism. Not every aspect of an ethno-racial divide or every inch of the fabric of social life is touched by a particular issue or source of conflict. Individuals within an ethno-racial category are not equally touched or equally moved by an issue. The configurations of interest clearly matter, as our analyses have shown time and again. But a plain clash of interests and overt group tension and conflict by no means ordain implacable and broad-spectrum group antagonism. Variations in the level or degree of personal stake in a matter and in the level of issue importance are among the complexities that lie between ethno-racial group membership and significant mobilization and contentiousness.

WHO GETS INVOLVED, AND WHY?

We are concerned not only with how actual protesters were perceived or how a representative sample of white Wisconsin residents rated the importance of the treaty dispute; also critical to us is whether individuals ever became directly active with respect to treaty rights. Our survey posed a series of four behavioral-report questions. We asked whether respondents had signed a petition, written a letter to a public official, given money to an organization, or attended a rally concerned with the treaty rights issue. The basic distribution of responses is shown in Figure 5.4.

Levels of involvement, on the whole, were low. Perhaps the single easiest task, signing a petition—usually meaning that respondents were approached by an activist on the issue and did not initiate involvement themselves—was the most common form of reported involvement in the treaty dispute, at about 12 percent statewide. Behaviors requiring greater personal initiative or cost, such as writing a letter to a public official, giving money, or actually attending a rally, were a good deal less common. In all, fewer than

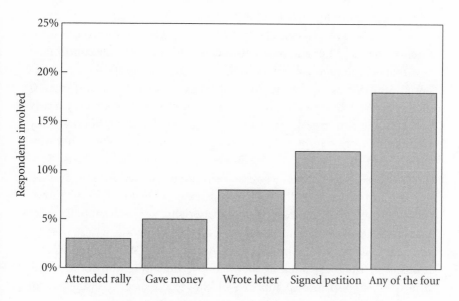

FIGURE 5.4 Involvement in the treaty rights dispute.
Source: Chippewa Indian Treaty Rights Survey, 1990.

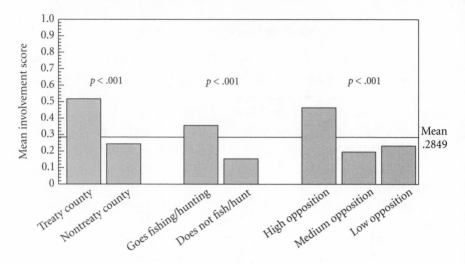

FIGURE 5.5 Cumulative involvement index by self-interest and
opposition to treaty rights.
Source: Chippewa Indian Treaty Rights Survey, 1990.

one in five of our respondents reported involvement in at least one of the
four types of dispute-related behaviors.

We created an overall cumulative involvement index and used this measure to assess whether and how self-interest and issue attitude contributed
to actual behavioral involvement in the treaty rights dispute. Figure 5.5 reports mean scores on the involvement index for each of the self-interest
measures. We found significantly higher rates of involvement, very nearly
by a factor of two in each case, among those who either lived in the treaty
counties or who were involved in fishing and hunting, as compared with
their nontreaty-county or nonfisherman/nonhunter counterparts. Self-
interest clearly prefigured the level of behavioral involvement in the issue.

Issue attitude mattered as well in this case. As Figure 5.5 also shows,
those most intensely opposed to the treaty rights were substantially more
likely to be involved than were others. The treaty controversy was not sym-
metrical in its behavioral implications. Among white Wisconsin residents,
it was primarily those thinking they had lost something who got involved;
principled support of the Chippewa did not lead to action on the part of
those in favor of the treaty rights.

There is good reason to expect issue importance to play a major role
in predicting actual involvement. Furthermore, it may be the case that self-

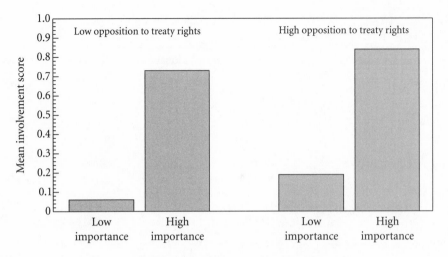

FIGURE 5.6 Mean score on the cumulative involvement index by
centrality and opposition to treaty rights.
Source: Chippewa Indian Treaty Rights Survey, 1990.

interest, issue attitude, and importance combine to tell a fuller story about
both who gets actively involved and why. As a first effort at gaining some
leverage in understanding these interconnections, Figure 5.6 shows cumulative involvement-index scores by attitude importance for those strongly
opposed to the treaty rights and those whose opposition was low. The
results suggest a key interaction. High-importance respondents were far
more likely to be actively involved, almost irrespective of issue attitude. Indeed, the high-importance respondents were very active, reaching mean
involvement-index scores that point to taking part in at least three of
the four possible behaviors. But there is also some trend in the direction
of strong treaty opponents being more active, above and beyond what
one would expect given knowledge of the importance of the treaty rights
dispute.

We tried to reach a more definitive assessment of the sources of behavioral involvement by estimating an OLS regression model of the determinants of the cumulative involvement index. For this purpose, we included
the respondents' level of interest in politics as an additional control variable. As Model 2 in Table 5.4 shows, interest in politics, opposition to
treaty rights, involvement in fishing and hunting, and residence in the
treaty counties all enhanced the overall level of involvement in the treaty

TABLE 5.4 OLS regression predicting involvement in the treaty rights dispute (cumulative behaviors index)

	Model 1	Model 2	Model 3	Model 4
Constant	.618**	−.126	−.176	−.142
	(.196)	(.237)	(.222)	(.235)
Age	−.001	−.001	−.001	−.001
	(.003)	(.003)	(.002)	(.002)
No H.S. diploma	.056	.108	.109	.110
	(.140)	(.136)	(.127)	(.128)
Some college	.171	.208*	.198*	.200*
	(.092)	(.089)	(.084)	(.084)
BA degree or more	.001	.123	.167	.170
	(.101)	(.100)	(.094)	(.094)
Female	−.279***	−.238***	−.211**	−.210**
	(.074)	(.073)	(.068)	(.068)
Income	−.018	−.011	−.011	−.012
	(.022)	(.022)	(.020)	(.020)
Interest in politics	.443**	.442**	.365**	.364**
	(.149)	(.146)	(.137)	(.137)
Opposition to treaty rights		.581***	.468**	.414*
		(.166)	(.156)	(.198)
Goes hunting/fishing		.169*	.045	.047
		(.086)	(.082)	(.082)
Treaty county		.187*	.147*	.146*
		(.077)	(.072)	(.072)
High importance			.636***	.543*
			(.074)	(.225)
High importance*treaty rights				.129
				(.295)
Adjusted R-squared	.040	.097	.208	.206
N	530	530	530	530

*p < .05   **p < .01   ***p < .001

Source: Chippewa Indian Treaty Rights Survey, 1990.

rights dispute. In addition, men were clearly more active than women. About half of the roughly 10 percent of the variance explained in behavioral involvement is attributable to the combination of issue attitude and self-interest measures.

Model 3 shows the results after adding the issue importance measure. Including importance more than doubles the amount of variance explained, to just over 20 percent. Doing so also reduces the magnitude of the self-interest measures, indicating that part of the impact of self-interest on involvement is indirect via its impact on issue importance (particularly so for involvement in fishing and hunting). We also tested for the possibility of an interaction between high importance and treaty rights attitude, but this coefficient did not reach statistical significance ($b = .129$, $se = .295$). The single strongest determinant of actual behavioral involvement was issue importance.

We also sought to examine how importance affected other political judgments. In particular, did individuals who saw the treaty rights issue as highly important translate this view into other judgments about prominent political actors? Did importance, in short, condition the translation of issue attitudes into other political perceptions and evaluations? To address this possibility we examined how our respondents evaluated four key political figures in Wisconsin during the treaty rights dispute: Governor Tommy Thompson, a Republican; Tom Loftus, speaker of the state assembly and the most prominent Democrat in Wisconsin at the time; Attorney General Donald Hanaway; and Judge Barbara Crabb, the Federal District Court judge who handled the treaty-related litigation.

Governor Thompson had been a critic of the treaty rights. He pushed for a "buy-out" of the rights at one point, and tried to convene the state's congressional delegation to pressure the U.S. Senate to invalidate the treaties. But he had no direct authority over the federal treaties, and furthermore he had the obligation to preserve order and ensure compliance with the law. Speaker Loftus had at one point attempted to criticize Thompson's handling of the treaty dispute, as part of his own bid to run for governor, but he had quickly backed away from the challenge. Attorney General Hanaway's office represented the state in the litigation with the Chippewa, and of course Judge Crabb was regularly issuing rulings on the scope and limits of the treaty rights. Thompson was easily the most well known of the group and Hanaway and Crabb the least.

Our results show only a weak correlation between evaluations of

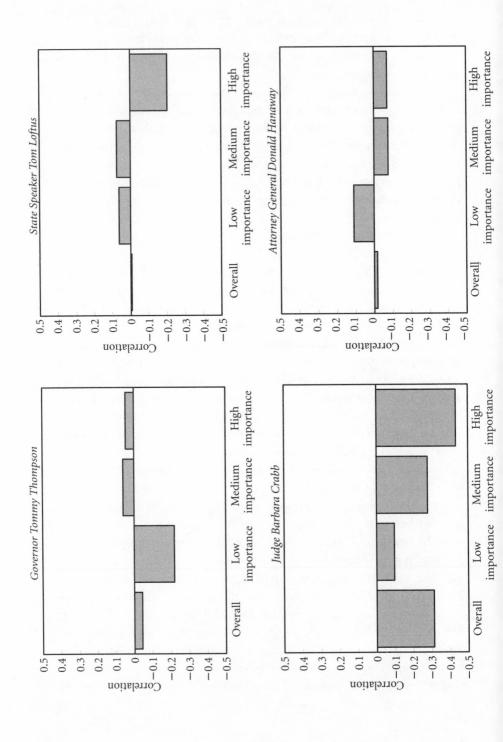

Thompson and attitudes on the treaty rights ($r = -.045$, not significant). See Figure 5.7. The correlation is larger and negative in direction among those with low issue importance. There is a slight tendency for the correlations to run in the opposite direction among those with medium and high issue importance. This mixed set of results makes sense in light of the fundamentally ambivalent role that Thompson played: treaty critic but enforcer of the law. A mixed picture also emerges for Hanaway. On the one hand, he could be viewed as carrying the state's legal struggle against the Chippewa as they pressed for affirmation of the treaty rights. On the other hand, he too is obliged to maintain law and order and to see to it that the court rulings are obeyed. This ambivalent role—on some level a legal antagonist to the Chippewa but also an upholder of their right to spearfish—resulted in a very muted overall correlation between his ratings and attitudes on the treaty rights. But among those with low issue importance, as evaluations of Hanaway became more positive, opposition to the treaty rights declined. Among those with medium to high issue importance, the correlations moved in the opposite direction, indicating that as opposition to the treaty rights increased ratings of Hanaway declined.

The results are somewhat clearer for Loftus and especially for Judge Crabb, particularly among high-issue-importance respondents. For Loftus, among those rating the treaty rights as highly important, as treaty opposition increased, his ratings declined ($r = -.205$, $p < .01$). The pattern for Crabb is clearer still. Among those rating the issue as high in importance, evaluations of Judge Crabb became much more negative as opposition to the treaty rights rose.[3]

On the whole, the results tend to support the idea that issue importance enhances the translation of attitudes into judgments about related political actors and issues. The main ambiguities in the results correspond well to the ambivalent roles that some of the political actors had to play and to the larger nature and context of the dispute. On the latter, the institutional locus of responsibility for the issue was the federal courts. State and local elected officials, especially given the complete unwillingness of the U.S.

FIGURE 5.7 Correlation of evaluations of political figures with opposition to treaty rights, by issue importance.
Source: Chippewa Indian Treaty Rights Survey, 1990.

Senate to open serious debate on the standing of the treaties, had a very constrained set of options: namely, they were to uphold the law.

WHAT SHOULD THE STATE DO?

It is said that politics is the art of compromise. In the treaty rights dispute, the federal courts had ruled; the U.S. Senate had no intention of revisiting the treaty issue in Wisconsin, or in any other state or dispute, for that matter. The legal resolution of the matter would most likely take the form of some degree of co-management of the natural resources by the Chippewa and agencies of the state government. We asked our respondents whether, as a way for the state to resolve the dispute, they would favor or oppose "protection of the treaty rights but co-management of fish and other resources in the off-reservation areas by the Chippewa bands and the state?" A full 73 percent of the sample replied that they would favor co-management of the resources. This includes 56 percent of those who lived in the treaty counties (versus 75 percent of those in the remainder of the state) and 69 percent of those involved in fishing and hunting activities (versus 79 percent of those not involved in such pursuits).

There is a clear relationship between support for resource co-management and attitude on the treaty rights. But we should stress that even a majority of strong treaty-rights opponents (52 percent) favored co-management, as compared with 75 percent of moderate opponents and a solid 90 percent of those who rated their opposition as low. These results strongly imply an important measure of tolerance and respect for the law. That is, many people were willing to see a resolution of the issue that ran counter to their own underlying attitude and preferred outcome.

We are able to bring some direct evidence to bear on this issue of respect for the law. Our survey included two statements dealing with respect for the law that read as follows:

Individuals should obey court orders even if they feel the court ruling treats them unfairly.

If two individuals or organizations sign a legal contract, that contract should be binding on both parties even if one party decides they would like to change the contract.

Responses to both statements ranged from agree strongly to disagree strongly. These questions were asked early in the survey interview, prior to any specific questions on the treaty rights dispute. As might be expected, only a small fraction of respondents disagreed with the view that individuals should obey court orders (18 percent, combining "strongly disagree" and "somewhat disagree"), and an even smaller fraction (14 percent) disagreed with the idea that contracts should be legally binding on both parties, even if one side becomes discontented.

Agreement with very general statements of this kind, however, may have a platitudinous quality for many respondents. Since these items did come early in the questionnaire and thus were essentially "context free," it was relatively easy for respondents to endorse "the rule of law," having not yet been asked about a case in which their own preferences might diverge from prevailing legal rulings and circumstances. The key question then becomes, does adherence to these sorts of opinions have consequences for opinions on the treaty rights and, especially, the issue of state co-management of resources with the Chippewa?

Based on a combination of these two items, we created a simple index of respect for the rule of law, with scores ranging from a low of 0 to a high of 1. As might be expected given the generality of the questions, the rule-of-law index was not significantly related to either self-interest measure.[4] More tellingly, it was also unrelated to opposition to the treaty rights. Treaty-county residents, those involved in fishing and hunting, and even those openly opposed to the treaty rights were just as likely to support the rule of law as were those living in nontreaty counties, not taking part in fishing and hunting, and expressing support for the treaty rights. Neither self-interest in the treaty rights dispute nor opinion on the core dispute itself had in any measure undermined a basic general commitment to principles of obeying the courts and living up to contractual obligations. Thus responses to these questions appear to reveal an important normative position concerning the rule of law (Tyler 1990a,b).

This set of results bespeaks a dilemma for many treaty rights opponents: they opposed the Chippewa's exercising of their treaty rights but at the same time espoused commitment to the rule of law. If these views constitute more than mere platitudes, then even many treaty rights opponents should have been open to a political resolution of the matter in which the state and the Chippewa would manage the resources together, and indeed this was the case. Even when we restrict our attention to those who expressed high opposition to the treaty rights, we find that a solid majority of those expressing moderate support for the rule of law (57 percent) or high

TABLE 5.5 Logistic regression predicting support for co-management

	Model 1	Model 2	Model 3	Model 4	Model 5
Constant	1.98**	4.54***	4.42***	3.23***	.84
	(.66)	(.85)	(.87)	(1.02)	(2.09)
Age	−.02*	−.01	−.01	−.01	−.01
	(.01)	(.01)	(.01)	(.01)	(.01)
No H.S. diploma	−.12	−.31	−.44	−.46	−.47
	(.41)	(.44)	(.45)	(.45)	(.45)
Some college	.06	.17	.12	.10	.10
	(.25)	(.28)	(.29)	(.29)	(.29)
BA degree or more	.62*	.40	.35	.28	.31
	(.31)	(.34)	(.35)	(.35)	(.36)
Female	.62**	.66**	.56*	.62**	.61**
	(.21)	(.23)	(.24)	(.24)	(.24)
Income	−.12	−.12	−.14	−.14	−.15*
	(.06)	(.07)	(.07)	(.07)	(.07)
Treaty county	−.69**	−.06	.02	.01	−.02
	(.22)	(.25)	(.26)	(.26)	(.26)
Goes fishing/hunting	−.59*	−.29	−.22	−.14	−.11
	(.27)	(.29)	(.29)	(.30)	(.30)
Conservative	−.84	−.48	−.35	−.44	−.43
	(.54)	(.60)	(.61)	(.62)	(.62)
Negative affect toward Indians		.19	.24	.20	.23
		(.54)	(.55)	(.55)	(.55)
New Indian-stereotype scale		−1.43	−1.09	−1.01	−.86
		(.77)	(.78)	(.79)	(.79)
New group competition scale		−.37	−.04	.02	.12
		(.71)	(.75)	(.76)	(.76)
New political-threat scale		−4.47***	−3.54***	−3.57***	−3.69***
		(.84)	(.88)	(.89)	(.90)
Medium opposition to treaty rights			−.50	−.49	3.45
			(.45)	(.45)	(2.19)
High opposition to treaty rights			−1.19**	−1.22**	.91
			(.46)	(.46)	(2.01)

TABLE 5.5   (continued)

	Model 1	Model 2	Model 3	Model 4	Model 5
Rule-of-law scale				1.52*	5.32
				(.73)	(3.09)
Rule of law*medium opposition					−6.16
					(3.44)
Rule of law*high opposition					−3.41
					(3.20)
Pseudo *R*-squared	.09	.21	.23	.23	.24
N	447	447	447	447	447

*$p < .05$ **$p < .01$ ***$p < .001$

Source: Chippewa Indian Treaty Rights Survey, 1990.

support (64 percent)—the great bulk of all of our respondents—actually favored co-management.

In a further effort to assess the importance of respect for the rule of law in public reactions to the treaty rights dispute, we estimated a logistic regression model predicting support for co-management of the resources. The results are shown in Table 5.5. Model 1 shows that the self-interest measures are negatively related to support for co-management. When we then add the key racial attitude measures from Chapter 4—affect toward Indians, stereotypes, group competition, and political threat (the reformulated measures)—the amount of variance explained rises substantially. However, most of this is due to the impact of perceived political threat: the greater the sense of threat, the lower the level of support for co-management (which is consistent with group position theory). None of the other racial attitude measures has a significant direct effect in the context of the other variables in the model. Including these racial attitude measures accounts for the entirety of the self-interest effects, indicating that these racial attitudes completely mediate the effects of the self-interest measures on support for co-management.

Next we added the treaty-rights opposition measure (Model 3). This variable also has a strong negative effect on support for co-management. The greater the opposition to the treaty rights, the less the support for co-management. Important, however, as Model 4 shows, even when we add the rule-of-law index at the very last stage, it still has a clear positive impact on support for co-management. Even taking into account self-interest, the full battery of racial attitude measures, including political threat, and opposition to the treaty rights themselves, the rule-of-law measure is still a potent predictor of how people wanted to see the state government respond to the treaty rights dispute.

CONCLUSIONS

Many voices clamored to be heard on the treaty rights dispute. If the courtrooms provided one forum and attorneys one set of antagonists in the treaty dispute, at least as important was the forum of the boat landings in the North Woods of Wisconsin, where white outdoorsmen and Chippewa spearfishers and their sympathizers clashed over competing claims on the area's natural resources. Group conflict is not merely a matter of diverging viewpoints between members of different ethno-racial communities. At some point, and perhaps at the point that matters most, politics and group conflict enter the sphere of action (Hochschild 2000).

A full account of the treaty rights dispute cannot be based on the distribution of opinion on the treaty rights themselves. Organic to the emergence of the treaty dispute as a matter of significant and broad concern were the efforts at mobilization and protest, largely by opponents of spearfishing and the Chippewa's treaty rights but also by supporters of the Chippewa. These actions commanded much local and statewide attention—and on occasion even national media recognition. As a result of the scale of the protests, their recurrence, and the risk of violence involved, local, state, and even federal officials had to get involved in policing the boat landings. The deeds of activists were, in short, the locus of the conflict itself.

Protest is without a doubt both a pressure tactic and a communicative act. As to the latter, we know that many different views of the protests and protesters were in circulation. And powerful passions were indeed aroused on both sides during the conflict. A regular column titled the "Capitol Eye" in *Isthmus,* a liberal, Madison-based paper, ran an essay with the headline "Still Racists at Heart: The PR Efforts of Treaty Foes Can't Hide Their Intolerance" (April 27, 1990, p. 10). This view was very much shared by a reporter for the *Capital Times* who had covered the protests at the boat landings. Barbara Mulhern's column of May 3, 1990, opened with a description of the humble wooden boat of two Chippewa men who were heading out to go spearfishing and how modest their equipment seemed relative to that of the Department of Natural Resources officials who watched them closely. She wrote:

> Yet these men and their tribal brothers and sisters are the subject of three weeks of annual brouhaha by anti-Indian protesters who claim their overriding interest is to protect the white man's so-called fishing "rights."
>
> Yes, I call them anti-Indian protesters and not anti-treaty protesters because racism—not 19th century treaties—is what this conflict is all about. There's no doubt in my mind the supporters of such groups as Stop Treaty Abuse could easily find some other reason to hurl racist slurs at Wisconsin's Indians if they didn't have spearfishing to use as an excuse. ("Media Fan Spearfishing Fire," *Capital Times,* May 3, 1990)

A strongly contrary view was articulated in a letter written to the *Capital Times* earlier that same season. The writer said:

> I'm not going to protest at the boat landings this year. Not because I don't care about the injustice and hypocrisy of the treaty rights laws but because my presence at the landings will be counterproductive to solving the treaty rights problem. Besides, if I'm at the landings, I'll be called a red-neck racist by the downstate media, ACLU and Treaty Rights Advocates. . . . I will protest in respectful silence, on the lawn at the Oneida County Courthouse. I might even hold a lighted candle as a symbol of peace in honor of my Native American brothers and sisters whose ancestors years ago were so inhumanely treated. I might even carry a sign saying "I am not a racist, I just want equality." I might even be joined by a few hundred of my neighbors. (Letter to the editor, *Capital Times,* March 7, 1990)

And even more extreme views, one overtly antagonistic and another embracing exaggerated claims about damage to the natural resources, were voiced in the *Vilas County News-Review:*

> Were it not for [the Indian's] great "White Father," he would not be enjoying his "treaty rights," and the millions of dollars of NON TREATY benefits he has received over the last 150 years and is still receiving! It was the Indian who wanted to stay in this state, not cross the Mississippi, and it was the Indian who wanted the reservations. So why should the American government keep paying so they can stay there?

He might also remind himself that if it were not for the white man's money, his great sovereign nation of the Chippewa would slide right down the tubes. He needs the great "White Father's" gravy trains to survive; history has proven that he can't do it on his own. And "treaty rights" is nothing but another gravy train. (Letter to the editor, *Vilas County News-Review*, April 19, 1989)

The second item went on at even greater length:

As the fourth Chippewa spearfishing season brought a record high walleye harvest to add to the treaty rights controversy, it's getting to the point that "opening day" of the state fishing season is more a celebration of a season ended than a season starting.

Opening day now marks the official end of the slaughter—the date all off-reservation spearfishing by Chippewa Indians must end even if ice-out is delayed or the walleyes are still spawning. For many people, the sigh of relief that spearing is over weighs heavier on their mind than anticipation of fishing.

It wasn't always this way. Back in 1985 and 1986 when the tribes were harvesting a reasonable number of walleye for the sake of heritage or consumption, the controversy was a minor spring event prior to fishing.

But with the harvest of more than 25,000 walleye this year, the clash between cultures and controversy over resource depletion is so great that it becomes hard not to rejoice with vigor that the spearing is over for another year.

The first beer that gets tipped in celebration of this Saturday, at least for many anglers who live in northern Wisconsin, will be a toast to the return of sport fishing.

Walleyes will regain their honor as an elusive game fish, instead of a meal stuck on the spear of an Indian who has invaded their spawning grounds. Walleyes will adorn stringers and swim in live wells, but they won't be subject to death tubs where the blood and slime is so deep they could almost swim—if they had any life left in them. (Kurt Krueger, sports editorial, *Vilas County News-Review*, May 4, 1988)

These views of the protest well exemplify the extremes of opinion in the conflict.

Despite the importance of overt conflict and social protest to many issues in the domain of race and politics, much of the research in this area is vulnerable to the claim that it focuses on attitudes disconnected from the real, lived experience of most people. If it does, scholars run the risk of misunderstanding the salience, the meaning, the effects and consequences of what racial conflict there is. Precisely to avoid this trap, we decided to look far beyond issue attitudes, racial prejudice, and the routinely assessed respondent background characteristics. In Chapter 3 we paid special attention to issue salience and issue knowledge. In Chapter 4 we examined not only multiple item measures of several competing theories, but also drew on extensive open-ended responses to capture respondents' frames of reference. In this chapter we focused on what sense people made of the treaty protests, the degree to which they perceived the issue as personally important and why, the extent to which people became involved in the issue, and how they wanted to see their government officials resolve the issue. This set of concerns with political action, we believe, provides both substantial grounding for our analysis and takes this study of public opinion on the treaty dispute well beyond the ordinary boundaries of racial and political attitude studies.

The first and clearest finding from our analysis is that the anti-treaty protesters had a tarnished image. Despite claiming to be justly aggrieved— being in effect discriminated against by affirmation of the treaty rights— and engaged in a struggle to preserve natural resources, they were seen by many as driven by base motives, including racial prejudice and publicity seeking. The end result was a low level of regard throughout the state for the anti-treaty protesters, even among those who should have been their most natural constituents.

A second clear finding is that, despite all of the media attention and public salience garnered by the protests, activists were not successful in moving a large fraction of the public to regard the issue as one of intense personal importance. No more than one in four respondents rated the issue as "very important" or "one of the most important" issues to them. This was true even though large fractions of the respondents were involved in fishing and hunting activities and even though a heavy majority opposed the exercising of the treaty rights.

Third, with respect to actual behavioral involvement, we would stress that although a nontrivial number of people did become involved in the issue, the overall rate of activism was low. Fewer than one in five respondents had either signed a petition, written a letter, given money, or attended a rally concerned with the treaty dispute. Still, it says something about the general level of engagement with the issue that more than one in ten white Wisconsin residents did report at least signing a petition on the subject.

Fourth—to some degree as a result of the combination of low regard for the anti-treaty protesters, the lack of a more widespread feeling of personal importance for the issue, and limited behavioral involvement—a clear majority of white Wisconsin residents, including those opposed to the treaty rights, endorsed co-management of resources by the state and the Chippewa. This is an important result, as it suggests that even in the midst of a bitter racial conflict there may be sufficient wellsprings of commitment to the rule of law to sustain a court's defense of the rights of a racial minority group against a degree of mobilized opposition.

In this chapter concerned with political action, self-interest mattered for politics. It influenced interpretations of social protests, issue importance, actual involvement, and even how one wanted the state to resolve the matter. To be sure, self-interest was never an overarching or controlling factor in any of these outcomes, but by the same token, nor was its influence minor or irrelevant. It was always a significant factor in the mix. Sometimes the effects were quite substantial, as in the case of predicting issue importance. At other times its effects were modest and largely mediated by other attitudes and outlooks (such as support for co-management).

There is a more subtle and crucial point here. Some scholars of race politics have dismissed theoretical approaches that emphasize interests and group conflict because these are not the sole or overarching factors shaping issue attitudes (see Sniderman and Carmines 1997). Real individuals and real social conflicts are much more complex than such a standard of relevance would admit. The search for single-factor explanations—what Allport once labeled "simple and sovereign" accounts—has long been recognized as ill-fated. We do not seek one here.

There are larger lessons, still, in the patterns we have reported. It is not hard to envision alternative scenarios or outcomes in a matter where the courts have affirmed or advanced a minority-group claim seen to be at odds with majority expectations and interests. Activists *could* achieve greater public approval and esteem than the anti-treaty activists in this case received. Their claims *could* come to be judged broadly important by much of a relevant public. Many more people *could* be moved to get involved on an issue (or at least to give sympathetic support to those who are involved), including by electing protest activists to public office. And, of course, a search for policy or other practical solutions that would significantly vitiate the realization of minority-group objectives *could* prove to be more successful. In quite a profound sense, this type of scenario is what took place in the black-white conflict, at least with respect to school desegregation.

Chapter 6

RACE POLITICS AS GROUP POSITION

> The analyst of public opinion must begin, then, by recognizing the triangular relationship between the scene of action, the human picture of that scene, and the human response to that scene working itself out upon the scene of action.
>
> Walter Lippmann, *Public Opinion*, 1922

> A social problem is always a focal point for the operation of divergent and conflicting interests, intentions, and objectives. It is the interplay of these interests and objectives that constitutes the way in which a society deals with any one of its social problems.
>
> Herbert Blumer, "Social Problems as Collective Behavior," 1971

> The peaceful harvest of fish by the Chippewa is threatened by non-Indians who barrage the peaceful fishers with rocks and insults, and who use large motorboats trailing anchors to capsize the boats of the fishers. Because of this, the State of Wisconsin has pressured the Chippewa to give up their ancient rights to fish off of their reservation, and has pressed them to do so immediately. This pressure has sometimes been applied indirectly, sometimes directly, but always upon the Chippewa. And all because a small group creates disturbances in opposition to the Chippewa's federally recognized legal rights.
>
> Rennard Strickland, Stephen J. Herzberg, and Steven R. Owens, *Keeping Our Word: Indian Treaty Rights and Public Responsibilities*, 1990

The treaty rights dispute played out in the courts, at the boat landings of the North Woods, and at the bar of public opinion. For white Wisconsin residents the controversy was a matter of regular television and newspaper coverage; discussions among family members, friends, and acquaintances; and often intensely held positions. From its inception, the issue took shape along the long-standing ethno-racial divide between whites and Native

208

Americans. This division was importantly challenged and reconfigured by the efforts of the Chippewa to breathe new life into their treaty-reserved rights to hunt, fish, and gather in their former territories. The treaty rights dispute thus emerged, was understood, and was contested as a matter of racial politics. As such, it was also grist for sociologists in their effort to better understand the interplay of race and politics in the United States.

The racialization of the dispute was often clear and direct. As such, understanding and controlling the expression of racial prejudice figured as a concern in the media and in the declarations of government officials. A 1990 article in the *Wisconsin State Journal* quoted Governor Tommy Thompson:

> "There is no silver bullet out there that is going to solve it," Thompson said. "It's education; it's interaction; and it's an understanding of different cultures that have been opposed for 150 years, and we have to break that down. There is no simple solution to this thing."
>
> "You have to day-after-day work at it, try to tear down the barriers of racism and hatred, try to develop a feeling of trust on both sides and an understanding of the various cultures," Thompson said. "That's not going to happen overnight." ("Proposal Called Immature," *Wisconsin State Journal*, April 8, 1990, p. 1b)

Yet this sort of commonsense or lay understanding of prejudice gives us only limited purchase on the full nature of the dispute and how and why prejudice figured in. There is a good deal more involved in the treaty rights conflict, and in most other matters of racialized political controversy, than bigotry and misunderstanding, and it is in probing that deeper complexity that some larger theoretical lessons may be learned.

Our research began with the very general question of how and why ethno-racial divisions become politicized—and racialized—disputes. From the outset, our approach to this question has proceeded on three levels. At first we focused on a racialized political controversy involving the rights of a Native American group: the Ojibwa, or Chippewa, Indians of Wisconsin. Second, we sought to elaborate and test the group position theory of prejudice. And we did so with an explicit eye toward direct comparison and contrast with the other major theories about race in politics. Third, we made use of a unique statewide survey of public opinion as our primary vehicle for assessing the dynamics of the treaty rights dispute and the competing theoretical accounts. In summarizing our results here, we will take up these considerations in reverse order.

For the bulk of our work we relied on sample survey data, on an examination of public opinion. In the design of the survey itself and in our analyses, several steps were taken to move well beyond simplistic "yes or no" or "favor or oppose" responses to a small number of questions. To begin with, we oversampled respondents in the areas most directly affected by the dispute. To make for a meaningfully engaged public opinion, we made sure that respondents had sufficient familiarity with the dispute—and the vast majority of white Wisconsinites plainly did. We took the further step of assessing the level of real issue knowledge that people brought to the dispute, and found disappointingly low levels of real understanding about the treaty rights. This low level of knowledge, we were able to show, played a part in the effects of prejudice in the life of the treaty dispute.

Beyond this, for the major issue-attitude of response to the treaty rights, as well as for measures of each major theoretical construct, we employed multiple item measures to ensure, as far as possible, a full and fair test of each perspective. Moreover, we made extensive use of open-ended questions to better gauge the frames of reference that respondents actually brought to the questions. These open-ended comments not only gave "voice" to our respondents and made clear the extent to which people understood our questions and had relatively well-defined views on the dispute but also helped to clarify key issues otherwise left ambiguous by correlations and cross-tabulations (Kane and Schuman 1991). Important leverage derived from open-ended questions has played a part in other recent survey-based studies of the personal experience of racial discrimination (Bobo and Suh 2000; Suh 2000) and in assessments of the social-psychological roots of racial residential segregation (Krysan and Farley 2002). In general, our results and these other studies underscore the virtue of "qualifying a quantifying analysis" (Krysan 1999; see also Schuman 1966).

And we took seriously the need to extend our concern to the sphere of action, assessing especially the perceived importance of the issue and the extent to which individuals actually became involved in the dispute. These results help place the ultimate political impact of public opinion in a fuller, more rigorously grounded social context. In particular, they move our

TABLE 6.1 Summary of results

	Statewide	Nontreaty county	Treaty county
Treaty issue salient	84%	82%	93%
Oppose off-reservation hunting	59	56	79
Oppose off-reservation fishing	70	67	86
Oppose off-reservation logging	64	60	85
Correct answer on three knowledge questions	9	9	9
Positive rating of anti-treaty protestors	25	24	32
Treaty is a very important/ important issue	22	20	34
Any of the four behaviors	18	16	30
All four behaviors	1	1	2
Agree with obeying court orders	82	82	80
Favor co-management	73	75	56

Source: Chippewa Indian Treaty Rights Survey, 1990.

work beyond the realm of just examining an atomistic public. Accordingly, this effort helped illuminate the forms, extent, and some of the dynamics of behavioral engagement with the treaty dispute.

Table 6.1 summarizes a number of the key patterns from the survey. The issue was a highly salient one, particularly among those in the treaty counties but throughout the state as well. Each aspect of the treaty rights—off-reservation hunting, fishing, or logging—elicited solid majority opposition. The role of self-interest is clear, with northern, treaty-county respondents more likely to oppose each type of treaty-protected right than those inhabiting the lower two-thirds of the state. Yet, to reiterate, these opinions did not rest on a foundation of accurate knowledge about the exercising of the treaty rights, as few people were well informed.

But high salience, objection to the treaty rights, and low levels of knowledge do not exhaust the relevant considerations for understanding the larger politics and fate of the dispute. We also found that comparatively

few respondents held those individuals and groups most vigorously pressing the case against the treaty rights—the anti-treaty activists and protesters—in high esteem. Indeed, on the whole, the motives of anti–treaty
rights activists were seen as disreputable and, arguably, seriously discredit-
ing. A correspondingly small fraction of the sample felt the issue was of
high personal importance. A smaller fraction still actually became directly
involved, through their own behavior, in the treaty dispute. On the one
hand, it is worth noting that a nontrivial number of the total sample did
engage in at least one treaty-relevant political behavior (such as signing a
petition). On the other hand, even in the treaty-affected counties, only a
very small handful of people took part in the full range of political behaviors—petition signing, letter writing, donating money, and taking part in a
rally—asked about in the survey.

Important to the social climate in which the treaty dispute played out
were the generally strong prevailing norms regarding compliance with
court orders. These norms had a bearing, we think, on the openness of
many white Wisconsin residents to a resolution of the treaty dispute in
which the state and the Chippewa would effectively co-manage the natural
resources. The overall picture is complex, and only briefly summarized by
the selected results of Table 6.1, but we also believe it is highly illuminating
with regard to the "career and life course" of the treaty rights dispute.

It has become too easy in the social sciences, perhaps especially so in
some quarters within sociology, to dismiss systematic survey research as
unable to tap complex points of view, identify underlying social processes,
and inform broader social theory (Esposito and Murphy 1999; Feagin
1999; Wellman 1977). These claims contain a much larger measure of mis-
information and ideology than they do truth or good science. The limitations of media polls and isolated research articles do not define the limits
of well-designed, well-contextualized, and carefully analyzed survey data.
And as the material in Chapters 3 and 4 should make clear, in-depth interviews are not the only vehicles for allowing the subjects of social research
to speak in their own words, and to do so vividly, candidly, and in sometimes distressingly frank terms. Likewise, the results in Chapter 5 do much
to mitigate the concern that understanding attitudes tells us little about
likely patterns of social behavior. What surveys then add is the capacity to
better gauge the reach, representativeness, and sources of points of view in
a manner that even a very large number of in-depth interviews can rarely
achieve. We do not claim, and would indeed dispute, that systematic social

surveys constitute the only valid and reliable path to knowledge and theory development in the social sciences. Instead, we hope we have provided a strong example of how such an approach can serve as one valuable tool for generating critical information; for illuminating the human meaning of key social issues, events, and actors; and for advancing tests of our theoretical ideas.

THE THEORETICAL DEBATES

Although we do not conclude that there is a simple and sovereign way of explaining the treaty dispute, we also do not feel that each of the theories considered here has equal merit or relevance in accounting for public opinion in this case. We assessed the empirical viability of five different theories that offer a way to think about an apparently racialized political dispute: self-interest, the injustice frame, orthodox or classical prejudice, symbolic racism, and the group position model. Two of these—self-interest and the injustice frame—are often viewed as "nonracial" and reasoned, if not largely rational, bases for objecting to change in the racial status quo. The other three approaches all invoke ideas about prejudice, but with important differences in how racial prejudice is understood.

Self-interest proved to be a very robust factor in our assessment of public opinion on the treaty dispute. Living in an area where the treaty rights had legal and material force, and involvement in those outdoor activities most directly impinged on by the treaty rights were important influences on virtually every major outcome we analyzed. This includes issue salience, issue knowledge, core attitudes on the treaty rights, anti–Native American stereotypes and affect, group competition, perceived political threat, issue importance, behavioral involvement, and views on how the state should resolve the issue. On one level, this is consistent with what some symbolic-politics theorists have found in the past. After a careful and extensive review of the literature, political scientists Jack Citrin and Donald Green concluded that "the degree to which self-interest influences policy preferences does vary across issues. Specifically, the research literature indicates that the role of self-interest is enhanced when the personal consequences of choices are: 1. visible, 2. tangible, 3. large, and 4. certain" (1990, p. 18), the implication being that this is a rare combination of circumstances. Yet we do not regard the dynamics of the Wisconsin treaty controversy as particularly idiosyncratic or unusual in the course of racial politics in the

United States. That is, the array of circumstances and conditions were by no means exceptional.

This does not mean that we would expect self-interest to be any more routinely influential in politics than Sears and Funk (1990) or Citrin and Green (1990) suggest in their reviews of the literature, though certainly once one moves below the level of intrinsically broad national issues to state- and local-level concerns, the force of "interests" in politics is likely to grow (Kaufmann 1998). And of course our full theoretical framework cannot be read as advancing a purely utilitarian or instrumentalist conception of political attitudes and behavior. Meaningful group identities and attachments (Tuan 1999b), no matter how malleable in the final analysis, are constitutive elements of the theory we propose here. What does matter for future research, we think, is sensible conceptualization, measurement, tests, and interpretations of when and why self-interest may exert political influence. And the guiding logic should recognize that "the critical elements in this regard refer to the nature of the stakes and the ability of citizens to perceive the personal costs and benefits involved" (Citrin and Green 1990, p. 22). These patterns are quite likely to be perceived and organized along lines of extant ethno-racial divisions and to differ in response to individual variation in proximity to the impact or consequences of social change.

We did not find support, however, for a direct, economic version of a self-interest hypothesis. Individual economic status was not an important determinant of views on the treaty rights. Concern over personal finances and economic situation also had little bearing on the treaty dispute. To the extent there was any class basis to the attitudes we examined, it appears that a slightly more affluent segment of treaty-county residents opposed the treaty rights, quite possibly those who owned small businesses. Despite the weakness of the results for an economic-class version of the self-interest hypothesis, we would not go so far as to dismiss claims that the sense of economic marginality felt by many northern Wisconsin residents was an ingredient in the dispute. It is certainly plausible that in an area of greater affluence, with fewer livelihoods and lifestyles dependent on access to natural resources, the basic social foundation for an intense and sustained dispute over the assertion of Native American treaty rights might not have been in place. Here it is important to be mindful that our survey took place long after the initial challenge to state fish and game regulations by the Tribble brothers (1974) and seven years after the pivotal Voigt decision (1983) upholding the Chippewa treaty rights. Also, it is worth noting that many of the key anti-treaty activists appear to have been local small-business owners, who arguably had the most to lose if the Chippewa's exercising of their treaty rights had proved to have ill effects on natural resources or tourism. That general context of economic marginality should, we think, be borne in mind, especially as a potential early seedbed for what became a long period of open conflict and dispute.

These results strongly temper the view from the injustice frame. A pure sense of grievance or injustice, tied strictly to concern about practical consequences of the treaty rights or to a violation of general principles, was difficult to find. Closely attached to most claims of pragmatic harm to natural resources or tourism was a litany of bigoted, anti-Indian stereotypes. This we inferred from the strong dependence of the injustice frame questions on anti-Indian affect, stereotypes, and lack of knowledge about the treaty rights. One can see it even more directly in open-ended responses to the spearfishing question, to the symbolic-racism question about special privileges, and to the getting-ahead-at-the-expense-of-the-non-Indians item among the group competition measures. To paraphrase Gordon Allport, one can scarcely distinguish the pure note of just grievance from the surrounding cacophonous and bitter jangle of manifest prejudice. The frequent, almost indiscriminate blend of the two was as clear in our results as it often was at the boat landings when anti-treaty protesters heckled, demeaned, and challenged the Chippewa spearfishers.

Despite this emphasis on prejudice, we believe these results should just as surely be read as identifying important qualifications for the symbolic politics account of why prejudice enters into politics. To be sure, the classical theory of prejudice, with its emphasis on negative affect and stereotyping, proves useful throughout our efforts to understand attitudes on the treaty rights. But affect and stereotyping alone plainly do not exhaust the array of sentiments expressed and aroused in connection with these issues.

Although our results are more sanguine for the symbolic racism theory than for the injustice frame approach, a number of serious problems emerge here as well. Our data certainly pinpoint the fusion of antiminority affect and reverence for the work ethic so long identified by symbolic racism researchers as a key feature of modern racial prejudice. But feelings and beliefs about critical trait differences have always been central to theories of prejudice, and the work ethic has been a pivotal aspect of white American self-identity from the earliest days of the republic (if not prior to its establishment). And what is more, not only was advocacy of such beliefs tied in important ways to self-interest in the treaty dispute, but it also typically carried with it an overt sense of fraternal deprivation. This sense of deprivation encompassed a perceived status loss for some and a perceived direct resource loss for numerous others. None of these patterns is consistent with the theory of symbolic racism. Indeed, they strongly contradict the theory's core explanatory logic.

We identified critical conceptual and empirical overlaps in the ideas invoked by the injustice frame, symbolic racism, and group position models. Our preference is for the group position model, for three reasons. First, only the group position model expressly weds a concern with the emotional and unreasoned aspects of intergroup attitudes and beliefs—affective group boundaries and attachments, and stereotyping—with the more instrumental and reasoned aspects of group conflict, such as the configurations of interests involved in a particular issue. This blending of what scholars over the past two to three decades have often framed as antithetical lines of analysis is not a post-hoc accommodation to the patterns found in the data. It reflects both Blumer's early explicit development of the theory (discussed in Chapter 1) and our own ideas about the nature of ethnoracial divisions (see Prologue).

Second, the group position model provides the most felicitous template for grappling with the critical changes in the history of white–Native American relations. In particular, the sometimes sharp changes in images of and ideas about Native Americans—going from benign and innocent primitives to blood-thirsty savages, for example, or from a defeated and indolent people to treaty-asserting, angry "red men"—exhibit a link to the needs and interests of important segments of white America that is all too clear to be attributed to mere psychological processes of perception or even group socialization. What is involved, we maintain, is perception and socialization within an evolving social context in which the needs, objectives, and interests of groups may change and call forth new ideas to justify or challenge a new configuration of "group positions."

Third, the empirical evidence overall strongly favors the logic of the group position model. The open-ended responses repeatedly, sometimes implicitly but often enough very explicitly, invoke ideas about challenges to group status and position. The dependence of all of the key racial-attitudes measures on self-interest also points in the direction of the group position theory. And the fact that the single most proximate predictor of issue attitudes proves to be perceived threat from the activist segment of an out-group is, again, organic to the group position theory.

When members of the Lac Courte Oreilles band of the Chippewa defied state fish and game regulations, it was a declaration of intent to alter the prevailing group positions. The Chippewa decided to move from the ranks of those whose historical rights and claims had been nullified to those whose rights would be visibly, aggressively validated and exercised. These actions, when finally upheld as legal by the courts, occasioned powerful feelings of violation among most white Wisconsinites regarding their "sense of group position," particularly among those residing in the North Woods.

THE TREATY DISPUTE

It is essential to note that the treaty dispute, unlike a number of other is-sues in American race politics, came to a close with the rights of the mi-nority group not only legally validated but also operative, even if not widely exercised by members of the Chippewa bands. The treaty rights were not the subject of a steady "war of attrition" in which the minority group claim or right was eventually narrowed, short-circuited, evaded, or gradually driven out of existence. This stands in contrast to matters like court-ordered school desegregation, where desegregation was argu-ably never realized on a national basis, the legal and political pressure for reform has completely evaporated, and rates of segregated schooling re-main high. Similarly, although minority set-aside contracts, special col-lege admission programs, and "goals and timetables" once governed the workplace and institutions of higher learning, affirmative action is not the controlling policy force it once was in terms of expanding realized op-portunities for racial and ethnic minorities. Even the legal and moral basis for affirmative action continues to be challenged in electoral referenda (such as Proposition 209 in California and a similar measure in Washing-ton State), in the courts, and in intellectual tracts (see Thernstrom and Thernstrom 1997). The result has been an inexorable diminution in the day-to-day vitality and administrative practice of affirmative action.

The success of the treaty rights case is ironic, furthermore, in that this was an instance of members of a historically disadvantaged ethno-racial minority acting to secure government protection for the *preservation* of a group cultural *difference*. Unlike blacks in the desegregation and affirmative action efforts, this minority group was not aspiring to fuller inclusion in the mainstream or seeking the diminution of group differences. Yet there was a strong legal and arguably moral basis for the claim, and today the treaty rights survive and are no longer the source of sustained bitter controversy and dispute.

A few critical features of this dispute should, therefore, be borne in mind. The Wisconsin treaty rights issue differed from other issues of racial politics in that the members of the minority group numbered so few. The entire Native American population in the state of Wisconsin is very small, and the Chippewa represent a smaller fraction still. The issue itself did not directly and manifestly impinge on economic opportunity—that is, it did not involve immediate access to jobs or to education and schooling or the direct transfer of financial resources—and of course the court rulings in the case made sure that the Chippewa could not fish, hunt, or log for commercial purposes. The court also ruled that non-Indians would always have substantial access to the underlying natural resources as well. And in the end, some uses of reservations and treaty rights, as in the eventual establishment of popular gaming casinos, have worked to the financial benefit of whites in surrounding communities as well as to Native Americans. The full mix of considerations—especially the size of the Native American population, the court rulings that spoke to the rights of all groups and completely undercut core claims of treaty opponents, and what eventually came to be regarded as beneficial uses of other aspects of Chippewa treaty rights (gaming casinos)—made a positive resolution of the dispute possible.

ON RACIALIZED POLITICS

Racialized politics, especially when played out on the national stage, can be very conspicuous. The most notorious case in recent memory involved the 1988 presidential campaign and the "Willie Horton" ad campaign (Kinder and Sanders 1996). The Bush campaign ads drew attention to a black convict who, while on a weekend furlough from prison, savagely attacked a white, middle-class couple. As political scientist Tali Mendelberg's (2001) careful analysis has shown, the Willie Horton television ads deliberately manipulated popular antiblack sentiment among an important segment of white voters. The ads in question did little to rouse thinking about crime and criminal justice issues or to make these considerations more central to judgments about the candidates. Instead, they brought hostile racial attitudes into greater currency.

Emphasizing the Horton ads, however, can make the racialization of politics seem a more episodic and isolated occurrence than we suspect it is in fact. There are strong reasons to believe that race and racial considerations are woven more deeply into the fabric of American politics than such an impression would allow (Mills 1997; R. Smith 1993). Perhaps the clearest domain in which race is at least an implicit (and often explicit) factor is welfare policy. Historical accounts (Quadagno 1994; Lieberman 1998) and detailed studies of public opinion (Gilens 1999; Fox 2004) both point out the powerful fashion in which race prefigures and shapes welfare policy debates and policymaking.

But race is an important factor in other major policy domains as well. Racial prejudice has proven to be a durable and substantial predictor of whites' support for punitive criminal justice policies. This pattern holds true even though no explicit racial cue is present in survey questions dealing with, say, the harshness of U.S. courts or whether or not to impose the death penalty (Johnson 2001; Hurwitz and Peffley 2005). Indeed, Devon Johnson's research based on national data from the General Social Survey revealed no sign that the strength of the association between racial prejudice and whites' criminal justice views had diminished over the span of years from 1977 to 1993. Antiblack prejudice is a direct and durable feature of the seemingly insatiable public taste for punitive criminal justice policies.

In all these cases, we believe the theory of group position and the dynamics it identifies are relevant. Take the changing criminal justice policies as one illustration. In this area, the issue of crime was first elevated to the status of a major topic for national political debate during the height of the black civil rights protests, when Republican presidential candidate Barry Goldwater made restoring "law and order" a major theme of his 1964 campaign. Though Goldwater was unsuccessful in his presidential bid, the model was established, and four years later Richard Nixon's "southern strategy" and law-and-order appeals honed Goldwater's message to a fine and ultimately successful edge. From then on, the wedding of implicit but real white apprehension about black demands for change to an explicit appeal focusing on an anticrime and law-and-order discourse would be a staple feature of Republican politics at state and national levels (Beckett 1997). And there should be no ambiguity about the outcome: the increasingly harsh tilt of criminal justice policies over the past three decades has weighed disproportionately on African American communities. Blacks now make up roughly half of all those incarcerated, and blacks are now heading to prison at a rate nearly ten times that for whites (Blumstein 2001). The racial consequences of the policy change have been so extreme that they have prompted some eminent scholars to regard the new "mass imprisonment" or "carceral state" as replacing the ghetto itself as a mechanism of black social control and oppression (Garland 2001; Wacquant 2001). We do not propose to develop a full analysis of these dynamics here. Rather, our point is that the heavy hand of racialized politics and the protection of group position can be seen operating in the domain of criminal justice and related public policy as well (Bobo and Johnson 2004).

We submit that the group position model is expressly integrative, dealing in a coherent and credible way with affect, stereotypes, interests, group competition, and perceived threats. The model is also mindful of elite and active segments of groups, of an observant public, and of the constitutive importance of both history and the contemporary array of interests at stake in an issue. The theory's breadth and synthetic nature make it a powerful approach, one applicable to many circumstances. Yet it has its limits. In particular, the full sense of group position is most likely to be a political force during times of change in intergroup relations or when there is direct mobilization and conflict over group rights and entitlements, which tends to occur when groups are brought together for the first time or when significant alterations occur in the power relationship between groups. In addition, the full group-position framework is more likely to matter in circumstances in which intimate interpersonal relations of friendship and family ties across the salient group boundary are infrequent. If these conditions do not obtain, all else being equal, then an atmosphere indicating a high degree of settled consensus, perhaps even an enveloping shroud of paternalism, is likely to characterize patterns of intergroup attitudes and beliefs (Jackman 1994). Under such a scenario, perceptions of group competition and threat are likely to be inchoate and weak. But other contextual factors, such as group size and the presence of third parties who may alter a balance of power via strategic alliances, also influence how the struggle for group position plays out.

One fruitful line of future inquiry will involve a more explicit linking of cultural-sociology approaches to race and the social psychology of race and prejudice. In her very powerfully argued book *The Dignity of Working*

Men: Morality and the Boundaries of Race, Class, and Immigration (2000), cultural sociologist Michele Lamont finds that for white working-class men in the United States, race is a crucial source of identity. These men define themselves as worthy people of integrity and status, in part by asserting a boundary between themselves (and people like them) and African Americans. The white working men Lamont interviewed believed that blacks lacked the work ethic, discipline, and sense of propriety that they possessed. The particular claim to honor or status made by Lamont's interviewees, it is interesting to note, has strong resonance with notions from the sense of group position and even with the particulars of the discourse concerning the treaty rights. For example, Lamont writes of one of her interviewees:

> Vincent is a workhorse. He considers himself "top gun" at his job and makes a very decent living. His comments on blacks suggest that he associates them with laziness and welfare and with claims to receiving special treatment at work through programs such as affirmative action. He says: "Blacks have a tendency to . . . try to get off doing less, the least possible . . . to keep the job, where whites will put in that extra oomph. I know this is a generality and it does not go for all, it goes for a portion. It's this whole unemployment and welfare gig. A lot of blacks on welfare have no desire to get off it. Why should they? It's free money. I can't stand to see my hard-earned money [said with emphasis] going to pay for someone who wants to sit on his ass all day long and get free money." (Lamont 2000, pp. 60–61, parenthetical in original)

As Lamont concludes about a number of the white working men she interviewed: "They underscore a concrete link between the perceived dependency of blacks, their laziness, and the taxes taken from their own paychecks" (p. 62). To a great degree, she finds important parallels between the identities and attitudes of white working men in the United States and the French working men she has interviewed elsewhere about their attitudes toward Muslim immigrants to France.

While the language used is that of behavioral traits (laziness) and violations of values (the Protestant work ethic), coupled with moral condemnation, the group comparisons, sense of loss and threat, and identity-engaging elements are clearly those of the group position model. Indeed, it was precisely this sort of mix that concerned social psychologist Eliot Smith in his critique of symbolic racism theory. In assessing what measures of symbolic racism really revealed, he wrote: "These items and the definition all involve appraisals of an out-group as violating in-group norms or obtaining illegitimate advantages, leading to the emotion of anger" (E. Smith 1993, pp. 308–309). Conceptualizing such responses as the venting of abstract, vague resentment, he said, missed the critical point, that "the focus in the model advanced here is not the intrinsically negative qualities attributed to blacks themselves (which are the theoretical key in concepts of prejudice as a negative attitude) but *appraisals of the threats posed by blacks to the perceiver's own group*" (p. 309, emphasis in original).

We should underscore that the sorts of remarks Lamont records—the intermingling of moralizing critiques with a sense of loss and threat—are not isolated findings. Not only do they strongly resonate with our results from the Chippewa Indian Treaty Rights Survey, but they also directly parallel what the eminent sociologist Mary Waters observed in her study of white business managers and employers of Caribbean immigrants to the United States. Wrote Waters: "Most white respondents were much more able to tap into their negative impressions of black people, especially 'underclass' blacks whom they were highly critical of. These opinions were not just based on disinterested observation. There was a direct sense among many whites that they personally were being taken advantage of and threatened by the black population" (Waters 1999, p. 177). The full array of these results implies, as Lamont argues, that people draw from a set of culturally available repertoires of discourse in understanding themselves and their relations to members of other social groups. Perhaps especially striking is the extent to which very similar vocabularies have emerged in Western European countries dealing with immigrants and guest workers (Pettigrew 1998); a sense of fraternal deprivation has consistently emerged as one of the strongest elements of intergroup attitudes in a range of Western European nations (Meertens and Pettigrew 1997; Pettigrew et al. 1998). And in Canada, social psychologist Victoria Esses and her colleagues used measures of competition and threat closely similar to those developed in Bobo and Hutchings (1996) and found them to be potent predictors of support for restrictive immigration policies (Esses, Jackson, and Armstrong 1998; Esses et al. 1999).

Here it is important to note again that critical focal points for the sense of fraternal deprivation are the leadership segments of those groups pressing to improve the relative position of a disadvantaged group. Theoretically, "claims makers" are elemental to racialized politics and the struggle for group position (see Blumer 1971): that is, those activists who assert demands, contest the status quo, articulate a case for change, and engage in various actions to draw attention to their demands and advance their objectives. Much of the public's attention and sense of threat focuses on these claims makers. This was readily evident in the treaty rights dispute, as for example in artifacts like the flyer announcing the "First Annual Indian Shoot," in which the maximum of 100 points was to be awarded for shooting an "Indian tribal lawyer" (see Figure P.1). It was also evident in the analysis of our survey data, in the potent direct effects of political threat measures on opposition to treaty rights.

Artifacts and results such as these have a direct parallel in the context of black-white relations, in whites' attitudes toward black civil rights leaders and the part those attitudes played in shaping opposition to school busing and other race-targeted social policies (Bobo 1983, 1988a, 1988b). Recent work by political scientist Taeku Lee (2002) has shown just how preoccupied many white Americans were with civil rights leaders such as the Reverend Martin Luther King, Jr. In their recent examination of white racial attitudes, media scholars Robert Entman and Andrew Rojecki (2000) identify the same blend of emotion-laden criticism and competitive threat in views of black leaders that we have stressed throughout our discussion of the sense of group position. They write:

> Here was the first and decisive element in the shift from ambivalence to animosity—the mention of Black leaders, and especially Jesse Jackson, who embodied the idea of opportunism and selfishness. His name came up spontaneously in a third of the interviews as the respondents became increasingly impatient with and emotional about Black problems. . . . Here was a key indirect indication of a media-related factor, the negative image of Black leadership and its association with a zero-sum view of Black-White politics. (Entman and Rojecki 2000, p. 37)

Assuming that the group position model is right, as we believe it is, then leaders, "claims makers" like Jesse Jackson, should loom large in public opinion. Indeed, such figures should be very proximally associated with the particular issue positions, policies, or outcomes at stake. This happens not because categories such as "tribal lawyer" and "civil rights leader" constitute abstract racial resentments or provide merely incidental cognitive markers that cue some more fundamental racial prejudice. Rather, group leaders—the claims they make, the cases they press, and the tactics and strategies they pursue—are all part and parcel of the larger, visible, public-stage struggle over group position. Reactions to such claims makers constitute a key aspect of the sense of threat and challenge to group position.

We believe that this full array of patterns—here and in our findings—supports both the broad relevance of the group position model and the cultural vocabulary surrounding group difference and entitlement in Western, white, capitalist, industrial democracies. Exploration of these parallels should be a high priority for future research. And one lesson from our treaty rights project is that, so far as possible, such research should be well grounded in the specific features of particular settings and controversies. As Walter Lippmann reminded us, a full study of public opinion moves well beyond the "pictures in people's heads" to include a grounding concern with the scene of action and the dynamics of political contestation.

As we see it, prejudice enters politics as part of a struggle for group position. In the first instance, the struggle is occasioned by an upset, change, or challenge to prior patterns of group relations. Next, extant patterns of feelings and beliefs about the characteristics of out-group members become part of the foundation for mobilizing claims about violations of appropriate "group positions." These feelings and beliefs find most consequential expression as perceptions of competition and threat from the out-group, with a focus on the activist, "claims-making," openly challenging segments of that group. And through all of this, there are likely to be segments of the majority or dominant group whose interests and status prompt them to take a leading role in defining what the appropriate group arrangements should be.

This full complex of social processes can and should be the subject of systematic social research, of a formal assessment of alternative lines of explanation, and of cross-cultural and comparative application.

Appendixes

Notes

References

Index

Appendix A

QUESTION WORDING IN THE
CHIPPEWA INDIAN TREATY RIGHTS SURVEY

QUESTIONS DISCUSSED IN CHAPTER 3

ISSUE ENGAGEMENT

Salience: Now we have some questions about the issue of the treaty rights of Chippewa Indians in the state of Wisconsin. Have you heard or read anything about the controversy over Indian treaty rights? (yes or no)

News coverage (if yes above): Since January, have you seen any newspaper articles or stories that dealt with Indian treaty rights? (yes or no)

KNOWLEDGE

Cooperate: As far as you know, do the Chippewa Indians cooperate with the state in monitoring the fishing and deer hunting of tribal members? (yes or no)

Fish-rearing program: To your knowledge, do any of the Chippewa Indian bands have fish-rearing and stocking programs? (yes or no)

Unlimited fishing: As far as you know, do court rulings on Chippewa Indian treaty rights allow the Chippewa unlimited fishing rights in northern Wisconsin? (yes or no)

TREATY RIGHTS ATTITUDES

Spearfishing: In general, do you strongly favor, favor, oppose, or strongly oppose off-reservation spearfishing by Chippewa Indians?

Open-ended follow-up: Why do you feel that way?

Hunting: Do you strongly favor, favor, oppose, or strongly oppose off-reservation hunting rights for Chippewa Indians?

227

Logging: Do you strongly favor, favor, oppose, or strongly oppose off-reservation timber harvesting rights for Chippewa Indians?

SUBJECTIVE FINANCIAL SECURITY

Financial satisfaction: We are interested in how people are getting along financially these days. So far as you and your family are concerned, would you say that you are pretty well satisfied with your present financial situation, more or less satisfied, or not satisfied at all?

Better or worse: During the past few years, has your financial situation been getting better, getting worse, or has it stayed the same?

POLITICAL INTEREST AND IDEOLOGY

Interest: People differ in how much interest they have in politics in the state of Wisconsin. How interested are you in state politics? Are you very interested, somewhat interested, only slightly interested, or not at all interested?

Ideology: We hear a lot of talk these days about liberals and conservatives. I'm going to read you a seven-point scale on which the *political* views that people might hold are arranged. The scale is: 1, extremely liberal; 2, liberal; 3, slightly liberal; 4, moderate to middle of the road; 5, slightly conservative; 6, conservative; and 7, extremely conservative. Where would you place yourself on this scale?

STEREOTYPES

Now I have some questions about different groups in society. I'm going to describe a 7-point scale that I'd like you to use to describe the characteristics of people in different groups. In the first statement, a score of 1 means that you think people in that group tend to be rich. A score of 7 means that you think people in that group tend to be poor. A score of 4 means that you think the group has absolutely no leaning one way or the other, and of course you may choose any number in between 1 and 7 that comes closest to where you think people in the group stand.

Rich or Poor

Whites: Where would you rate whites in general on this scale, where 1 meant "tend to be rich," and 7 meant "tend to be poor"?

Indians: Where would you rate Indians in general, where 1 meant "tend to be rich," and 7 meant "tend to be poor"?

Blacks: Where would you rate blacks in general, where 1 meant "tend to be rich," and 7 meant "tend to be poor"?

Respect for Nature

The next set of characteristics asks if people in each group tend to have great respect for nature or tend to have no respect for nature.

Whites: Where would you rate whites in general on this scale, where 1 meant "tend to have great respect for nature," and 7 meant "tend to have no respect for nature"?

Indians: Where would you rate Indians in general, where 1 meant "tend to have great respect for nature," and 7 meant "tend to have no respect for nature"?

Blacks: Where would you rate blacks in general, where 1 meant "tend to have great respect for nature," and 7 meant "tend to have no respect for nature"?

Lazy or Hardworking

The next set asks if people in each group tend to be lazy or tend to be hardworking.

Whites: Where would you rate whites in general on this scale, where 1 meant "tend to be hardworking," and 7 meant "tend to be lazy"?

Indians: Where would you rate Indians in general on this scale, where 1 meant "tend to be hardworking," and 7 meant "tend to be lazy"?

Blacks: Where would you rate blacks in general on this scale, where 1 meant "tend to be hardworking," and 7 meant "tend to be lazy"?

Live Off Welfare

The next series asks whether people in each group tend to prefer to be self-supporting or tend to prefer living off of welfare.

Whites: Where would you rate whites in general on this scale, where 1 meant "tend to prefer to be self-supporting," and 7 meant "tend to prefer living off of welfare"?

Indians: Where would you rate Indians in general on this scale, where 1 meant "tend to prefer to be self-supporting," and 7 meant "tend to prefer living off of welfare"?

Blacks: Where would you rate blacks in general on this scale, where 1 meant "tend to prefer to be self-supporting," and 7 meant "tend to prefer living off of welfare"?

GROUP AFFECT

Now we would like to get your opinion on several groups and organizations in our society. For each group I will ask you to tell me if you have strongly negative feelings toward the group, somewhat negative feelings, no feeling in either direction, somewhat positive feelings, or strongly positive feelings. If we come to a group that you don't recognize at all, you don't need to rate that group. Just tell me, and we'll move on to the next one.

Feelings toward Chippewa: How would you rate Chippewa Indians as a group? (strongly negative feelings, somewhat negative feelings, no feeling in either direction, somewhat positive feelings, strongly positive feelings)

QUESTIONS DISCUSSED IN CHAPTER 4

INJUSTICE FRAME

Now we'd like to get your reactions to some opinions that have been expressed over the treaty rights issue. Please tell me whether you strongly agree, agree somewhat, neither agree nor disagree, disagree somewhat, or strongly disagree with each statement.

Two classes: First, court rulings on Indian treaty rights create two classes of people with different and unequal rights. (strongly agree, agree somewhat, neither agree nor disagree, disagree somewhat, or strongly disagree)

Hurt supply of fish: Indians' use of their off-reservation treaty fishing rights damages the supply of fish for non-Indian fisherman. (strongly agree, agree somewhat, neither agree nor disagree, disagree somewhat, or strongly disagree)

Hurt tourism: Off-reservation fishing by Indians is hurting the tourism business in northern Wisconsin. (strongly agree, agree somewhat, neither agree nor disagree, disagree somewhat, or strongly disagree)

Need treaties: Indian treaty rights are as necessary today as they were more than 100 years ago. (strongly agree, agree somewhat, neither agree nor disagree, disagree somewhat, or strongly disagree)

SYMBOLIC RACISM

Less attention: Indians have been getting less attention from the government than they deserve. (strongly agree, agree somewhat, neither agree nor disagree, disagree somewhat, or strongly disagree)

Work for living: Most Indians work hard to make a living just like everyone else. (strongly agree, agree somewhat, neither agree nor disagree, disagree somewhat, or strongly disagree)

Take advantage: Most Indians take unfair advantage of privileges given to them by the government. (strongly agree, agree somewhat, neither agree nor disagree, disagree somewhat, or strongly disagree)

Open-ended follow-up: Can you tell me why you feel that way?

GROUP POSITION

Group Competition Items

Hurt whites: Court rulings that protect the rights of Indians usually hurt the rights of non-Indians. (strongly agree, agree somewhat, neither agree nor disagree, disagree somewhat, or strongly disagree)

Same goals: Indians in Wisconsin share many basic values and goals with non-Indians. (strongly agree, agree somewhat, neither agree nor disagree, disagree somewhat, or strongly disagree)

Little influence: Indians have too *little* influence on federal policy concerned with treaty rights (strongly agree, agree somewhat, neither agree nor disagree, disagree somewhat, or strongly disagree)

Get ahead at others' expense: Many Indians have been trying to get ahead economically at the expense of many non-Indians. (strongly agree, agree somewhat, neither agree nor disagree, disagree somewhat, or strongly disagree)

Open-ended follow-up: Can you tell me why you feel that way?

Perceived Threat

(See introduction above for Group Affect questions.) How would you rate:

Chippewa leaders: Chippewa tribal leaders? (strongly negative feelings, somewhat negative, no feeling in either direction, somewhat positive, strongly positive feelings)

Chippewa fishers: Chippewa who exercise their off-reservation fishing rights? (strongly negative feelings, somewhat negative, no feeling in either direction, somewhat positive, strongly positive feelings)

Pro-treaty protesters: People who protest at boat landings in support of spearfishing? (strongly negative feelings, somewhat negative, no feeling in either direction, somewhat positive, strongly positive feelings)

QUESTIONS DISCUSSED IN CHAPTER 5

WHY PROTESTS HAPPEN

Prejudice: There has been a lot of controversy over Indian treaty rights, including people protesting against the practice of spearfishing. Do you think these protests happen because some protesters are prejudiced against Indians? (yes or no)

Unfair: Do you think these protests happen because some protesters believe it is unfair for some people to have rights that other people don't have? (yes or no)

Media: Do you think these protests happen because the media blows the problem out of proportion? (yes or no)

Hurt fish: Do you think these protests happen because some protesters believe off-reservation spearfishing may permanently damage the supply of fish? (yes or no)

ISSUE IMPORTANCE

Importance: Compared with how you feel on other public issues, would you say that Indian treaty rights is one of the *most* important issues to you, a very important issue, a somewhat important issue, or not too important?

Governor vote: How important was a candidate's position on Indian treaty rights when you decided how to vote in the election for governor? Is it one of the most important issues you would consider, a very important issue, somewhat important, or not too important?

BEHAVIORAL INVOLVEMENT

Letter: Have you ever contacted or written a letter to a public official expressing your views on Indian treaty rights? (yes or no)

Money: Have you ever given money to an organization concerned with the treaty rights issue? (yes or no)

Petition: Have you ever signed a petition circulated by a group or organization concerned with the treaty rights issue? (yes or no)

Rally: Have you ever taken part in a meeting, rally, or march concerning the treaty rights issue? (yes or no)

NEGATIVE AFFECT TOWARD PROTESTERS

Anti-treaty protesters: How would you rate your feelings about people who protest at boat landings in opposition to spearfishing? (strongly negative feelings, somewhat negative feelings, no feeling in either direction, somewhat positive feelings, strongly positive feelings)

EVALUATIONS OF POLITICAL FIGURES

I'd like to get your feelings toward some of our political leaders. I'll read the name of a person, and I'd like you to tell if you have strong negative feelings toward the person, somewhat negative feelings, no feelings in either direction, somewhat positive feelings, or strongly positive feelings toward that person. If we come to a person whose name you don't recognize at all, you don't need to rate that person.

Thompson: First, how would you rate Tommy Thompson? (strongly negative feelings, somewhat negative feelings, no feelings in either direction, somewhat positive feelings, strongly positive feelings)

Loftus: Next, how would you rate Tom Loftus? (strongly negative feelings, somewhat negative feelings, no feelings in either direction, somewhat positive feelings, strongly positive feelings)

Hanaway: Next, how would you rate Donald Hanaway? (strongly negative feelings, somewhat negative feelings, no feeling in either direction, somewhat positive feelings, strongly positive feelings)

Crabb: And how would you rate Barbara Crabb? (strongly negative feelings, somewhat negative feelings, no feelings in either direction, somewhat positive feelings, strongly positive feelings)

ATTITUDE ON RESOURCE CO-MANAGEMENT

Different groups have proposed dealing with the treaty rights issue in different ways. Now I'm going to ask you about each of several proposals. Please tell me whether you favor or oppose each possibility.

Co-management: Protection of the treaty rights by *co-management* of fish and other resources in the off-reservation areas by the Chippewa bands and the state? (favor or oppose)

Appendix B

FACTORIAL STRUCTURE OF PREJUDICE

We used confirmatory factor analysis to assess the pattern of correlation among responses to our questions about opposition to Chippewa treaty rights; prejudice driven by perceptions of competition, threat, or lost privilege; and racial stereotyping by whites of the Chippewa.[1]

The questions were asked to uncover respondents' attitudes. In essence, attitudes are unobservable and not subject to direct measurement, but are assumed to cause variations in responses to direct measures such as the survey questions. No individual survey question serves as a perfect, or error-free, measure of the attitude that causes it to vary. Thus the variation in response to any single question arises from the effect of the underlying attitude (true variation) and the effect of other processes (error variation). The processes generating error variation may be intentional, so as to mislead the interviewer about the respondent's true attitude, or unintentional, as a result of failure to understand the question or confusion about how to respond accurately.

Because of the variation caused by error, several questions asked about the same attitude will usually yield responses that are correlated, but not perfectly so. Questions asked about different but closely related attitudes will also be correlated, but are expected to be less correlated than questions about the same attitude. The reduction in correlation when error is present, compared with what would be observed if error were not present, may lead to the spurious conclusion that attitudes are not measurable, or that specific attitudes are not related to other attitudes or behaviors. Occasionally errors may result in correlations that inflate the apparent relationship between different attitudes or between attitudes and behaviors. This situation may arise if responses to different questions are systematically varied, such as when a respondent consistently tries to suppress answers he believes would be negatively judged by others. When errors are correlated

235

there is, unfortunately, no simple way to predict the consequence. But the modeling of measurement error provides some leverage in ruling out unlikely explanations of the responses obtained in the survey.

We thus undertook confirmatory factor analysis of the structure of racial attitudes driving opposition to Chippewa treat rights in order to shed light on the extent to which responses to survey questions could be usefully interpreted by reference to factors deriving from the different theoretical models of interethnic attitudes: classic prejudice (stereotyping),[2] the injustice frame, symbolic racism, and group position (group competition and political threat). Within the confirmatory framework, we did statistical testing of alternative models to examine which best accounted for the observed correlation of respondents' answers to seventeen attitude questions (described in Chapters 3 and 4). The alternative models are distinguished by the assumptions they make regarding (1) the number of factors affecting the survey responses, (2) whether there is correlation between the factors, (3) whether survey responses are affected by more than one factor, and (4) whether errors in responses are correlated. These assumptions are used with the sample data to predict the correlation of the survey responses to the attitude questions. The predicted correlations are compared with the observed correlations. Discrepancies between the predicted and observed correlations arise when model assumptions are inconsistent with the data. The sum of discrepancies over the matrix of correlations representing the full set of attitude measures is captured by *LR*, the likelihood ratio statistic (Long 1983, pp. 63–68), which is distributed as a chi-square, with degrees of freedom (*df*) determined as the difference in the number of independent parameters of a hypothesized model and the model of the null hypothesis. The likelihood ratio statistic of the model is compared with the critical value at the alpha level of significance *(p)* of the chi-square distribution, with *df* degrees of freedom. The models were fit using the LISREL program (version 7.16; Joreskog and Sorbom 1989). The program includes additional measures to aid the search for better-fitting models, and our analysis relied on the modification index (Long 1983, p. 69).

SINGLE PREJUDICE–TOLERANCE CONTINUUM

We examined a series of theoretically motivated models to see which best described the underlying pattern of correlation. The initial model examined in the analysis specified that only one factor accounted for variation

TABLE B1   Single-factor model loadings

Survey question	Single anti-Chippewa construct factor loading (standard error)
Respect nature	.370 (.047)
Lazy	.419 (.046)
Welfare dependent	.487 (.045)
Two classes	.236 (.048)
Hurt fish	.637 (.043)
Hurt tourism	.671 (.042)
Need treaty	.432 (.046)
Unfair advantage	.737 (.041)
Government attention	.547 (.045)
Indian influence	.413 (.046)
Work hard	.622 (.043)
Rights hurt	.582 (.044)
Same goal	.469 (.046)
Get ahead	.509 (.045)
Chippewa leaders	.602 (.044)
Chippewa spearfishers	.759 (.041)
Sympathy protests	.339 (.047)

in the seventeen items, with no correlation of response errors. Substantively, this model suggests that there is a single underlying continuum on which the attitudes can be arranged, running from high prejudice at one extreme to high tolerance at the other. Had this model fit the data, it would have totally undermined the usefulness of any of the other racial attitude constructs suggested by the different theoretical models. Instead, it would have sufficed to interpret the responses as reflecting a very general anti-Chippewa sentiment.

This model did a quite poor job of accounting for the data ($LR = 529.21$, $df = 119$ [$p = .000$]). The factor loadings, which measure the relationship between the separate survey questions and the factor, are shown in Table B.1.

We did not simply dismiss the single-factor model. We considered several possible minor alterations to see if the model was within the realm of statistical plausibility. With a single factor specification, the only way to substantially improve the fit of the model is to allow response errors to

TABLE B2 Theoretical pluralism multifactor model loadings

Survey question	Factor 1	Factor 2	Factor 3	Factor 4	Factor 5
Respect nature	.348 (.051)				
Lazy	.725 (.049)				
Welfare dependent	.770 (.049)				
Two classes		.294 (.050)			
Hurt fish		.721 (.044)			
Hurt tourism		.748 (.044)			
Need treaty		.438 (.048)			
Unfair advantage			.762 (.042)		
Government attention			.568 (.045)		
Indian influence			.425 (.044)		
Work hard			.622 (.047)		
Rights hurt				.626 (.048)	
Same goal				.501 (.049)	
Get ahead				.561 (.048)	
Chippewa leaders					.654 (.044)
Chippewa spearfishers					.880 (.042)
Sympathy protests					.373 (.048)

Note: Loadings of .2 or less not shown.

correlate. A review of the modification indexes showed that the greatest improvement in fit would likely come from allowing response errors to two stereotype questions to correlate: "lazy" and "welfare dependent." We fit several additional models, allowing this error correlation and others suggested by the modification indexes. What rapidly became apparent, not surprisingly, was that many of the significant error correlations occurred in relationships between items designed to measure the alternative racial-attitude constructs posited as factors in opposition to Chippewa treaty rights. Rather than further exploring the impact of error correlations, we shifted to a multifactor specification.

THEORETICAL PLURALISM

Our second effort treated the core concepts in each theory as if they were all necessary to provide an adequate description of the underlying data. Thus the initial multifactor model specified five factors: stereotypes (1), injustice frame (2), symbolic racism (3), group competition (4), and political threat (5), as outlined in Table B.2 (and in Figure 4.6 earlier). Under the model, no response error correlations were allowed, and items were not affected by more than one factor. The factors were allowed to correlate. The fit of this model was somewhat better than the single-factor model but would still not be considered an adequate explanation of the data ($LR =$ 327.15, $df = 109$ $[p = .000]$).

A review of the modification indexes suggested that fit could be improved by allowing items to load on multiple factors, as well as by allowing response errors to correlate. The suggestion of multifactor loadings, combined with an estimated high degree of correlation among the five specified factors (shown in Table B.3), gives rise to serious questions about the

TABLE B3 Estimated factor correlations for theoretical pluralism specification

Factor	Factor 1	Factor 2	Factor 3	Factor 4	Factor 5
1	1.000				
2	0.666	1.000			
3	0.474	0.799	1.000		
4	0.540	0.901	0.842	1.000	
5	0.457	0.807	0.793	0.762	1.000

distinctiveness of the constructs, and their ultimate empirical necessity in classifying survey respondents with respect to attributes that explain opposition to Chippewa treaty rights.

A FINAL GROUP POSITION MODEL

These considerations are consistent with the specification of fewer factors to account for the structure of racial attitudes. The attitude questions·were remapped to the three-factor structure specified in Table B.4, with correlation among the factors. The fit of this model proved to be somewhat worse ($LR = 409.79$, $df = 116$ [$p = .000$]), but it was easily improved by allowing the "unfair advantage" question to load on both the new stereotype and new group-competition factors. With the addition of this single factor loading, the fit improved ($LR = 366.68$, $df = 115$ [$p = .000$]), and the factor structure remained relatively simple, although still not adequate to explain the observed data. Further improvements in the fit were achieved by allowing for correlated response errors. After sequential estimation of eight error correlations, the likelihood ratio had been reduced to 164.16 ($df = 107$ [$p = .000$]). Five of these involved correlated errors within factors; the remaining three occurred across factors. The progression of improvement in fit is shown in Table B.4.

At this point, examination of the modification indexes suggested that smaller improvements to fit would be achieved by allowing for error correlations between items on different factors. As the returns were diminishing, and the odds of capitalizing on sampling error were increasing, we ceased to estimate additional errors. Review of the error correlations allowed in the models shows that five of the eight (those added in Models 3, 4, 6, 7, 8) occurred within constructs, while the remaining three carried across constructs (those added in Models 5, 9, 10). These may have arisen from method effects, intentional bias, or other unspecified sources.

Results for the three-factor model, with one cross-factor loading and eight correlated errors, are given in Table B.5. Factor 1 represents the new stereotype construct, Factor 2 represents the new group competition construct, and Factor 3 represents the new political threat construct.

Substantively, as argued in Chapter 4, this means that the injustice frame and symbolic racism models have not survived as clear theoretical constructs. Symbolic racism divides into stereotyping, group competition, and political threat. And the injustice frame items, likewise, also divide into stereotyping, group competition, and political threat.

TABLE B4 Chi-squared results for different three-factor models

Model	LR	df	p	LR change	df	p
1. 3-factor	409.79	116	.000			
2. Model 1 plus unfair advantage cross-factor loading	366.68	115	.000	43.11	1	.000
Correlated error models						
3. Model 2 plus lazy–welfare	285.48	114	.000	83.20	1	.000
4. Model 3 plus influence–government attention	238.98	113	.000	56.50	1	.000
5. Model 4 plus work hard–government attention	222.10	112	.000	16.88	1	.000
6. Model 5 plus two classes–hurt fish	210.36	111	.000	11.74	1	.000
7. Model 6 plus hurt fish–hurt tourism	199.29	110	.000	11.07	1	.000
8. Model 7 plus influence–need treaty	187.57	109	.000	11.72	1	.000
9. Model 8 plus two classes–need treaty	174.63	108	.000	12.94	1	.000
10. Model 9 plus same goal–get ahead	164.16	107	.000	10.47	1	.000

TABLE B5 Final group position three-factor model loadings

Survey question	Factor 1	Factor 2	Factor 3
Respect nature	.422 (.050)		
Lazy	.481 (.049)		
Welfare dependent	.508 (.049)		
Two classes		.241 (.050)	
Hurt fish		.652 (.046)	
Hurt tourism		.700 (.045)	
Need treaty			.446 (.047)
Unfair advantage	.272 (.080)	.531 (.077)	
Government attention			.532 (.046)
Indian influence			.388 (.048)
Work hard	.731 (.046)		
Rights hurt		.629 (.045)	
Same goal	.547 (.048)		
Get ahead		.533 (.046)	
Chippewa leaders			.658 (.044)

TABLE B5 (continued)

Survey question	Factor 1	Factor 2	Factor 3
Chippewa spearfishers			.846
			(.041)
Sympathy protests			.377
			(.048)

Note: Loadings of .2 or less not shown.

Although the loading of the unfair-advantage question on the stereo-type factor is statistically significant, it is a relatively unreliable indicator of that construct; likewise, the two-classes question is the least reliable indica-tor of the group competition construct.

The three facets of racial attitudes represented by the construct are strongly related in the Chippewa treaty rights context (see Table B.6). Re-sults presented for scales based on these constructs demonstrate that they have considerable predictive power individually and in combination.

Finally, the estimated error correlations are shown in Table B.7. All the coefficients are statistically different from zero at the .05 level or lower. The positive direction indicates that respondent errors of reporting are consis-tent across the variables. Respondents are likely to over- or underreport their true response on each pair of variables. It is on the basis of these anal-yses that we specified and estimated the final models examined in Chapter 4 (Table 4.8).

TABLE B6   Estimated factor correlations for final three-factor group position model

Factor	Factor 1	Factor 2	Factor 3
1	1.000		
2	0.732	1.000	
3	0.720	0.843	1.000

TABLE B7 Error correlations under final three-factor group position model

Questions	Correlation	Standard error
Lazy–welfare	.329	.043
Influence–government attention	.242	.038
Work hard–government attention	.121	.031
Two classes–hurt fish	.135	.036
Hurt fish–hurt tourism	.103	.033
Influence–need treaty	.132	.037
Two classes–need treaty	.141	.040
Same goal–get ahead	.114	.036

NOTES

1. Although in their empirical work Carmines and Stimson develop a definitive assessment of the transformation of partisan alignments in the United States, their theoretical treatment of race is sparse and problematic. They expressly regard race and the black-white divide as just incidentally the issue that proved to be the main impetus to redefining partisan allegiances. From our vantage point, race is necessarily and organically—given the constitution and historical development of American institutions and culture—one of only a very few issues with the capacity to have so profoundly reorganized American politics.

2. Ellis's (2001) Pulitzer Prize–winning discussion of "the silence" in his book *The Founding Brothers* is perhaps the most telling example of the inextricable importance of race. He recounts just how explicitly—and in an overtly political fashion—the founding brothers accepted black slavery, despite recognizing the powerful contradiction it represented to the spirit of the revolutionary struggle they had just waged.

1. LINKING PREJUDICE AND POLITICS

1. Different labels for the concept have been advanced by different advocates of the core theory. McConahay settled on the designation "modern racism" (McConahay, Hardee, and Batts 1981). Kinder settled on the designation "racial resentment" (Kinder and Sanders 1996). But Sears has continued to employ the label symbolic racism, and so have many others (Sears et al. 1997). We continue that usage here and intend it to encompass this full range of constructs.

2. Recognition of this point at the outset might have done much to avoid some misspent energy during the "race versus class" debate of the 1980s. Although seldom stated so directly, the quasi-autonomous and permeative effects of social conceptions of race are exactly what figured in many early critiques

of William Julius Wilson's (1978) "declining significance of race" thesis (see Pettigrew 1980, 1981; Willie 1989). Many counterproductive features and limitations in this and closely allied exchanges might have been avoided if sociological analysts of race issues had attended to the social-psychological, microsocial aspects of racial phenomena as well as the structural, institutional, and macrosocial aspects.

3. This was done to ensure that a substantial proportion of the interviews would be conducted with individuals living in the areas most affected by the treaty rights issue. The nineteen oversampled counties were: Bayfield, Douglas, Ashland, Iron, Price, Rusk, Sawyer, Taylor, Barron, Burnett, Polk, Washburn, Chippewa, Forest, Oneida, Vilas, Langdale, Lincoln, and Marathon.

4. The open-ended items follow one of the key treaty-rights issue attitude questions, one of the symbolic racism questions, and one of the group competition questions.

3. BETWEEN PREJUDICE AND SELF-INTEREST

1. At least since Converse's seminal paper (1964), there has been a concern with the problem of "nonattitudes" in surveys of public opinion. As others have noted, there can be a fine line between attitudes and nonattitudes (Schuman and Presser 1981), because even on topics on which respondents may have little information, often an effort is made to link the issue to other broad orientations, such as liberal versus conservative or views on the role of government, that make the expression of opinions more than just guessing.

2. The "most important problem" question was also coded for second mentions. Taking this possibility into account, a total of 6 percent of the sample made any mention of the treaty rights dispute.

3. Newspapers and other media sources throughout the state reported for several years on the small fraction of the overall harvest taken by the Chippewa. This point is noted in the GLIFWC reports (see Great Lakes Indian Fish and Wildlife Commission 1990). The authoritative "Inouye Report" provides compelling evidence on this point (U.S. Department of the Interior and Bureau of Indian Affairs, *Casting Light upon the Waters: A Joint Fishery Assessment of the Wisconsin Ceded Territory,* 1991).

4. The three knowledge items are significantly and positively intercorrelated (approximately $+.176$ on average) and thus may be used as a cumulative index of knowledge on the treaty issue.

5. We examined the correlation between opposition to treaty rights and education and then statistically removed the effect of knowledge.

6. These correlations are comparable to those obtained in other surveys. The 1990 General Social Survey (Davis and Smith 1990), a national survey, in-

cluded stereotype trait rating questions and questions on racial intermarriage in reference to blacks and to Hispanics, similar to those asked in our survey. For white respondents to the General Social Survey, we found a significant correlation between an antiblack stereotype scale (composed of items on the trait dimensions of lazy/hardworking, violence-prone/not violence-prone, unintelligent/intelligent, prefer to live off welfare/prefer to be self-supporting) and the intermarriage with blacks question ($r = -.31, p < .001$) and for a parallel anti-Hispanic stereotyping scale and intermarriage with Hispanics question ($r = -.34, p < .001$).

7. This pattern of result parallels Russell Middleton's (1976) classic examination of the importance of authoritarianism to North-South difference in prejudice. He found higher levels of antiblack prejudice among Southern whites than among non-Southern whites. However, there was no regional difference in level of general authoritarianism. Thus he argued: "The South and the non-South also differed very little on psychological variables—authoritarianism, anomie and psychic distress. If prejudice were primarily a function of such characteristics, we would expect consistent regional differences in each type of prejudice. The fact that anti-black prejudice was far higher in the South but the other types of prejudice were not suggests that there was a special subcultural tradition of anti-black prejudice in the region" (Middleton 1976, p. 110).

8. The results are no more encouraging when examined separately within the treaty and nontreaty counties. The single largest correlation is -14. ($p < .05$) between the "better or worse" item and treaty rights opposition among nontreaty-county respondents. Given the expectation that the effect should help account for the high opposition among treaty-county respondents, the finding that strongest correlation exists for those farthest removed from the treaty dispute contradicts the economic self-interest argument.

4. DISENTANGLING RACIALIZED POLITICS

1. This is not to minimize the amount of open (or, more often, subtle) bigotry that characterized a number of the anti-treaty groups and their leaders. For example, Larry Peterson, the founder of PARR (Protect America's Rights and Resources) was highly critical of the federal government for "keeping Indians Indian" by keeping them "sitting on their porches looking for something to do" (quoted in *Isthmus*, March 30, 1990, p. 1). And Dean Crist, leader of Stop Treaty Abuse, was quoted as saying: "You know, I was listening to [former Ku Klux Klan leader] David Duke speak the other day, and he was good, very good. . . . What he was saying was the same stuff we have been saying. It was like he might have been reading it from S.T.A. literature" (*Wisconsin State Jour-*

nal, January 14, 1990). And legal scholar Rennard Strickland and his colleagues were unambiguous in their criticism of these anti-treaty spokesmen and their tactics, writing: "All of these groups focus their attention on the exercise of treaty rights, but use racist literature, hate-group organizing techniques and propaganda to convince non-Indians that their livelihood is threatened by Chippewa treaties" (Strickland, Herzberg, and Owens 1990, pp. 15–16).

2. These results are similar to those obtained from national surveys containing indicators of symbolic racism. For example, data from the 1986 National Election Study show 59 percent of whites agreeing with the idea that "if blacks would only try harder they could be just as well off as whites"; 59 percent rejecting the idea that blacks "have gotten less than they deserve"; and 59 percent rejecting the idea that "government officials usually pay less attention to a request or complaint from a black person than from a white person" (Kinder and Sanders 1996, p. 107).

3. These results are highly comparable to those reported by Kinder and Sanders (1996, pp. 109–110 and related note 50, p. 322) for their national data on measures of "racial resentment" toward blacks. Our CITRS average inter-item correlation is slightly higher than the .36 they report for their 1986 NES data, but our alpha is slightly lower (.71 versus .78) and mainly reflects the smaller number of items. Our figures are likewise comparable to those that Sears et al. report (1997, p. 26) for four different surveys—three national surveys and one for Los Angeles County—containing symbolic racism measures.

4. The items are narrow and conservative in that, under group position theory as Blumer first developed it, challenges to the sense of group position are indeed emotionally arousing and engaging. Yet, to sharpen the distinction from symbolic racism for the purposes of this test (and other tests; see Bobo and Hutchings 1996; Bobo and Johnson 2000), we erred on the side of a decidedly cognitive (not affect-infused) measure of perceived group competition. Future research should not reify these particular items but should move ahead to incorporate the more emotional tone in the wording of the question, as suggested by the extensive open-ended comments reviewed in this and the previous chapter.

5. The reliability figure is lower than that found among whites by Bobo and Hutchings (1996, p. 960n9) in their 1992 Los Angeles County survey. The difference is most likely traceable to two considerations. First, the present measure is based on fewer items. Second, the Los Angeles County survey measures were more tightly focused on the tangibles of housing, economic outcomes, and political clout.

6. We conducted both exploratory and confirmatory factor analyses in connection with these specifications. Exploratory factor analysis with oblique rotation yields only four latent constructs with eigenvalues greater than 1.0. This is true whether we use all eighteen items in column one of Table 4.8 (see also Figure

4.5), or seventeen, omitting the single affect measure. The underlying factor-structure results roughly correspond to the affect, stereotype, competition, and threat constructs (but not in terms of each exact item). The differences usually involve multiple factor loadings. We also performed extensive confirmatory factor analysis and did obtain satisfactory results for the organization shown in Figure 4.5. However, slightly different specifications of a four-construct set of dimensions are also viable. Since, as is typically the case with factor analyses, these results speak no more unequivocally than the analyses presented and reviewed in the main body of the text, we do not belabor the specific results here. Our remapping of constructs is essentially sustained by these analyses (see Appendix B).

7. We also estimated a model of opposition to the treaty rights using the original stereotyping, injustice frame, symbolic racism, group competition, and political threat scales. The overall amount of variance explained was identical. Injustice frame ($b = .28, p < .001$), symbolic racism ($b = .24, p < .001$), and political threat ($b = .26, p < .001$) all had highly significant direct effects. Neither stereotyping ($b = .05$) nor group competition ($b = .05$) had significant direct effects. Although this is certainly one way of specifying the model, we believe it is theoretically and empirically flawed. Recall that the content of the original injustice frame and symbolic racism measures overlaps heavily with stereotyping, group competition, and threat, and that they are all responsive to self-interest considerations—making such a version of the model empirically uninterpretable and highly misleading in terms of theory.

5. PROTEST, MOBILIZATION, AND MASS COMPLIANCE

1. A plausible case can be made that the protests, fear of disorder, and general climate of opinion influenced the court rulings. The decisions holding that the Chippewa could not hunt, fish, or log for commercial purposes or on private land, that they, too, were bound by the state's determinations of safe-harvest limits, and that non-Indian anglers were entitled to half of the safe harvest (particularly the latter) could all be read as significant curtailments of the Chippewa's rights.

2. We should reiterate that there were also those who protested in support of the treaty rights and the Chippewa spearfishers. For example, a front-page story in the *Wisconsin State Journal* ran under the headline "Treaty Backers Plan Protest" (*Wisconsin State Journal*, April 8, 1990). Similarly, a story a month earlier described how long-time peace activists were taking up the Chippewa cause ("Minocqua, Not Managua: Local Activists to Watch for Peace at Landings," *Wisconsin State Journal*, March 18, 1990, p. 1A). These examples notwithstanding, the vast majority of the media coverage focused on anti–treaty rights activists, groups, and actions.

3. We also examined likely voting patterns in the gubernatorial election, using a difference-score approach (i.e., Thompson rating minus Loftus rating) as a vote-preference measure. In a multivariate OLS model, opposition to the treaty rights had no significant effect on support for Thompson over Loftus, nor did the self-interest measures of treaty county and involvement in fishing and hunting. Importance of the treaty rights dispute had no direct influence, and, moreover, there was no significant interaction of issue importance with treaty rights opposition. That is, even among those rating the treaty dispute as highly important, treaty rights attitudes had no impact on preference for Thompson over Loftus. In the end, the significant predictors were political ideology and party identification, with conservatives and Republicans favoring Thompson over Loftus. The lack of an effect for treaty rights opposition, and the failure of the interaction with issue importance, mainly reflect the fact that the treaty dispute never became a matter of sustained partisan engagement.

4. This is consistent with Tyler's (1990a,b) discussion of a normative perspective on why people obey the law. Under the instrumental perspective, individuals obey the law because there is something in it for them or because it at least avoids the imposition of costs or sanctions. Under a normative perspective, people obey the law because it accords with important general norms and values they hold. If the items in the rule-of-law index had been strongly related to the self-interest measures, this would have suggested, consistent with the instrumental approach, that views of the law are tied to the stakes people have in particular situations, outcomes, or circumstances.

APPENDIX B

1. A basic introduction to these methods is given in Long (1983), while the original exposition of the confirmatory model is found in Joreskog (1967, 1969).

2. The Chippewa affect item was not included in these models, since we had only the single item with which to tap the construct of general group affect.

REFERENCES

Adorno, T., et al. 1950. *The Authoritarian Personality.* New York: Harper.

Allport, Gordon W. 1954. *The Nature of Prejudice.* Reading, MA: Addison-Wesley.

Almaguer, Tomas. 1994. *Racial Faultlines: The Historical Origins of White Supremacy in California.* Berkeley: University of California Press.

Altemeyer, Bob. 1988. *Enemies of Freedom: Understanding Right-Wing Authoritarianism.* San Francisco: Jossey-Bass.

Arey, Bette B. 1991. *Chippewa Off-Reservation Treaty Rights: Origins and Issues.* State of Wisconsin, Legislative Reference Bureau, Research Bulletin 91-1 (December 1991).

Armstrong, Virginia Irving. 1971. *I Have Spoken: American History through the Voices of Indians.* Chicago: Swallow Press.

Attewell, Paul. 1974. "Ethnomethodology since Garfinkel." *Theory and Society* 1:179–210.

Axtell, James. 1974. "Through a Glass Darkly: Colonial Attitudes toward the Native Americans." *American Indian Culture and Research Journal* 1 (1): 17–28.

Bataille, Gretchen M., and Charles L. P. Silet. 1983. "Economic and Psychic Exploitation of American Indians." *Explorations in Ethnic Studies* 6 (2): 8–23.

Beckett, Katherine. 1997. *Making Crime Pay: Law and Order in Contemporary American Politics.* New York: Oxford University Press.

Begley, Thomas M., and Henry Alker. 1982. "Anti-busing Protest: Attitudes and Action." *Social Psychology Quarterly* 45:187–197.

Benford, Robert D., and David Snow. 2000. "Framing Processes and Social Movements: An Overview and Assessment." *Annual Review of Sociology* 26:611–639.

Berger, Thomas R. 1985. *Village Journey: The Report of the Alaska Native Review Commission.* New York: Hill and Wang.

Berkhofer, Robert F. 1978. *The White Man's Indian: Images of the American Indian from Columbus to the Present.* New York: Vintage.

Blauner, Robert. 1972. *Racial Oppression in America.* New York: Harper & Row.

———. 1989. *Black Lives, White Lives: Three Decades of Race Relations in America.* Berkeley: University of California Press.

Blumer, Herbert. 1946. "Collective Behavior." Pp. 167–222 in *New Outlines of the Principles of Sociology,* ed. A. M. Lee. New York: Barnes and Noble.

———. 1948. "Public Opinion and Public Opinion Polling." *American Sociological Review* 13:542–555.

———. 1955a. "Attitudes and the Social Act." *Social Problems* 3:59–65.

———. 1955b. "Reflections on Theory of Race Relations." Pp. 3–21 in *Race Relations in World Perspective,* ed. A. W. Lind. Honolulu: University of Hawaii Press.

———. 1956. "Sociological Analysis and the 'Variable.'" *American Sociological Review* 22:683–690.

———. 1958a. "Race Prejudice as a Sense of Group Position." *Pacific Sociological Review* 1:3–7.

———. 1958b. "Recent Research on Race Relations." *International Social Science Bulletin* 10:403–477.

———. 1965a. "The Future of the Color Line." Pp. 322–336 in *The South in Continuity and Change,* ed. J. C. McKinney and E. T. Thompson. Durham, NC: Seeman.

———. 1965b. "Industrialization and Race Relations." Pp. 228–249 in *Industrialization and Race Relations: A Symposium,* ed. G. Hunter. New York: Oxford University Press.

———. 1969. *Symbolic Interactionism.* Berkeley: University of California Press.

———. 1971. "Social Problems as Collective Behavior." *Social Problems* 18:298–306.

Blumer, Herbert, and Troy Duster. 1980. "Theories of Race and Social Action." Pp. 211–238 in *Sociological Theories: Race and Colonialism,* UNESCO. Poole, England: Sydenhams Printers.

Blumstein, Alfred. 2001. "Race and Criminal Justice." Pp. 21–31 in *American Becoming: Racial Trends and Their Consequences,* vol. 2, ed. N. Smelser, W. J. Wilson, and F. Mitchell. Washington, DC: National Academy Press.

Bobo, Lawrence D. 1983. "Whites' Opposition to Busing: Symbolic Racism or Realistic Group Conflict?" *Journal of Personality and Social Psychology* 45:1196–1210.

———. 1988a. "Attitudes toward the Black Political Movement: Trends, Meaning, and Effects on Racial Policy Preferences." *Social Psychology Quarterly* 51:287–302.

———. 1988b. "Group Conflict, Prejudice, and the Paradox of Contemporary Racial Attitudes." Pp. 85–114 in *Eliminating Racism: Profiles in Controversy,* ed. P. A. Katz and D. A. Taylor. New York: Plenum.

———. 1991. "Social Responsibility, Individualism, and Redistributive Policies." *Sociological Forum* 6:71–92.

———. 1997. "Race, Public Opinion, and the Social Sphere." *Public Opinion Quarterly* 61:1–15.

———. 1999. "Prejudice as Group Position: Microfoundations of a Sociological Approach to Racism and Race Relations." *Journal of Social Issues* 55:445–472.

———. 2000a. "Race and Beliefs about Affirmative Action: Assessing the Effects of Interests, Group Threat, Ideology, and Racism." Pp. 137–164 in *Racialized Politics: The Debate on Racism in America,* ed. D. O. Sears, J. Sidanius, and L. Bobo. Chicago: University of Chicago Press.

———. 2000b. "Reclaiming a DuBoisian Perspective on Racial Attitudes." *Annals of the American Academy of Political and Social Science* 568:186–202.

———. 2001. "Racial Attitudes and Relations at the Close of the Twentieth Century." Pp. 264–301 in *America Becoming: Racial Trends and Their Consequences,* vol. 1, ed. N. Smelser, W. J. Wilson, and F. Mitchell. Washington, DC: National Academy Press.

Bobo, Lawrence D., and Vincent L. Hutchings. 1996. "Perceptions of Racial Group Competition: Extending Blumer's Theory of Group Position to a Multiracial Social Context." *American Sociological Review* 61:951–972.

Bobo, Lawrence D., and Devon Johnson. 2000. "Racial Attitudes in a Prismatic Metropolis: Mapping Identity, Stereotypes, Competition, and Views on Affirmative Action." Pp. 81–166 in *Prismatic Metropolis: Inequality in Los Angeles,* ed. L. D. Bobo et al. New York: Russell Sage Foundation.

———. 2004. "A Taste for Punishment: Black and White Americans' Views on the Death Penalty and the War on Drugs." *Du Bois Review* 1:151–180.

Bobo, Lawrence D., and James R. Kluegel. 1993. "Opposition to Race-Targeting: Self-Interest, Stratification Ideology, or Racial Attitudes?" *American Sociological Review* 58:443–464.

———. 1997. "Status, Ideology, and Dimensions of Whites' Racial Beliefs and Attitudes: Progress and Stagnation." Pp. 93–120 in *Racial Attitudes in the 1990s: Continuity and Change,* ed. S. A. Tuch and J. K. Martin. New York: Praeger.

Bobo, Lawrence, James R. Kluegel, and Ryan A. Smith. 1997. "Laissez-Faire Racism: The Crystallization of a Kinder, Gentler Anti-Black Ideology." Pp. 15–41 in *Racial Attitudes in the 1990s: Continuity and Change,* ed. S. A. Tuch and J. K. Martin. Westport, CT: Praeger.

Bobo, Lawrence D., and Fredrick C. Licari. 1989. "Education and Political Tolerance: Testing the Effects of Cognitive Sophistication and Target Group Affect." *Public Opinion Quarterly* 53:285–308.

Bobo, Lawrence D., and Michael P. Massagli. 2001. "Stereotypes and Urban Inequality." Pp. 89–162 in *Urban Inequality in the United States: Evidence from Four Cities,* ed. A. O'Connor, C. Tilly, and L. D. Bobo. New York: Russell Sage Foundation.

Bobo, Lawrence D., and Ryan A. Smith. 1994. "Antipoverty Policy, Affirmative Action, and Racial Attitudes." Pp. 365–395 in *Confronting Poverty: Prescriptions for Change,* ed. S. H. Danziger, G. D. Sandefur, and D. H. Weinberg. Cambridge, MA: Harvard University Press.

Bobo, Lawrence D., and Susan A. Suh. 2000. "Surveying Racial Discrimination: Analyses from a Multiethnic labor Market." Pp. 523–560 in *Prismatic Metropolis: Inequality in Los Angeles,* ed. L. D. Bobo et al. New York: Russell Sage Foundation.

Bobo, Lawrence D., and Camille L. Zubrinsky. 1996. "Attitudes on Residential Integration: Perceived Status Differences, Mere In-group Preference, or Racial Prejudice?" *Social Forces* 74:883–909.

Bodenhausen, Galen C., Neil Macrae, and Jennifer Garst. 1998. "Stereotypes in Thought and Deed: Social Cognitive Origins of Intergroup Discrimination." Pp. 311–335 in *Intergroup Cognition and Intergroup Behaviors,* ed. C. Sedikides, J. Schopler, and C. A. Insko. Mahwah, NJ: Erlbaum.

Bonacich, Edna. 1972. "A Theory of Ethnic Antagonism: The Split Labor Market." *American Sociological Review* 37:547–559.

———. 1973. "A Theory of Middleman Minorities." *American Sociological Review* 398:583–594.

Boniger, David, Jon A. Krosnick, and Matthew K. Berent. 1995. "Origins of Attitude Importance: Self-Interest, Social Identification, and Value Relevance." *Journal of Personality and Social Psychology* 68:61–80.

Bonilla-Silva, Eduardo. 1997. "Re-thinking Racism: Toward A Structural Interpretation." *American Sociological Review* 62:465–480.

———. 2003. *Racism without Racists: Color-blind Racism and the Persistence of Racial Inequality in the United States.* Lanham, MD: Rowan & Littlefield.

Bordewich, Fergus M. 1996. *Killing the White Man's Indian.* New York: Anchor Books.

Boxberger, Daniel L. 1989. *To Fish in Common: The Ethnohistory of Lummi Indian Salmon Fishing.* Lincoln: University of Nebraska Press.

Bradburn, Norman M., and Seymour Sudman. 1988. *Polls and Surveys: Understanding What They Tell Us.* San Francisco: Jossey-Bass.

Brannon, Robert, et al. 1973. "Attitude and Action: A Field Experiment Joined to a General Population Survey." *American Sociological Review* 38:625–636.

Brown, Rupert. 1995. *Prejudice: Its Social Psychology.* Oxford: Blackwell.

Brubaker, Rogers. 1998. "Myths and Misconceptions in the Study of Nationalism." Pp. 272–306 in *The State of the Nation: Ernest Gellner and the Theory of Nationalism,* ed. J. Hall. New York: Cambridge University Press.

Brubaker, Rogers, and Frederick Cooper. 2000. "Beyond 'Identity.'" *Theory and Society* 29:1–47.

Burstein, Paul. 1985. *Discrimination, Jobs, and Politics: The Struggle for Equal Employment Opportunity in the United States since the New Deal.* Chicago: University of Chicago Press.

Campbell, Donald T. 1967. "Stereotypes and the Perception of Group Differences." *American Psychologist* 22:817–829.

Carmines, Edward G., and James A. Stimson. 1989. *Issue Evolution: Race and the Transformation of American Politics.* Princeton, NJ: Princeton University Press.

Chaudhuri, Joyotpaul. 1985. "American Indian Policy: An Overview." Pp. 15–34 in *American Indian Policy in the Twentieth Century*, ed. V. Deloria. Norman: University of Oklahoma Press.

Citrin, Jack, and Donald P. Green. 1990. "The Self-Interest Motive in American Public Opinion." *Research in Micropolitics* 3:1–28.

Citrin, Jack, Donald P. Green, and David O. Sears. 1990. "White Reactions to Black Candidates: When Does Race Matter?" *Public Opinion Quarterly* 54:74–96.

Citrin, Jack, et al. 1990. "The 'Official English' Movement and the Symbolic Politics of Language in the United States." *Western Political Quarterly* 43:535–559.

Cohen, Fay G. 1986. *Treaties on Trial: The Continuing Controversy over the Northwest Indian Fishing Rights.* Seattle: University of Washington Press.

Conover, Pamela Johnston. 1984. "The Influence of Group Identifications on Political Perception and Evaluation." *Journal of Politics* 46:760–785.

———. 1988. "The Role of Social Groups in Political Thinking." *British Journal of Political Science* 18:51–76.

Conover, Pamela Johnston, and Stanley Feldman. 1984. "Group Identification, Values, and the Nature of Political Beliefs." *American Politics Quarterly* 12:151–175.

Converse, Philip E. 1964. "The Nature of Belief Systems in Mass Publics." Pp. 206–261 in *Ideology and Discontent*, ed. D. E. Apter. New York: Free Press.

Cornell, Stephen. 1988. *Return of the Native: American Indian Political Resurgence.* New York: Oxford University Press.

Cornell, Stephen, and Douglas Hartmann. 1998. *Ethnicity and Race: Making Identities in a Changing World.* Thousand Oaks, CA: Pine Forge Press.

Danziger, Edmund Jefferson. 1979. *The Chippewas of Lake Superior.* Norman: University of Oklahoma Press.

Davis, James A. 1987. *Social Differences in Contemporary America.* New York: Harcourt, Brace, Jovanovich.

Davis, James A., and Tom W. Smith. 1990. *General Social Survey Cumulative Codebook: National Data Program for the Social Sciences.* Chicago: National Opinion Research Center.

Dawson, Michael C. 1994. *Behind the Mule: Race and Class in African American Politics.* Princeton, NJ: Princeton University Press.

———. 2000. "Slowly Coming to Grips with the Effects of the American Racial Order on American Policy Preferences." Pp. 344–358 in *Racialized Politics: The Debate on Racism in America*, ed. D. O. Sears, J. Sidanius, and L. D. Bobo. Chicago: University of Chicago Press.

Delli Carpini, Michael X., and Scott Keeter. 1996. *What Americans Know about Politics and Why It Matters.* New Haven, CT: Yale University Press.

Deloria, Vine. 1985. "The Evolution of Federal Indian Policy Making." Pp. 239–256 in *American Indian Policy in the Twentieth Century*, ed. V. Deloria. Norman: University of Oklahoma Press.

Deloria, Vine, and Clifford M. Lytle. 1983. *American Indians, American Justice.* Austin: University of Texas Press.

Department of Natural Resources. n.d. *A Brief Chronology of the Chippewa Treaty Rights Issue.* State of Wisconsin, Department of Natural Resources, Bureau of Fisheries Management, Office of Tribal Cooperative Management and North Central District Staff.

Downs, Anthony. 1957. *An Economic Theory of Democracy.* New York: Harper & Row.

Drinnon, Richard. 1980. *Facing West: The Metaphysics of Indian-Hating and Empire-Building.* Minneapolis: University of Minnesota Press.

Duckitt, John. 1992. *The Social Psychology of Prejudice.* New York: Praeger.

Dudziak, Mary. L. 2000. *Cold War Civil Rights: Race and the Image of American Democracy.* Princeton, NJ: Princeton University Press.

Duneier, Mitchell. 1992. *Slim's Table: Race, Respectability, and Masculinity.* Chicago: University of Chicago Press.

Ellis, Joseph J. 2001. *Founding Brothers: The Revolutionary Generation.* New York: Knopf.

Enloe, Cynthia. 1985. "The Growth of the State and Ethnic Mobilization: The American Experience." Pp. 79–88 in *Majority and Minority: The Dynamics of Race and Ethnicity in American Life,* ed. Norman R. Yetman. Boston: Allyn and Bacon.

Entman, Robert M., and Andrew Rojecki. 2000. *The Black Image in the White Mind: Media and Race in America.* Chicago: University of Chicago Press.

Esposito, Luigi, and John W. Murphy. 1999. "Desensitizing Herbert Blumer's Work on Race Relations: Recent Applications of His Group Position Theory to the Study of Contemporary Race Prejudice." *Sociological Quarterly* 40:397–410.

Esses, Victoria M., Lynne M. Jackson, and Tamara L. Armstrong. 1998. "Intergroup Competition and Attitudes toward Immigrants and Immigration: An Instrumental Model of Group Conflict." *Journal of Social Issues* 54:699–724.

Esses, Victoria M., et al. 1999. "Economic Threat and Attitudes toward Immigrants." Pp. 212–229 in *Immigrant Canada: Demographic, Economic, and Social Challenges,* ed. S. S. Halli and L. Driedger. Toronto: University of Toronto Press.

Farley, Reynolds, et al. 1994. "Stereotypes and Segregation: Neighborhoods in the Detroit Area." *American Journal of Sociology* 100:750–780.

Feagin, Joe R. 1999. "Soul-Searching in Sociology: Is the Discipline in Crisis?" *Chronicle of Higher Education,* October 15, 1999, B4.

Fishbein, Martin, and Icek Ajzen. 1975. *Belief, Attitude, Intention, and Behavior: An Introduction to Theory and Research.* Reading, MA: Addison-Wesley.

Fiske, Susan T. 1998. "Stereotyping, Prejudice, and Discrimination." Pp. 357–411 in *Handbook of Social Psychology,* vol. 2, ed. D. T. Gilbert, S. T. Fiske, and G. Lindzey. New York: McGraw-Hill.

Fixico, Donald L. 1993. "Encounter of Two Different Worlds: The Columbus-Indian Legacy of History." *American Indian Culture and Research Journal* 17 (3): 17–31.

Fortunate Eagle. 1992. *Alcatraz! Alcatraz! The Indian Occupation of 1969–1971.* Berkeley: Heyday Books.

Fossett, Mark A., and K. Jill Kiecolt. 1989. "The Relative Size of Minority Populations and White Racial Attitudes." *Social Science Quarterly* 70:820–835.

Fox, Cybelle. 2004. "The Changing Color of Welfare?: How Whites' Attitudes toward Latinos Influence Support for Welfare." *American Journal of Sociology* 110:580–625.

Franklin, John Hope, and Alfred A. Moss, Jr. 1988. *From Slavery to Freedom: A History of Negro Americans,* 6th ed. New York: Knopf.

Fredrickson, George M. 1971. *The Black Image in the White Mind: The Debate on Afro-American Character and Destiny, 1817–1914.* New York: Harper & Row.

———. 1999. "Models of American Ethnic Relations: A Historical Perspective." Pp. 23–34 in *Cultural Divides: Understanding and Overcoming Group Conflict,* ed. D. A. Prentice and D. T. Miller. New York: Russell Sage Foundation.

Fredrickson, George M. and Dale T. Knobel. 1982. "A History of Discrimination." Pp. 30–87 in *Prejudice,* ed. T. F. Pettigrew, G. M. Fredrickson, and N. Glazer. Cambridge, MA: Belknap Press of Harvard University Press.

Gans, Herbert J. 1999. "The Possibility of a New Racial Hierarchy in the Twenty-first Century United States." Pp. 371–390 in *The Cultural Territories of Race: Black and White Boundaries,* ed. M. Lamont. New York and Cambridge, MA: Russell Sage Foundation and Harvard University Press.

Garland, David, ed. 2001. *Mass Imprisonment: Social Causes and Consequences.* Thousand Oaks, CA: Sage.

Gerstle, Gary. 2001. *American Crucible: Race and Nation in the Twentieth Century.* Princeton, NJ: Princeton University Press.

Gibson, James R. 1976. *Imperial Russia in Frontier America: The Changing Geography of Supply of Russian America, 1784–1867.* New York: Oxford University Press.

Gilens, Martin I. 1999. *Why Americans Hate Welfare: Race, Media, and the Politics of Antipoverty Policy.* Chicago: University of Chicago Press.

Giles, Michael W., and Arthur S. Evans. 1986. "The Power Approach to Intergroup Hostility." *Journal of Conflict Resolution* 30:469–486.

Glaser, James M. 1994. "Back to the Black Belt: Racial Environment and White Racial Attitudes in the South." *Journal of Politics* 56:21–41.

———. 2003. "Social Context and Inter-Group Political Attitudes: Experiments in Group Conflict Theory." *British Journal of Political Science* 33:607–620.

Glazer, Nathan. 1975. *Affirmative Discrimination: Ethnic Inequality and Public Policy.* New York: Basic Books.

Great Lakes Indian Fish and Wildlife Commission. 1990. *A Guide to Understanding Chippewa Treaty Rights.* Odanah, WI: Great Lakes Indian Fish and Wildlife Commission.

———. 1994. *A Guide to Understanding Chippewa Treaty Rights,* updated ed. Odanah, WI: Great Lakes Indian Fish and Wildlife Commission.

Green, Donald Philip, and Jonathan Cowden. 1992. "Who Protests: Self-Interest and White Opposition to Busing." *Journal of Politics* 54:471–496.

Gross, Emma. 1989. *Contemporary Federal Policy toward American Indians.* New York: Greenwood Press.

Hanaway, Donald. 1990. *History of the Chippewa Treaty Rights Controversy.* State of Wisconsin, Department of Justice, Attorney General's Office (March 1990).

Herbst, Susan. 1993. *Numbered Voices: How Opinion Polling Has Shaped American Politics.* Chicago: University of Chicago Press.

Hochschild, Jennifer L. 1984. *The New American Dilemma: Liberal Democracy and School Desegregation.* New Haven, CT: Yale University Press.

———. 2000. "Lumpers and Splitters, Individuals and Structures: Comments on Racialized Politics." Pp. 324–343 in *Racialized Politics: The Debate on Racism in America,* ed. D. O. Sears, J. Sidanius, and L. D. Bobo. Chicago: University of Chicago Press.

Horsman, Reginald. 1981. *Race and Manifest Destiny: The Origins of American Racial Anglo-Saxonism.* Cambridge, MA: Harvard University Press.

House, James S. 1981. "Social Structure and Personality." Pp. 525–561 in *Social Psychology: Sociological Perspectives,* ed. M. Rosenberg and R. H. Turner. New York: Basic Books.

Huber, Joan, and William H. Form. 1973. *Income and Ideology: An Analysis of the American Political Formula.* New York: Free Press.

Huddy, Leonie, and David O. Sears. 1995. "Opposition to Bilingual Education: Prejudice or the Defense of Realistic Interests?" *Social Psychology Quarterly* 58:133–143.

Hughes, Michael. 1997. "Symbolic Racism, Old-Fashioned Racism, and Whites' Opposition to Affirmative Action." Pp. 45–75 in *Racial Attitudes in the 1990s: Continuities and Change,* ed. S. A. Tuch and J. K. Martin. Westport, CT: Praeger.

Hurwitz, Jonathan, and Mark Peffley. 2005. "Playing the Race Card in the Post–Willie Horton Era: The Impact of Racial Code Words on Support for Punitive Crime Policy." *Public Opinion Quarterly* 69:99–112.

Hutchings, Vincent L. 2003. *Public Opinion and Democratic Accountability: How Citizens Learn about Politics.* Princeton, NJ: Princeton University Press.

Hyman, Herbert, H. Charles R. Wright, and John S. Reed. 1975. *The Enduring Effects of Education.* Chicago: University of Chicago Press.

Jackman, Mary R. 1976. "The Relation between Verbal Attitude and Overt Behavior: A Public Opinion Application." *Social Forces* 54:646–668.

———. 1977. "Prejudice, Tolerance, and Attitudes toward Ethnic Groups." *Social Science Research* 6:145–169.

———. 1994. *The Velvet Glove: Paternalism and Conflict in Gender, Class, and Race Relations.* Berkeley, CA: University of California Press.

Jackman, Mary R., and Michael J. Muha. 1984. "Education and Intergroup Attitudes: Normative Enlightenment, Superficial Democratic Commitment, or Ideological Refinement?" *American Sociological Review* 49:751–769.

Jennings, Francis. 1975. *The Invasion of America: Indians, Colonialism, and the Cant of Conquest.* Chapel Hill: Institute of Early American History and Culture, University of North Carolina.

Johnson, Devon. 2001. "Punitive Attitudes on Crime: Economic Insecurity, Racial Prejudice, or Both?" *Sociological Focus* 24:33–54.

Jordan, Winthrop D. 1968. *White over Black: American Attitudes toward the Negro, 1550–1812.* Chapel Hill: University of North Carolina Press.

Joreskog, K. G. 1967. "Some Contributions to Maximum Likelihood Factor Analysis." *Psychometrika* 32:443–482.

———. 1969. "A General Approach to Confirmatory Factor Analysis." *Psychometrika* 34:183–202.

Joreskog, K. G., and D. Sorbom. 1989. LISREL. Mooresville, IN: Scientific Software.

Jorgensen, Joseph G. 1978. "A Century of Political Economic Effects on American Indian Society, 1880–1980." *Journal of Ethnic Studies* 6 (3): 1–82.

Kane, Emily W., and Howard Schuman. 1991. "Open Survey Questions as Measures of Personal Concern with Issues: A Reanalysis of Stouffer's Communism, Conformity, and Civil Liberties." *Sociological Methodology* 21:81–96.

Katz, Irwin. 1991. "Gordon W. Allport's *The Nature of Prejudice.*" *Political Psychology* 12:125–157.

Kaufmann, Karen M. 1998. "Racial Conflict and Political Choice: A Study of Mayoral Voting Behavior in Los Angeles and New York." *Urban Affairs Review* 33:655–685.

———. 2004. *The Urban Voter: Group Conflict and Mayoral Voting Behavior in American Cities.* Ann Arbor: University of Michigan Press.

Kelman, Herbert. 1974. "Attitudes are Alive and Well and Gainfully Employed in the Sphere of Action." *American Psychologist* 29:310–324.

Keshin, Rita. 1974. "The Role of American Indians in Motion Pictures." *American Indian Culture and Research Journal* 1 (2): 25–28.

Killian, Lewis M. 1970. "Herbert Blumer's Contributions to Race Relations." Pp. 179–192 in *Human Nature and Collective Behavior: Papers in Honor of Herbert Blumer,* ed. T. Shibutani. Englewood Cliffs, NJ: Prentice Hall.

Kim, Claire Jean. 2000. *Bitter Fruit: The Politics of Black-Korean Conflict in New York City.* New Haven, CT: Yale University Press.

Kinder, Donald R. 1998. "Opinion and Action in the Realm of Politics." Pp. 778–867 in *The Handbook of Social Psychology,* 4th ed., ed. D. Gilbert, S. Fiske, and G. Lindzey. New York: Random House.

Kinder, Donald R., and Tali Mendelberg. 2000. "Individualism Reconsidered: Principles and Prejudice in Contemporary American Opinion." Pp. 44–74 in *Racialized Politics: The Debate on Racism in America,* ed. D. O. Sears, J. Sidanius, and L. Bobo. Chicago: University of Chicago Press.

Kinder, Donald R., and Lynn M. Sanders. 1996. *Divided by Color: Racial Politics and Democratic Ideals.* Chicago: University of Chicago Press.

Kinder, Donald R., and Howard Schuman. 2004. "Racial Attitudes: Developments and Divisions in Survey Research." Pp. 365–392 in *A Telescope on Society: Survey Research and Social Science in the 20th and 21st Centuries,* ed. J. House et al. Ann Arbor: University of Michigan Press.

Kinder, Donald R., and David O. Sears. 1981. "Prejudice and Politics: Symbolic Racism versus Racial Threats to the Good Life." *Journal of Personality and Social Psychology* 40:414–431.

Kiser, Edgar, and Michael Hechter. 1991. "The Role of General Theory in Comparative Historical Sociology." *American Journal of Sociology* 97:1–30.

———. 1998. "The Debate on Historical Sociology: Rational Choice and Its Critics." *American Journal of Sociology* 104:785–816.

Klinkner, Philip, and Rogers Smith. 1999. *The Unsteady March: The Rise and Decline of Racial Equality in America.* Chicago: University of Chicago Press.

Kluegel, James R., and Eliot R. Smith. 1986. *Beliefs about Inequality: Americans' Views of What Is and What Ought to Be.* New York: Aldine de Gruyter.

Kohn, Melvin L. 1989. "Social Structure and Personality: A Quintessentially Sociological Approach to Social Psychology." *Social Forces* 68:26–33.

Krysan, Maria. 1998. "Privacy and the Expression of White Racial Attitudes: A Comparison across Three Contexts." *Public Opinion Quarterly* 62:506–544.

———. 1999. "Qualifying a Quantifying Analysis on Racial Equality." *Social Psychology Quarterly* 62:211–218.

———. 2000. "Prejudice, Politics, and Public Opinion: Understanding the Sources of Racial Policy Attitudes." *Annual Review of Sociology* 26:135–168.

Krysan, Maria, and Reynolds Farley. 2002. "The Residential Preferences of Blacks: Do They Explain Persistent Segregation?" *Social Forces* 80:937–980.

Lacy, Michael G. 1985. "The United States and American Indians: Political Relations." Pp. 83–104 in *American Indian Policy in the Twentieth Century,* ed. V. Deloria. Norman: University of Oklahoma Press.

Lal, Barbara. 1986. "The 'Chicago School' of American Sociology, Symbolic Interactionism, and Race Relations Theory." Pp. 280–298 in *Theories of Race and Ethnic Relations,* ed. J. Rex and D. Mason. New York: Cambridge University Press.

———. 1995. "Symbolic Interaction Theories." *American Behavioral Scientist* 38:421–441.

Lamont, Michele. 2000. *The Dignity of Working Men: Morality and the Boundaries of Race, Class, and Immigration.* Cambridge, MA: Harvard University Press.

LaPiere, Richard T. 1934. "Attitudes vs. Actions." *Social Forces* 13:230–237.

Law, John, and Peter Lodge. 1978. "Structure as Process and Environmental Constraint." *Theory and Society* 5:373–386.

Lee, Jennifer. 2002. "From Civil Relations to Racial Conflict: Merchant-Customer Interactions in Urban America." *American Sociological Review* 67:77–98.

Lee, Taeku. 2002. *Mobilizing Public Opinion: Black Insurgency and Racial Attitudes in the Civil Rights Era.* Chicago: University of Chicago Press.

LeVine, Robert A., and Donald T. Campbell. 1971. *Ethnocentrism: Theories of Conflict, Ethnic Attitudes, and Group Behavior.* New York: John Wiley & Sons.

Lieberman, Robert C. 1998. *Shifting the Color Line: Race and the American Welfare State.* Cambridge, MA: Harvard University Press.

Lieberson, Stanley. 1961. "A Societal Theory of Race and Ethnic Relations." *American Sociological Review* 26:902–910.

———. 1991. "Small N's and Big Conclusions: An Examination of the Reasoning in Comparative Studies Based on a Small Number of Cases." *Social Forces* 70:307–320.

Lippmann, Walter. 1922. *Public Opinion.* New York: Free Press.

Loew, Patty. 1990. *Spring of Discontent.* Ann Arbor: University of Michigan Media Resource Center. Video.

Long, J. Scott. 1983. *Confirmatory Factor Analysis: A Preface to LISREL.* Sage University Paper Series on Quantitative Applications in the Social Sciences 07-033. Beverly Hills and London: Sage Publications.

Lurie, Nancy Oestrich. 1978. "The Indian Claims Commission." *Annals of the American Academy of Political and Social Science* 436:97–110.

Lyman, Stanford M. 1990. *Civilization: Contents, Discontents, Malcontents, and Other Essays in Social Theory.* Fayetteville: University of Arkansas Press.

McAdam, Doug. 1982. *Political Process and the Development of Black Insurgency, 1930–1970.* Chicago: University of Chicago Press.

McClendon, McKee J. 1985. "Racism, Rational Choice, and White Opposition to Racial Change: A Case Study of Busing." *Public Opinion Quarterly* 49:214–233.

McClendon, McKee J., and Fred P. Pestello. 1982. "White Opposition: To Busing or to Desegregation." *Social Science Quarterly* 63:70–82.

———. 1983. "Self-Interest and Public Policy Attitude Formation: Busing for School Desegregation." *Sociological Focus* 16:1–12.

McCloskey, Herbert, and Alida Brill. 1983. *Dimensions of Tolerance: What Americans Believe about Civil Liberties.* New York: Russell Sage Foundation.

McConahay, John B. 1982. "Self-Interest versus Racial Attitudes as Correlates of Anti-busing Attitudes in Louisville: Is It the Buses or the Blacks?" *Journal of Politics* 44:692–720.

————. 1986. "Modern Racism, Ambivalence, and the Modern Racism Scale." Pp. 91–125 in *Prejudice, Discrimination, and Racism*, ed. J. F. Dovidio and S. Gaertner. Orlando: Academic Press.

McConahay, John B., Betty B. Hardee, and Valerie Batts. 1981. "Has Racism Declined in America?: It Depends on Who Is Asking and What Is Asked." *Journal of Conflict Resolution* 25:563–579.

McKee, James B. 1993. *Sociology and the Race Problem: The Failure of a Perspective.* Chicago: University of Illinois Press.

Meertens, R., and Thomas F. Pettigrew. 1997. "Is Subtle Prejudice Really Prejudice?" *Public Opinion Quarterly* 61:54–71.

Mendelberg, Tali. 2001. *The Race Card: Campaign Strategy, Implicit Messages, and the Norm of Equality.* Princeton, NJ: Princeton University Press.

Middleton, Russell. 1976. "Regional Differences in Prejudice." *American Sociological Review* 41:94–117.

Mills, Charles W. 1997. *The Racial Contract.* Ithaca, NY: Cornell University Press.

Moloney, Francis X. 1967. *The Fur Trade in New England 1620–1676.* Hamden, CT: Archon Books.

Morris, Aldon D. 1984. *The Origins of the Civil Rights Movement: Black Communities Organizing for Change.* New York: Free Press.

Nagel, Joane. 1996. *American Indian Ethnic Renewal.* New York: Oxford University Press.

Nash, Gary. 1974. *Red, White, and Black: The Peoples of Early America.* Englewood Cliffs, NJ: Prentice Hall.

Newcomb, Theodore M. 1948. "Public Opinion and Public Opinion Polling: Discussion." *American Sociological Review* 13:549–552.

O'Brien, Sharon. 1989. *American Indian Tribal Governments.* Norman: University of Oklahoma Press.

O'Connor, Alice. 2001. *Poverty Knowledge: Social Science, Social Policy, and the Poor in Twentieth-Century U.S. History.* Princeton, NJ: Princeton University Press.

Omi, Michael, and Howard Winant. 1986. *Racial Formation in the United States from the 1960s to the 1980s.* New York: Routledge.

Page, Benjamin I., and Robert Y. Shapiro. 1992. *The Rational Public: Fifty Years of Trends in American Policy Preferences.* Chicago: University of Chicago Press.

Pearce, Roy Harvey. 1957. "The Metaphysics of Indian-Hating." *Ethnohistory* 4:27–40.

Peffley, Mark, and Jon Hurwitz. 1998. "Whites' Stereotypes of Blacks: Sources and Political Consequences." Pp. 58–99 in *Perception and Prejudice: Race and Politics in the United States*, ed. J. Hurwitz and M. Peffley. New Haven, CT: Yale University Press.

Pettigrew, Thomas F. 1971. "When a Black Candidate Runs for Mayor: Race and

Voting Behavior." Pp. 99–105 in *People and Politics in Urban Society*, ed. H. Hahn. Beverly Hills, CA: Sage.

———. 1980. "The Changing–Not Declining Significance of Race." *Contemporary Sociology* 9:19–21.

———. 1981. "Race and Class in the 1980s: An Interactive View." *Daedalus* 110:233–255.

———. 1982. "Prejudice." Pp. 1–29 in *Prejudice*, ed. T. F. Pettigrew, G. Fredrickson, and N. Glazer. Cambridge, MA: Belknap Press of Harvard University Press.

———. 1998. "Reactions to the New Minorities of Western Europe." *Annual Review of Sociology* 24: 77–103.

———. 2002. "Summing Up: Relative Deprivation as a Key Social Psychological Concept." Pp. 351–373 in *Relative Deprivation: Specification, Development, and Integration*, ed. I. Walker and H. J. Smith. New York: Cambridge University Press.

Pettigrew, Thomas F., and D. A. Alston. 1988. *Tom Bradley's Campaigns for Governor: The Dilemma of Race and Political Strategies*. Washington, DC: Joint Center for Political Studies.

Pettigrew, Thomas F., et al. 1998. "Out Group Prejudice in Western Europe." *European Review of Social Psychology* 8:241–273.

Petty, Richard, Daniel T. Wegener, and L. R. Fabrigar. 1997. "Attitudes and Attitude Change." *Annual Review of Psychology* 48:609–647.

Pinderhughes, Howard. 1993. "The Anatomy of Racially Motivated Violence in New York City: A Case Study of Youth in Southern Brooklyn." *Social Problems* 40:478–492.

Price, Vincent L. 1989. "Social Identification and Public Opinion: Effects of Communicating Group Conflict." *Public Opinion Quarterly* 53:197–224.

———. 1992. *Communication Concepts 4: Public Opinion*. Newbury Park, CA: Sage.

Prothro, James W., and Charles M. Grigg. 1960. "Fundamental Principles of Democracy: Bases of Agreement and Disagreement." *Journal of Politics* 22:276–294.

Prucha, Francis P. 1984. *The Great Father: The United States Government and the American Indians*. Lincoln: University of Nebraska Press.

Quadagno, Jill. 1994. *The Color of Welfare: How Racism Undermined the War on Poverty*. New York: Oxford University Press.

Quillian, Lincoln. 1995. "Prejudice as a Response to Perceived Group Threat: Population Composition and Anti-Immigrant and Racial Prejudice in Europe." *American Sociological Review* 60: 586–611.

———. 1996. "Group Threat and Regional Change in Attitudes toward African Americans." *American Journal of Sociology* 102:816–860.

Rieder, Jonathan. 1985. *Canarsie: The Jews and Italians of Brooklyn against Liberalism.* Cambridge, MA: Harvard University Press.

Rose, Arnold M. 1956. "Intergroup Relations vs. Prejudice: Pertinent Theory for the Study of Social Change." *Social Problems* 4:173–176.

Roth, Byron M. 1990. "Social Psychology's 'Racism.'" *The Public Interest* 98:26–36.

Sachdev, Itesh, and Richard Y. Bourhis. 1991. "Power and Status Differences in Minority and Majority Group Relations." *European Journal of Social Psychology* 21:1–24.

Satz, Ronald N. 1991. *Chippewa Treaty Rights: The Reserved Rights of Wisconsin's Chippewa Indians in Historical Perspective.* Madison: Wisconsin Academy of Sciences, Arts, and Letters.

Schuman, Howard. 1966. "The Random Probe: A Technique for Evaluating the Validity of Closed Questions." *American Sociological Review* 31:218–222.

————. 1972. "Attitudes vs. Actions versus Attitudes vs. Attitudes." *Public Opinion Quarterly* 36:347–354.

————. 1982. "Artifacts Are in the Mind of the Beholder." *American Sociologist* 17:21–28.

————. 1995. "Attitudes, Beliefs, and Behaviors." Pp. 68–89 in *Sociological Perspectives on Social Psychology,* ed. K. S. Cook, G. A Fine, and J. S. House. Boston: Allyn & Bacon.

Schuman, Howard, and John Harding. 1963. "Sympathetic Identification with the Underdog." *Public Opinion Quarterly* 27:230–241.

————. 1964. "Prejudice and the Norm of Rationality." *Sociometry* 27:353–371.

Schuman, Howard, and Graham Kalton. 1985. "Survey Methods." Pp. in *The Handbook of Social Psychology,* 3rd ed., ed. G. Lindzey and E. Aronson. New York: Random House.

Schuman, Howard, and Stanley Presser. 1981. *Questions and Answers in Attitude Surveys: Experiments on Question Form, Wording, and Context.* New York: Academic Press.

Schuman, Howard, et al. 1997. *Racial Attitudes in America: Trends and Interpretations,* rev. ed. Cambridge, MA: Harvard University Press.

Sears, David O. 1986. "College Sophomores in the Lab: Influences of a Narrow Database on Social Psychological Views of Human Nature." *Journal of Personality and Social Psychology* 51:515–530.

————. 1987. "Political Psychology." *Annual Review of Psychology* 38:229–255.

————. 1988. "Symbolic Racism." Pp. 53–84 in *Eliminating Racism: Profiles in Controversy,* ed. P. A. Katz and D. A. Taylor. New York: Plenum.

Sears, David O., and Harris M. Allen. 1984. "The Trajectory of Local Desegregation Controversies and Whites' Opposition to Busing." Pp. 123–151 in *Groups in Contact: The Psychology of Desegregation,* ed. N. Miller and M. B. Brewer. New York: Academic Press.

Sears, David O., and Jack Citrin. 1985. *Tax Revolt: Something for Nothing in California*. Cambridge, MA: Harvard University Press.

Sears, David O., Jack Citrin, and Richard Kosterman. 1987. "Jesse Jackson and the Southern White Electorate in 1984." Pp. 209–225 in *Blacks in Southern Politics*, ed. R. P. Steed, L. W. Moreland, and T. A. Baker. New York: Praeger.

Sears, David O., and Carolyn L. Funk. 1990. "Self-Interest in Americans' Political Opinions." Pp. 147–170 in *Beyond Self-Interest*, ed. J. Mansbridge. Chicago: University of Chicago Press.

Sears, David O., P. J. Henry, and Rick Kosterman. 2000. "Egalitarian Values and Contemporary Racial Politics." Pp. 75–117 in *Racialized Politics: The Debate on Racism in America*, ed. D. O. Sears, J. Sidanius, and L. Bobo. Chicago: University of Chicago Press.

Sears, David O., and Donald R. Kinder. 1985. "Whites' Opposition to Busing: On Conceptualizing and Operationalizing Group Conflict." *Journal of Personality and Social Psychology* 48:1148–1161.

Sears, David O., and John B. McConahay. 1973. *The Politics of Violence: The New Urban Blacks and the Watts Riot*. Boston: Houghton Mifflin.

Sears, David O., et al. 1997. "Is It Really Racism?: The Origins of White Americans' Opposition to Race-Targeted Policies." *Public Opinion Quarterly* 61:16–53.

———. 1999. "Cultural Diversity and Multicultural Politics: Is Ethnic Balkanization Inevitable?" Pp. 35–79 in *Cultural Divides: Understanding and Overcoming Group Conflict*, ed. D. A. Prentice and D. T. Miller. New York: Russell Sage Foundation.

———. 2000. "Race in American Politics." Pp. 1–43 in *Racialized Politics: The Debate on Racism in America*, ed. D. O. Sears, J. Sidanius, and L. Bobo. Chicago: University of Chicago Press.

Selznick, Gertrude J., and Stephen Steinberg. 1969. *The Tenacity of Prejudice: Anti-Semitism in Contemporary America*. Westport, CT: Greenwood Publishers.

Sheatsley, Paul B. 1983. "Questionnaire Construction and Item Writing." Pp. 195–230 in *Handbook of Survey Research*, ed. P. Rossi, J. D. Right, and A. B. Anderson. New York: Academic Press.

Sherif, Muzafer, et al. 1988 (1961). *The Robbers Cave Experiment: Intergroup Conflict and Cooperation*. Middletown, CT: Wesleyan University Press.

Sidanius, Jim, and Felicia Pratto. 1999. *Social Dominance: An Intergroup Theory of Social Hierarchy and Oppression*. New York: Cambridge University Press.

Sidanius, Jim, Felicia Pratto, and Lawrence D. Bobo. 1994. "Social Dominance Orientation and the Political Psychology of Gender: A Case of Invariance?" *Journal of Personality and Social Psychology* 67:998–1011.

———. 1996. "Racism, Conservatism, Affirmative Action, and Intellectual Sophistication: A Matter of Principled Conservatism or Group Dominance?" *Journal of Personality and Social Psychology* 70:476–490.

Sidanius, Jim, et al. 2000. "It's Not Affirmative Action, It's the Blacks: The Continuing Relevance of Race in American Politics." Pp. 191–235 in *Racialized Politics: The Debate on Racism in America,* ed. D. O. Sears, J. Sidanius, and L. D. Bobo. Chicago: University of Chicago Press.

Simpson, George E., and J. Milton Yinger. 1985. *Racial and Cultural Minorities: An Analysis of Prejudice and Discrimination,* 5th ed. New York: Harper & Row.

Sitkoff, Harvard. 1981. *The Struggle for Black Equality, 1954–1980.* New York: Hill and Wang.

Sivacek, J., and W. D. Crano. 1982. "Vested Interest as a Moderator of Attitude-Behavior Consistency." *Journal of Personality and Social Psychology* 43:210–221.

Smith, A. Wade. 1981. "Racial Tolerance as a Function of Group Position." *American Sociological Review* 46:558–573.

Smith, Eliot R. 1993. "Social Identity and Social Emotions: Towards New Conceptualizations of Prejudice." Pp. 297–315 in *Affect, Cognition, and Stereotyping,* ed. D. Mackie and D. Hamilton. San Diego: Academic Press.

Smith, Eliot R., and Colin Ho. 2002. "Prejudice as Intergroup Emotion: Integrating Relative Deprivation and Social Comparison Explanations of Prejudice." Pp. 332–348 in *Relative Deprivation: Specification, Development and Integration,* ed. I. Walker and H. J. Smith. New York: Cambridge University Press.

Smith, Rogers M. 1993. "Beyond Tocqueville, Myrdal, and Hartz: The Multiple Traditions in America." *American Political Science Review* 87:549–566.

Sniderman, Paul M., and Edward Carmines. 1997. *Reaching Beyond Race.* Cambridge, MA: Harvard University Press.

Sniderman, Paul M., and Michael G. Hagen. 1986. *Race and Inequality: A Study in American Values.* Chatham, NJ: Chatham House.

Sniderman, Paul M., and Tom Piazza. 1993. *The Scar of Race.* Cambridge, MA: Harvard University Press.

Sniderman, Paul M., and Philip E. Tetlock. 1986a. "Reflections on American Racism." *Journal of Social Issues* 42:173–187.

———. 1986b. "Symbolic Racism: Problems of Motive Attribution in Political Analysis." *Journal of Social Issues* 42:129–150.

Snipp, C. Matthew. 1989. *American Indians: The First of This Land.* New York: Russell Sage Foundation.

Sowell, Thomas. 1984. *Civil Rights: Rhetoric or Reality?* New York: Morrow.

Spicer, Edward H. 1980. *The American Indians: Dimensions of Ethnicity.* Cambridge, MA: Harvard University Press.

Steinback, David C. 1977. "White Nationalism and Native Cultures." *American Indian Culture and Research Journal* 2 (1): 9–13.

Steinberg, Stephen. 1980. *The Ethnic Myth: Race, Ethnicity, and Class in America.* New York: Atheneum.

———. 1989. *The Ethnic Myth: Race, Ethnicity, and Class in America,* expanded ed. Boston: Beacon Press.

―――. 1995. *Turning Back: The Retreat from Racial Justice in American Thought and Policy.* Boston: Beacon Press.

Stephan, Walter G., and David Rosenfield. 1982. "Racial and Ethnic Stereotypes." Pp. 92–136 in *In the Eye of the Beholder: Contemporary Issues in Stereotyping,* ed. A. G. Miller. New York: Praeger.

Stephan, Walter G., and Cookie White Stephan. 1984. "The Role of Ignorance in Intergroup Relations." Pp. 229–257 in *Groups in Contact: The Psychology of Desegregation,* ed. N. Miller and M. B. Brewer. New York: Academic Press.

Stinchcombe, Arthur L., and D. Garth Taylor. 1980. "On Democracy and Integration." Pp. 157–186 in *School Desegregation: Past, Present, and Future,* ed. W. G. Stephan and J. R. Feagin. New York: Plenum.

Stone, Jonathan. 1985. *Racial Conflict in Contemporary Society.* Cambridge, MA: Harvard University Press.

Stouffer, Samuel A. 1955. *Communism, Conformity, and Civil Liberties.* New York: Doubleday.

Strickland, Rennard, Stephen J. Herzberg, and Steven R. Owens. 1990. *Keeping Our Word: Indian Treaty Rights and Public Responsibilities: A Report on a Recommended Federal Role Following Wisconsin's Request for Federal Assistance.* Madison: University of Wisconsin Law School.

Suh, Susan A. 2000. "Women's Perceptions of Workplace Discrimination: Impacts of Racial Group, Gender, and Class." Pp. 561–596 in *Prismatic Metropolis: Inequality in Los Angeles,* ed. L. D. Bobo et al. New York: Russell Sage Foundation.

Tajfel, Henri. 1969. "Cognitive Aspects of Prejudice." *Journal of Social Issues* 25:79–97.

―――. 1981. *Human Groups and Social Categories.* London: Cambridge University Press.

―――. 1982. "The Social Psychology of Intergroup Relations." *Annual Review of Psychology* 33:1–39.

Takaki, Ronald T. 1979. *Iron Cages: Race and Culture in 19th-Century America.* Seattle: University of Washington Press.

―――. 1994. "Reflections on Racial Patterns in America." Pp. 24–36 in *From Different Shores: Perspectives on Race and Ethnicity in America,* ed. R. Takaki. New York: Oxford University Press.

Taub, Richard P., D. Garth Taylor, and Jan D. Dunham. 1984. *Paths of Neighborhood Change: Race and Crime in Urban America.* Chicago: University of Chicago Press.

Taylor, D. Garth. 1986. *Public Opinion and Collective Action: The Boston School Desegregation Conflict.* Chicago: University of Chicago Press.

Taylor, Marylee C. 1998. "How White Attitudes Vary with the Racial Composition of Local Populations: Numbers Count." *American Sociological Review* 63:512–535.

Tetlock, Philip E. 1994. "Political Psychology or Politicized Psychology: Is the Road to Scientific Hell Paved with Good Moral Intentions? *Political Psychology* 15:509–529.

Thernstrom, Stephan, and Abigail Thernstrom. 1997. *America in Black and White: One Nation, Indivisible.* New York: Simon & Schuster.

Thornton, Russell. 1987. *American Indian Holocaust and Survival: A Population History since 1492.* Norman: University of Oklahoma Press.

Tocqueville, Alexis de. 1969 (1848). *Democracy in America.* New York: Harper and Row.

Trimble, Joseph E. 1988. "Stereotypical Images, American Indians, and Prejudice. Pp. 181–202 in *Eliminating Racism,* ed. Phyllis A. Katz and Dalmas A. Taylor. New York: Plenum Press.

Tuan, Mia. 1995. "Korean and Russian Students in a Los Angeles High School: Exploring the Alternative Strategies of Two High-Achieving Groups." Pp. 107–130 in *California's Immigrant Children: Theory, Research, and Implications for Educational Policy,* ed. R. G. Rumbaut and W. A. Cornelius. San Diego: Center for U.S.-Mexican Studies, University of California, San Diego.

———. 1999a. *Forever Foreigners or Honorary Whites? The Asian Ethnic Experience Today.* New Brunswick, NJ: Rutgers University Press.

———. 1999b. "Neither Real Americans nor Real Asians? Multigenerational Asian Ethnics Navigating the Terrain of Authenticity." *Qualitative Sociology* 22:105–125.

Turner, Ralph H. 1969. "The Public Perception of Protest." *American Sociological Review* 34:815–831.

———. 1988. "Personality in Society: Social Psychology's Contribution to Sociology." *Social Psychology Quarterly* 51:1–10.

Tyler, S. Lyman. 1973. *A History of Indian Policy.* Bureau of Indian Affairs. Washington, DC: U.S. Government Printing Office.

Tyler, Tom R. 1990a. "Justice, Self-Interest, and the Legitimacy of Legal and Political Authority." Pp. 171–182 in *Beyond Self-Interest,* ed. J. Mansbridge. Chicago: University of Chicago Press.

———. 1990b. *Why People Obey the Law.* New Haven, CT: Yale University Press.

U.S. Commission on Civil Rights. 1989. *Discrimination against the Chippewa Indians in Northern Wisconsin: Summary Report of the Wisconsin Advisory Committee.* Washington DC: U.S. Government Printing Office.

U.S. Department of the Interior. 1991. *Casting Light upon the Waters: A Joint Fishery Assessment of the Wisconsin Ceded Territory.* Minneapolis: Bureau of Indian Affairs.

Useem, Bert. 1980. "Solidarity Model, Breakdown Model, and the Boston Antibusing Movement." *American Sociological Review* 45:357–369.

Vizenor, Gerald. 1972. *The Everlasting Sky: New Voices from the People Named the Chippewa.* New York: Crowell-Collier Press.

———. 1984. *The People Named the Chippewa.* Minneapolis: University of Minnesota Press.

Wacquant, Loic. 2001. "Deadly Symbiosis: When Ghetto and Prison Meet and

Mesh." Pp. 82–120 in *Mass Imprisonment: Social Causes and Consequences*, ed. D. Garland. Thousand Oaks, CA: Sage.

———. 2002. "Scrutinizing the Street: Poverty, Morality, and the Pitfalls of Urban Ethnography." *American Journal of Sociology* 107:1468–1532.

Waldinger, Roger. 1996. *Still the Promised City?: African Americans and the New Immigrants in Post-Industrial New York*. Cambridge, MA: Harvard University Press.

Walsh, Edward J. 1981. "Resource Mobilization and Citizen Protest in Communities around Three Mile Island." *Social Problems* 29:1–21.

Waters, Mary C. 1990. *Ethnic Options: Choosing Identities in America*. Berkeley: University of California Press.

———. 1999. *Black Identities: West Indian Immigrant Dreams and American Realities*. Cambridge, MA: Harvard University Press.

Weigel, Russel H., and L. Newman. 1976. "Increasing Attitude-Behavior Correspondence by Broadening the Scope of the Behavior Measure." *Journal of Personality and Social Psychology* 33:793–802.

Wellman, David T. 1977. *Portraits of White Racism*. New York: Cambridge University Press.

Weyler, Rex. 1983. *Blood of the Land: The Government and Corporate War against the American Indian Movement*. New York: Everest House.

White, Robert H. 1990. *Tribal Assets: The Rebirth of Native America*. New York: Henry Holt and Company.

Williams, Robin M. Jr. 1965. "Social Change and Social Conflict: Race Relations in the United States, 1944–1964." *Sociological Inquiry* 35:8–25.

Willie, Charles V. 1989. "The Inclining Significance of Race." Pp. 10–21 in *The Caste and Class Controversy on Race and Poverty: Round Two of the Willie/Wilson Debate*, ed. C. V. Willie. Dix Hills, NY: General Hall.

Wilson, William J. 1973. *Power, Racism, and Privilege: Race Relations in Theoretical and Sociohistorical Perspectives*. New York: Free Press.

———. 1978. *The Declining Significance of Race: Blacks and Changing American Institutions*. Chicago: University of Chicago Press.

Winant, Howard. 2000. "Race and Race Theory." *Annual Review of Sociology* 26:169–185.

Woodward, Julian 1948. "Public Opinion and Public Opinion Polling: Discussion." *American Sociological Review* 13:552–554.

Young, Jason, et al. 1987. "Personal Agendas and the Relationship between Self-Interest and Voting Behavior." *Social Psychology Quarterly* 50:64–71.

Zaller, John R. 1992. *The Nature and Origins of Mass Opinion*. New York: Cambridge University Press.

Zuberi, Tukufu. 2001. *Thicker Than Blood: How Racial Statistics Lie*. Minneapolis: University of Minnesota Press.

INDEX

Adorno, Theodore, 15, 114
Affirmative action, 2, 19, 23, 31, 38, 217
African Americans (blacks), vii, 8, 29, 37, 39, 59, 217–218; affect toward, 29; compared with Indians, 3–4, 120–121; electoral candidates, 18; intermarriage with, 115; stereotypes of, 29, 114, 123
Age effects, 118
Ajzen, Icek, 17
Alaska Native Claim Settlement Act (1971), 62
Alker, Henry, 18–19
Almaguer, Tomas, 13, 16, 38
Altemeyer, Bob, 114
Allport, Gordon W., 7, 15, 29, 44, 106, 215
Alston, D., 18
Anti-Semitism, 114
Appropriation Act (1871), 55
Armstrong, Virginia, 54
Arey, Bette, 75
Asian Americans, 8, 23
Attewell, Paul, 16
Attitudes, 264n1; Blumer critique, 14–15; issue centrality or importance, 46, 186–189, 232–233; complexity of, 16, 21; defined, 16; relation to behavior, 16–18, 193–195, 210
Authoritarianism, 15, 114, 247n7
Axtell, James, 67

Bataille, Gretchen, 65, 67
Beckett, Katherine, 219
Begley, Thomas, 18
Behavioral involvement, 46, 191, 194, 210–211; measures, 191–192, 233; relation to

attitudes, 192–193; relation to issue importance, 192–194; relation to self-interest, 192, 193
Benford, Robert, 179
Berent, Matthew, 179
Berger, Thomas, 62, 63
Berkhofer, Robert F., 53, 65, 70
Bilingualism, attitudes toward, 7, 23
Blacks. *See* African Americans
Blauner, Robert, 10, 11, 12, 13
Blumer, Herbert, 13–16, 19–20, 30, 31, 33, 35–44, 116, 129, 151, 159, 180, 208, 216, 223
Blumstein, Alfred, 220
Boat landings, 1, 81, 83, 84, 93, 133, 208
Bobo, Lawrence D., 8, 12, 13, 14, 26, 32, 37, 44, 104, 106, 110, 118, 149, 150, 190, 210, 220, 223, 248nn4,5
Bodenhausern, Galen, 10
Boldt decision (Judge George Boldt), 62
Bonacich, Edna, 32
Boniger, David, 179
Bonilla-Silva, Eduardo, 10, 13, 14
Borgida, Eugene, 179
Bourhis, Richard Y., 113
Bradburn, Norman, 16
Bradley, Tom, 18
Brannon, Robert, 17
Brill, Alida, 108
Brown, Rupert, 140
Brubaker, Rogers, 9, 12, 44
Bureau of Indian Affairs, 58
Burstein, Paul, 19, 20
Busing, 2, 7, 8, 18–19, 28, 88, 107. *See also* School desegregation

271